TORIES AND THE WELFARE STATE

Tories and the Welfare State

A History of Conservative Social Policy since the Second World War

Timothy Raison

MACMILLAN

First published 1990

Published by
THE MACMILLAN PRESS LTD
Houndmills, Basingstoke, Hampshire RG21 2XS
and London
Companies and representatives
throughout the world

Printed and bound in Great Britain by
WBC Ltd, Bristol and Maesteg

British Library Cataloguing in Publication Data
Raison, Timothy
Tories and the welfare state: a history of conservative
social policy since the Second World War.
1. Great Britain. Political parties. Conservative Party.
Social policies, history
I. Title
361.6'1'0941
ISBN 0–333–47006–0

To the memory of my father,
Maxwell Raison

Contents

List of Tables and Figures

Preface

In the British system, the principal areas of government are broadly reflected in the three main Cabinet committees: one is concerned with overseas and defence policy, one with economic affairs and one with home affairs or social policy. The subject matter of this book lies in the realm of the third of those committees – in particular in education, health, housing, social security and some important aspects of the Home Office's work. Drawing boundary lines is obviously very difficult; indeed some would say that you *cannot* separate economic and social policy – for example, the interplay of tax and benefits. Perhaps in logic they are right: nevertheless, I hope that the reader will find some sort of unity in the development of social policy and the welfare state as I have treated them in this book.

At least the fact that I have handled the subject in terms of what the Conservative Party thought and did about it in the years since the Beveridge Report and the Butler Education Act should give it a coherent shape. It is, I believe, the first book to attempt to do this; and I have tried to write as a historian, rather than as an apologist, a polemicist – or even an occasional participator (though just once or twice there are hints of the last). Only in Chapters 11 and 12 do I deliberately switch from narrative to something more speculative and opinionated. And I immediately follow them by accepting David Butler's suggestion that I should include some tables of hard facts so that readers can assess for themselves something of what happened under different governments.

Naturally, the book has drawn on many sources, both written and oral. The former I have generally indicated as appropriate. As to the latter, there are a number of individuals to whom I am particularly indebted.

For a start, I am very grateful to Dr Sarah Street for her help in guiding me through the Conservative Party archives held at the Bodleian Library, Oxford, and to Alistair Cooke at Conservative Central Office, for facilitating permission for me to use and print extracts from these papers. Charles Bellairs at Central Office also gave me useful help: in particular, his two volumes recording Conservative social and industrial reform, published by the Conservative Political Centre, were invaluable. The House of Commons Library staff, especially Robert Twigger, were also enormously helpful, particularly over the factual tables. I am also indebted to the Conservative Central Office Library.

Let me also thank warmly the following individuals for their guidance and recollections: Lord Fraser of Kilmorack, Lord Joseph, Lord Thorneycroft, Sir Geoffrey Howe, Norman Fowler, Lord Harris of High Cross, Arthur Seldon, David Willetts and others at the Centre for Policy Studies, Sir Alfred Sherman, Brendon Sewill, and from Nuffield College, Oxford, David Butler, A. H. Halsey and Nevile Johnson. Needless to say, none of those whom I have thanked is responsible for my faults or errors. Above all I am grateful to my secretary, Annabel Linney, for her exceptional typing skill and good humour. I also thank Joy Greenfield for her help over the index and references.

April 1989   TIMOTHY RAISON

Acknowledgements

The author and publishers are grateful for permission to reproduce copyright material from the following sources:

Losing Ground, Charles Murray (New York: Basic Books); *The Case for Conservatism*, Quintin Hogg (Lord Hailsham) (Harmondsworth: Penguin Books); *Margaret Thatcher*, Russell Lewis (London: Routledge); *A Mission to Beat Poverty*, Hermione Parker, *Independent*, 13 June 1988; *Ruling Performance*, Peter Hennessy and Anthony Seldon (Oxford: Blackwell); *The Genesis of the British National Health Service*, John and Sylvia Jewkes (Oxford: Blackwell); *Conservatism and Social Services, Political Quarterly XXIV*, J. Enoch Powell (Political Quarterly Publishing Company); *The Life of Iain Macleod*, Nigel Fisher (London: André Deutsch); *The Middle Way*, Harold Macmillan (London: Macmillan); *The Tides of Fortune*, Harold Macmillan (London: Macmillan); *William Beveridge*, J. Harris (Oxford: Clarendon Press); Keith Joseph Interview, Anthony Seldon, *Contemporary Record* (Vol. 1, No. 1); Review of '*Bertrand Russell* by Alan Ryan, David Marquand, *Observer*, 10 July 1988; *The Local Right*, Nicholas Ridley (London: Centre for Policy Studies); *The Audit of War*, Correlli Barnett (London: Macmillan); *The Art of the Possible*, R. A. Butler (London: Hamish Hamilton); and the Controller of Her Majesty's Stationery Office for UK tables drawn from DHSS *Abstract of Statistics, Home Office Statistical Bulletin 7, British Labour Statistics Historical Abstracts 1886–1968* and *Social Trends, 1989*.

Every effort has been made to trace all the copyright-holders, but if any have been inadvertently overlooked the publishers will be pleased to make the necessary arrangement at the first opportunity.

1 1939–45: Coalition

Wars have a way of defining epochs in social policy as in other spheres, and the 1939–45 war provides as good a starting point as any for a study of modern Conservative social policy. I will not therefore say anything about the achievements of Peel, Disraeli or other earlier statesmen – save to recall the famous words of Disraeli at the Crystal Palace on 24 June 1872 when he laid down that it was one of the great objects of the Conservative Party 'to improve the condition of the People'.

That aim was usually there, but it is inescapable that World War Two gave an enormous fillip to it. It is true that Neville Chamberlain thought hard about social policy (as his father Joseph had done). Not only had he been a notable success as Minister of Health in the 1920s, at a time when that department ranged over much of housing, local government and even social security; he also continued to take an interest, even as Prime Minister, in the formation of social policy at the Conservative Research Department – of which he remained chairman right up until his death in 1940. Indeed, John Ramsden in *The Making of Conservative Party Policy* is able to say that 'from work already done in the Research Department, it seems likely that a Conservative manifesto of 1940 would have included family allowances and the inclusion of dependants of insured persons in health cover – about half the allowances that are usually traced to Beveridge'.[1] It would be surprising if Chamberlain, for all his international preoccupations, were not abreast of this.

Nor, of course, should we forget about the campaigning of Harold Macmillan. His 1938 book *The Middle Way* was primarily economic in content, in some ways foreshadowing *The Industrial Charter* of 1947, but in his stress on economic security he was very much concerned with aspects of social policy. In his book he set out his thinking on the balance between social and individual responsibility.

It should be the responsibility of society to find the means of granting to every one of its citizens a guarantee of security in the enjoyment of minimum standards of food, clothing, and shelter in return for their willing offer to share in the labour necessary to produce them. That is to say, society has the responsibility of creating the social and economic organisation for the continuous supply of these minimum requirements; society has not the right to

1

abandon the individual because, as a result of faulty organisation, the labour which he is still willing to extend cannot temporarily be utilised.

The individual, on the other hand, must undertake certain duties and responsibilities to society. He must be willing to work. He must be willing to contribute to schemes of social insurance that society may devise to provide for the contingencies of sickness, disablement and retirement. He must contribute out of his income to the carrying out of other national responsibilities, such as the provision of public health, sanitation, amenity, and defence services by which society defends itself against disease, ugliness or destruction.[2]

Macmillan's ideas of the reciprocal duty to work would not have found favour with the Left today: it looks as though he would have supported the 'workfare' notion, of compulsory work in return for certain benefits. But there is one particular respect in which his thinking proved not to be prophetic: he was a firm believer in the idea of food as a social service and in the payment of certain benefits in the form of food. He wanted a national Nutrition Board. The state would pay for it to provide foodstuffs as a form of children's allowances to the poor, and the Insurance Fund would pay for foodstuffs for the unemployed, though where insurance benefit was exhausted the cost would be repaid by the state. Foodstuffs would also be provided as benefits for the dependants of the sick, for the disabled and to increase various pensions. The different insurance schemes might be unified under a single department, which would use the Nutrition Board as its agent.

In the event, the tide generally turned against benefits in kind, at least on this scale, and the first post-war Conservative government abandoned the concept of food as a social service with its bold decision to end food subsidies.

Macmillan anyway was a marginal figure as far as the pre-war Conservative government was concerned. By the time *The Middle Way* came out the crucial social problem of unemployment was easing – and political thinking was becoming more and more dominated by Hitler and the threat of war.

While unemployment had stirred consciences and led to the search for solutions, there is no doubt that the war, when it came, accelerated social reform.

There were a number of reasons why this should be so. Some were analysed by R. M. Titmuss in his *Problems of Social Policy*.[3] Titmuss himself quoted Anthony Eden as saying in 1939 that war 'exposed weaknesses ruthlessly and brutally ... which called for revolutionary changes in the economic and social life of the country'. In particular Titmuss stressed the way in which mass evacuation and the disturbance caused by the bombing of 1940 brought home to many people the weaknesses in services, the scale of poverty, the uneven nature of health care and so on. Human concern was coupled with a realisation that winning the war required healthy and as far as possible contented people – not only in the armed forces but on the home front as well. This in turn was tied up with the high level of mobilisation of resources, including people, and the fact that the war effort was essentially state-directed: for all the muddles endemic in any war, the state was seen as efficient at getting things done – and it was a recurring theme that if the state could tackle the great problems of war why could it not do the same for the problems of peace? As José Harris puts it in her biography of Beveridge 'This argument was strengthened by recollections of the withdrawal of government from social and economic life after the First World War – a withdrawal that had been accompanied by, if not necessarily responsible for, prolonged depression and unemployment'.[4]

Dr Harris points out, too, that as unemployment fell there was a switch of interest among social reformers from that problem to the problems of low wage earners (who did not share in the spiralling wages of workers in key industries), of those on fixed benefits, and of large families.

But there were also important political factors at work. The creation of the coalition government suspended the formal party battle. Common war aims were needed, and Conservatives – sometimes reluctantly and sometimes willingly – took on board ideas that had by and large been seen as the particular property of the left. Moreover, for all that it was a period of coalition, throughout the war the left campaigned more actively on social policy than did the right. In so far as there was a parliamentary opposition (except occasionally on the actual conduct of the war) it was predominantly Labour. In the country Labour was certainly much more active. Natural Conservatives of military age were mostly to be found in the armed forces; many natural socialists did their war work in munitions factories, mines or services like the fire service where there was often a high level of political and union activity. In the armed forces themselves, nevertheless, the education and current affairs programmes were ready vehicles for leftish material and instructors – while the newly booming paperbacks and publications like *Picture Post* and the *News*

Chronicle brought radical politics to millions. Even *The Times* of R. M. Barrington-Ward and E. H. Carr acquired a pinkish hue. Conservatives would occasionally grumble that while they were busy fighting the war, socialists were having a political field day – but the 1945 election result showed that there were many socialist-voting servicemen.

If the wartime *zeitgeist* was generally reformist and statist, that does not of course mean that all Conservatives submerged themselves in it readily and happily. Whether on grounds of long-held belief or of self-interest there were clearly those who resisted the *zeitgeist*. Some – including to a considerable extent Churchill himself – regarded it all as largely irrelevant to the real business of winning the war, as witness his comment to Butler in 1941: 'I certainly cannot contemplate a new Education Bill'. And others – like Sir Kingsley Wood, the Chancellor of the Exchequer – were alarmed at the scale of the financial commitment if the Beveridge proposals were accepted in full.

The fact remains, however, that it was under the coalition government, in which the Conservatives were the predominant partners, that the pattern of the post-war welfare state was shaped. The 1944 Education Act was R. A. Butler's achievement. The white paper setting out proposals for a national health service was presented to Parliament in 1944 by a Conservative Minister of Health, Henry Willink. And in the response to Beveridge Conservative ministers played a full, if sometimes reluctant, part.

The Beveridge report on *Social Insurance and Allied Services* started with an inter-departmental committee set up under Sir William Beveridge in June 1941 – the month in which Hitler attacked Russia.[5] According to Dr Harris, it was created almost by accident. Initially it was designed to survey existing schemes of social insurance and allied services, but in the following January it was allowed to consider new schemes. The other departmental members of the committee became simply assessors and advisers and the report became Beveridge's alone. It appeared as a white paper in December 1942. The impact of the report was startling. The report's main proposals were family allowances for second and subsequent children, full employment, a universal health service, a uniform system of contributory insurance, subsistence level benefits which would be related not just to survival but to perceived human needs and the reduction of public assistance, which would be transferred to the Exchequer. Universality was an important principle: Beveridge rejected the idea of graduated contributions for equal benefits (the 'Santa Claus state'), although he did see insurance as shifting resources from single people to married and from rich to poor.

Beveridge put considerable stress on the insurance principle. He dismissed the idea that benefits should be financed by a surcharge on taxation. This helped to win support for the report among Conservatives. Some of the insurance companies were not particularly keen on the extension of a state-run scheme, but in general Conservatives could respond to Beveridge's statement in his report that 'Benefit in return for contributions, rather than free allowances from the State, is what the people of Britain desire'. Beveridge was far from simply being interested in more and more state-funded welfare.

But in spite of the insurance principle implementation would clearly be costly. The first battle within the government came over the question of whether the report should be published. As Correlli Barnett records in *The Audit of War*, 'Kingsley Wood as Chancellor fired in a personal note to Churchill the day after this Cabinet meeting (on 16 November 1942) to urge in language almost of desperation that Beveridge's scheme is "ambitious and involves an impracticable financial commitment" and that therefore publication ought to be postponed'.[6]

Wood continued:

Whether the report is valuable will be of much argument. But it is certainly premature ... Many in this country have persuaded themselves that the cessation of hostilities will mark the opening of the Golden Age (many were so persuaded last time also). However this may be, the time for declaring a dividend on the profits of the Golden Age is the time when the profits have been realised in fact, not merely in the imagination.[7]

But great expectations had been aroused and to have refused publication would have been out of the question. In the event, no less than 800 000 copies of the report were sold.

There was still a feeling that the government was dragging its feet in endorsing Beveridge and this found reflection in the Commons debate on it which took place on 16, 17 and 18 February 1943, a few weeks after the report came out. The debate was opened by Arthur Greenwood, the Leader of the Opposition, with a speech welcoming the report, and Labour speakers supported it enthusiastically. The ex-civil servant, Sir John Anderson, Lord President of the Council, gave the government's first response. He supported the general line of development of the social services laid down in the report, but, as Aneurin Bevan put it (apparently not unfairly), he read his speech from a boring script. Sir Kingsley Wood did not go down very well either. Not unreasonably, he stressed the need for a 'sound and solid financial foundation'. His claim that 'the government are doing nothing to retard these proposals, but are doing everything that can be reasonably done at the present time to expedite them' did not however exactly mollify those who wanted a sense of urgency.

Reactions among Tory backbenchers varied. At one pole, Sir Herbert Williams said: 'I think the Beveridge Report as a whole is a very bad Report'. Sir Cuthbert Headlam was typical of a number in saying that he looked forward to the legislation being produced, but in not too great a hurry. Colonel Sir Charles MacAndrew said: 'I am sure that all of us are keen that everything should be done to assist social security ... But I am a little worried when I look at the cost ... To my mind, such expressions as "cut your coat according to your cloth" do mean something'.

Sir Austin Hudson favoured giving some home-grown products in kind rather than cash – but the Independent Eleanor Rathbone interrupted him to say that if mothers were given the cash they would have the sense to spend it on those products.

Mrs Cazalet Keir supported Beveridge. Henry Willink – not yet a minister – recognised 'a feeling of lack of confidence in the Government's determination, a feeling of dissatisfaction which has been expressed by many Members on the other side of the House, and by a considerable number on this'.

But the most eloquent Conservative was Quintin Hogg. Speaking on the second day of the debate, he said:

I am one of those who have come to the conclusion that the question of whether or not we recover after the war depends in the main not so much upon economic as moral decisions and upon our ability to continue the community spirit, new in time of peace but not unfamiliar on the battlefield or in time of war. As I see it, the Government have been guilty of what I can only describe as a major political blunder in not seizing upon that vital fact, either in the urgency or the tempo of what was said yesterday [by Sir John Anderson] or in the practical proposal of the institution of a Ministry of Social Security ... I do not think that present trend of either the Conservative or the Labour Party offers much hope for the future. I believe it is necessary to restate political problems in a form in which they are acceptable to the young.

Hogg was speaking in support of an amendment put down by another Conservative, Viscount Hinchingbrooke: the question of setting up a comprehensive ministry, advocated by Beveridge, was seen by them as something of a touchstone. But when it came to the vote at the end of the debate the Tories did not join those Socialists, led by James Griffiths, who voted for an amendment put down during the course of the debate expressing 'dissatisfaction with the now declared policy of His Majesty's Government towards the Report'. Nevertheless, the views of the young Turks in the Tory party were beginning to come over – not just Hogg and Hinchingbrooke, but also Peter Thorneycroft and Hugh Molson, active members of the recently founded Tory Reform Committee. It was notable that it was the younger Members, serving in the Forces, who felt most impatient with the attitudes of the 'Old Gang'.

The government was somewhat shaken by the episode and Churchill responded with a broadcast on 21 March 1943. While warning against unsustainable expenditure, he offered a four-year plan of reconstruction to cover five or six large measures of a practical character after the war from a new government. They would be compulsory national insurance, prevention of unemployment by government action, a broadening field for state ownership and enterprise, a housing drive, major reform in education and much improved health and welfare services.

Officials then settled down to the task of preparing white papers. Two on social insurance appeared in the autumn of 1944,[8,9] and one on a National Health Service in February of that year.[10] Beveridge was conspicuously left out of the follow-up process. Correlli Barnett says that Churchill's 'only recourse during the last two years of the war lay in trying to slow up the Whitehall machinery'. However, things moved on and the Family Allowance Bill received its second reading in March 1945 while the coalition government was still in being. The allowance was fixed at five shillings rather than Beveridge's proposed eight, but benefits in kind were provided on top of it and they, unlike the allowance, were not subject to taxation. There was a sharp clash over the government's initial proposal that the allowance should be paid to the father, but after the government conceded a free vote, partly under pressure from Eleanor Rathbone, it was decided that allowances would 'belong' to the mother. Although Eleanor Rathbone was an Independent, it was again largely Tory backbench pressure that helped to cause the government to change its stance.

The Beveridge Report was not only about cash benefits: it also called for the creation of a comprehensive health service. The Minister of Health in the middle years of the war was the National Liberal, Ernest

Brown. He was thinking in terms apparently of unifying all the health services in one unit of administration on a regional basis. The voluntary hospitals would probably be brought into this, and general practitioners were apparently to be full-time salaried servants.

The British Medical Association reacted sharply against this. Brown floundered and was replaced by Willink, who had made his mark in the Beveridge debate. In February 1944 he produced a White Paper.[10] This gave added responsibility to the Minister of Health. Services would be organised on the basis of joint county and county borough areas, but doctors would be paid on a per capita basis, except in health centres. These latter were a part of the progressive dream of the time – the Peckham health centre was the prototype. Nevertheless, their status was to be regarded as experimental, and the dream has never quite been fulfilled.

Willink introduced his proposals to Parliament in notably lyrical words. In the debate on the white paper on 16 March 1944 he said:

> Is it not right to think of a National Health Service as one of the main pillars upon which our post-war social structure must rest – education, health, housing, social insurance and there will, of course, be others? Big as this scheme is, it is really to be regarded, I feel, as part of a bigger process still, the process of reshaping the background of individual life in the country. It is really a counter-process to all the destructiveness of war. We have had other great public health landmarks in the past, but this dwarfs them all in its scope and conception. The health of the nation, the health of every citizen, young and old, is at the very root of national vigour and national enterprise.

Between the debate and the end of the coalition government discussion went on, notably about regional planning of the service. The terms and remuneration of the general practitioners were never fully resolved, but one way and another a good deal of ground had been covered by the end of the war. There was particular emphasis on good relations with the medical profession and the right to choose your own doctor.

It was not health, however, nor social security but education that received a complete legislative reform before the war had ended. The creator and impresario of the 1944 Education Act was of course R. A. Butler.

Butler's pre-war experience as a junior minister had been almost entirely to do with Foreign and Indian affairs. Nevertheless, while he was still at the Foreign Office in July 1940 he was asked by the Conservative Party chairman, Sir Douglas Hacking, to undertake a research programme into the currents of opinion within the country 'with a view eventually to adjusting the Party's outlook to the radically different trends of thought which prevail at a time like this'. As John Ramsden shows in *The Making of Conservative Party Policy*[11] Butler saw it as a first way into the problems of post-war reconstruction, and his long and fruitful influence on the party's research activities got under way. The following year, he was elected chairman of the party's newly formed Post War Problems Central Policy Committee, which first met on 24 July 1941.

Four days before, Butler had been appointed President of the Board of Education, though according to his biographer, Anthony Howard, he had known about the move for at least six weeks beforehand.[12] It was the prelude to a great achievement.

It is important to remember that Butler – for all the Butskell image – was always very much a Conservative. One who worked very closely with both Butler and Macmillan, Lord Fraser of Kilmorack, stresses that point, adding that Macmillan was not! There is an interesting letter among the Woolton papers at the Bodleian dating from September 1944 in which Butler takes issue with Woolton's argument that the Conservatives on the government's Reconstruction Committee had not pulled their weight. In particular Butler argues that the government's white paper following the Beveridge report 'stresses the features of thrift and gets back to placing the whole Beveridge scheme upon an insurance or subsistence basis. Conservatives in the country will prefer this attitude to that which Beveridge adopted'. Later he comments:

It would be wrong to say that the Conservative element has not sufficiently influenced the social reconstruction of the country in a proper manner – that is to say in the National interest and with a view to the trend of opinion at the present time.

He added, however, that 'Certainly if non-co-operating Conservatives are wanted, they can be found at three a penny!'.

However scornful or ambivalent Butler might seem to be about some of his fellow Conservatives, however pragmatic his instincts often were, however interested he was in (rational) reform, the milieu in which he

operated was the Conservative Party. It is impossible to imagine him
ever crossing the floor of the House. He always preferred to use his
own arts to keep the party sensible.

That said, however, the Education Act was very much a non-party
matter, both in content and in the way it was brought into being.
Chuter Ede, Butler's Labour parliamentary secretary, worked very
closely with him – and said of Butler during the Third Reading debate
of 11 and 12 May 1944:

I have been associated in the preparation of the Bill with a very great
man indeed … no man in the past, in this difficult and controversial
matter, has ever striven so wholeheartedly to understand the point
of view of people to whom, temperamentally, he was most opposed.

It was not party politicians but churchmen of differing denominations
that Chuter Ede would have had in mind, for it was the religious
settlement that caused most difficulty. But Butler was able to open his
speech on Second Reading on 19 January 1944 by saying:

I now commend the Bill to the House as one which is warmly
welcomed by the many active partners in the education service. It is
they, as a team, who have helped to fashion it during the last two
years.

He went on to say of the religious issue: 'We have been fortified by the
fact that we are a National government and are making an all-party
approach to this issue'. And his peroration struck a very non-partisan
note:

Hammered on the anvil of this war, the nation has been shaped to a
new unity of purpose. We must preserve this after victory is won, if
the fruits of victory are to be fully garnered, and that unity will, by
this Bill, be founded where it should be founded in the education
and training of youth.

On top of the religious settlement, the Act set out or confirmed the
pattern of post-war education as we have known it, at least up to the
1988 Baker Act. It transformed the Board of Education into a
ministry, it authorised the raising of the school-leaving age, it
abolished all maintained school fees, it encouraged nursery schools, it

set out the system of primary, secondary and further education, it provided for Central Advisory Councils (which have fallen into disuse) and it legislated for county colleges for part-time post-fifteen education (which have never come into being).

Above all, it was based on the notion of partnership between the Minister and the local education authorities (and the churches). The national system was to be under the control and direction of the minister but the LEAs were to manage it on the ground. Butler saw the minister as having a strong role. He resisted an amendment to leave out the words 'under his control and direction' from the first clause of the Bill, saying 'I do propose that the central authority shall lead boldly, and not follow timidly' – characteristically adding, however, that 'in no sense shall we take away the spirit of partnership which we desire from local authorities'.

The committee stage, taken on the floor of the House in March 1944, was not without interest. The Tory Reform Committee made an attempt to secure a limit to class sizes of say thirty, but were seen off. There was a strong Tory effort with an amendment proposed by Mrs Cazalet Keir to raise the school-leaving age to sixteen within twelve months of the passing of the Act, or three years at most. Butler stressed the administrative difficulty of providing the places – 'As it is, we have to find 391 000 extra school places to raise the age to 15 alone'. Sixteen would require 406 000 more. Nevertheless, the amendment was pressed and at least six Tories voted against the government, including Hogg and Hinchingbrooke.

One significant amendment which Butler brought in was the provision stressing 'the expediency of seeing that, so far as is compatible with the need for providing efficient instruction and training and the avoidance of unreasonable expense to the authority, provision is made for enabling children to be educated in accordance with the wishes of their parents'.

The most difficult amendment proved to be the one put down by Mrs Cazalet Keir, designed to establish the principle of equal pay for men and women teachers. It was debated on 28 March 1944. Thorneycroft seconded it in a spirited speech. Butler responded by saying that the issue was a matter for the Burnham Committee which dealt with teachers' pay, but that as a question of general national policy the government was not able to guarantee that equal pay for equal work as a general practice would be introduced, given the cost implications.

Butler then weighed in on the Tory rebels:

I am as much desirous of reform as anybody else, including any member of the Tory Reform Committee ... They have not taken my advice on one occasion hitherto and they have, with others, taken part in a division against the Government. In my view, a division against the Government is not just a demonstration; it is a serious thing; and if they decide to vote against the Government instead of taking the advice I have given a second time, the responsibility must be theirs.

Hogg responded with a not unconciliatory speech but affirmed that the amendment would be pressed. The whips seem to have done an inept job, and the outcome was a defeat for the government by 117 votes to 116.

This caused considerable upset. A rather inconclusive debate about confidence took place on 29 March 1944, and then the government decided to make the defeat of the relevant clause as it now stood a formal issue of confidence. The clause was rejected the following day by 425 votes to 23 – and, since it was an issue of confidence, Mrs Keir, Hogg, Thorneycroft, Hinchingbrooke and the other Tory rebels decided to vote with the government. As Hogg suggested in his speech, Butler may not have been very happy to have had to stamp down on the reformers; but he did so pretty toughly.

After that, the Bill sailed on to become an Act, and Butler was praised on all sides. Even Churchill – initially so unresponsive – respected and in an odd way even liked a man with whom he had little in common.

During the passage of the Bill Butler had had less time for party work, but after the burden lifted he was back at the task of preparing for the general election. He was aware that the party had been losing the ideological battle during the war. So were others, including Lord Woolton.

Woolton sprang to political fame as Minister of Food. In the latter part of the war he was Minister for Reconstruction. He was not at the time officially a Conservative (and incidentally always had a somewhat prickly relationship with Butler); but among his papers housed in the Bodleian Library is an interesting undated record of a talk he had with a Conservative backbench MP, Alexander Erskine-Hill.

Woolton's record reads:

I invited Erskine-Hill to consider whether the Conservative party were wise in letting all the measures that, during the war, have arisen along the lines of social reconstruction and are of good repute in the public mind be attributed to the socialist conception of life.

I asked him to consider whether, as a party, they agreed with me in the steps that I had taken to preserve infant health by making milk readily accessible to all nursing mothers, but insisting that those simple "luxuries" of the rich, such as orange juice and codliver oil, which have caused rickets to disappear from the nurseries of the well-to-do, were not an equal necessity for the children of the poor: I drew his attention to the importance of fortifying the health of our children by insisting on the provision of meals in schools.

I pointed out that in none of these things that this Ministry has instituted, simple and humble as they are, have the Conservative party ever raised a voice in the House of Commons in support. Yet probably no single factor has been so important in giving the country confidence in the administration of the Ministry of Food as this effort to look after child life ...

What a chance for the Conservative Party to become the advocates of a constructive system of caring for children.

Later on, in his outstanding stint as chairman of the Conservative party, Woolton was to concentrate on organisation and presentation, but the former warden of a settlement in Liverpool brought humanity as well as the skills of a major retailer to the job.

When the general election came in 1945, Conservative social policy as expressed in Churchill's *Declaration of Policy to the Electors*, which constitutes the manifesto, was very much a continuation of what had been developing under the coalition. Churchill certainly did not fight the campaign as a whole on a bi-partisan basis – he sought to frighten people from voting socialist; but his message to the electorate as far as social policy was concerned was cast as a follow-up to the broadcast of March 1943 in which he had offered a four-year plan. 'This plan has now been shaped, and we present it to the country for their approval'.

Education, of course, had been tackled with the Butler Act: the task now was its implementation. Top priority was to be given to housing. Building material costs were to be controlled and subsidies provided for public and private sector alike. The labour force was to be built up again – it had fallen from the pre-war million to under 400 000. At least 220 000 permanent new houses were to be built in the first two years. New types of factory-made permanent houses and equipment were being developed (early tastes of a *damnosa hereditas*!). Rent controls were to be continued on houses already controlled. And new proposals covering the law of compensation and betterment were to be brought forward – though their nature was not disclosed.

In social security, Churchill re-committed the party to a nation-wide and compulsory scheme of national insurance, based on the all-party white paper of 1944. In return for a single, consolidated contribution there would be a retirement pension of one pound for single people and 35 shillings for married couples. One way and another, the bulk of Beveridge would be implemented whichever party came to power.

One touch of generosity to an opponent that you would not expect to find in a modern manifesto of any party was a reference to the demobilisation proposals 'which Mr Bevin has elaborated with much wisdom'. And perhaps the most flowery language was to be found in the section on education: 'No system of education can be complete unless it heightens what is splendid and glorious in life and art. Art, science and learning are the means by which the life of the whole people can be beautified and enriched'. We have become a little more utilitarian since then!

In many respects, the programmes of Labour and the Conservatives were very similar – but that was hardly odd, given the generally harmonious collaboration of the war years. But it was Labour that appealed to the people – for all the respect and affection for Churchill, it was Attlee and his team who seemed more likely to bring about the world that ordinary people wanted. The Conservative Party was not yet seen as committed to the welfare state.

Historians may quarrel with the popular verdict. Correlli Barnett has certainly mounted a case which cannot just be shrugged off in saying that too much investment went into housing, too little into industrial re-equipment. He also attacks what he sees as the failure of the 1944 Education Act to tackle scientific and technical education – a task that was only really grappled with by David Eccles more than a decade later. Certainly our wartime enemies Germany and Japan saw more clearly than we did that before you can spend money you have to create it. Maybe Sir Kingsley Wood was right; but the *zeitgeist* could not be gainsaid.

2 1945–51: Parallel Lines

In *Ruling Performance*, a book edited by Peter Hennessy and Anthony Seldon about British governments from Attlee to Thatcher, Lord Fraser of Kilmorack draws on his unique backroom experience of Conservative policy-making to sum up the postwar period.[1] He writes:

> In a fundamental sense, there must always be a good deal of common ground between the main parties alternating in government in a free society. When in power, after all, they are governing the same country, with the same history, people, problems and elbow-room, or lack of it, within the same world. Because the two main parties coming out of the coalition government in 1945 had already hammered out, not without some hard bargaining and horse-trading, the broad policies for dealing after the war with those social problems that had been identified and prepared for during the war on the basis of the Beveridge Report, the Employment Policy White Paper and the Butler Education Act of 1944, there was for a time an unusual degree of apparent unity of aim. To say, however, that the situation after 1945 amounted to a 'consensus' is a myth of more recent origin. No one thought that at the time. The real position was like that of two trains, starting off from parallel platforms at some great London terminus and running for a time on broadly parallel lines but always heading for very different destinations.

This statement is a shrewd summary of the post-war period. So, too, is Lord Fraser's comment later in the same chapter that the British people began to suspect after a year or two that Labour had no real 'feel for freedom'. As Fraser puts it:

> It was this, and the emergence of R. A. Butler from a long ministerial apprenticeship to be the man primarily responsible for initiating and coordinating the new postwar Conservative policies, that began the containment of socialism and later its eventual reversal in changed economic and social conditions.

There was a real change of mood and ideas between the rather shell-shocked reaction to the 1945 defeat and the emergence of the One Nation approach in the famous pamphlet of 1950.

At times, consensus did seem to be the order of the day. In his speech on the Second Reading of the National Insurance Bill on 6 February 1946 – the Bill which set up the universal scheme proposed by Beveridge – Butler spoke as follows:

> We regard this plan as part of the mosaic or the pattern of the new society. When I heard [James Griffiths] the Right Honourable Gentleman reading out his clause 1, I could not but think of the similar satisfaction I had a short time ago in reading out clause 1 of the Education Bill. Both Bills have a certain similarity. They introduce a national scheme, for the first time, of a national scope to fulfil and satisfy national aspirations. I warmly share in the satisfaction that the Right Honourable Gentleman obviously felt in drawing the attention of the House to the drafting of that clause ... The Bill forms part of a series of Bills, starting with the Education Bill, which I may say foresaw the pattern of the new society long before this Parliament was even thought of – the Industrial Injuries Bill, the Family Allowances Bill and the Health Bill, to name only a few; and I was interested to hear that the Right Honourable Gentleman proposed to introduce a Bill dealing with assistance and similar matters at a later date. The whole philosophy behind these measures, in which, I must make it plain, we have played our part and shall play our part, is that the good things of life shall be more widely shared; we look forward to a society in which the more unfortunate members are free from the direst dread of penury and want.

As always, Butler was anxious to make it plain that the modern welfare state was not the exclusive creation of the Labour Party – understandably a constant (and legitimate) theme of much Conservative propaganda of that era. He did draw attention to the high cost of retirement pensions, and in particular the decision to make them available to many who had no contributions record, but there was no question of opposing the scheme.

The National Health Service Bill, which was debated on Second Reading on 30 April and 1 May 1946, faced the party with more difficult questions.

As we have seen, the shaping of the health service had had its difficulties under the coalition, but the tendency had been towards some sort of tie-up with local government and a reluctance simply to take over the voluntary hospitals. The question of how doctors were to be paid had never been quite settled, but Conservatives had accepted that a fully salaried service was not appropriate.

Aneurin Bevan built on the wartime work but he did make certain significant changes. In particular, he opted for a national hospitals service, with all responsibility ultimately lying with the minister, as opposed to a local government basis. He also decided to nationalise the voluntary hospitals. To the upset of many socialists, he decided to keep private practice and the pay beds – remarking that 'If the State owned a theatre it would not charge the same prices for different seats'. He did not introduce a full-time salaried service, though for the time being there was some vagueness as to what his intentions were. He was also very keen to set up health centres.

The Conservative leadership was faced with something of a dilemma. It must have felt that the Bill was popular, but it was sympathetic to the doctors, it had itself favoured a local government framework, and it supported the voluntary hospitals. It was decided therefore to vote against the Bill on a reasoned amendment. Willink moved it on the second day of the Second Reading debate:

> This House, while wishing to establish a comprehensive service, declines to give a Second Reading to a Bill which prejudices the patient's right to an independent family doctor; which retards the development of the hospital services by destroying local ownership, and gravely menaces all charitable foundations by diverting to purposes other than those intended by the donors the trust funds of the voluntary hospitals; and which weakens the responsibility of local authorities without planning the health services as a whole.

This last point was a criticism of the tripartite system by which hospitals, local health services and GP services came in under separate management.

During the debate various Tories criticised the government. There was suspicion of health centres and support for small hospitals. (Bevan had favoured units of 1000 beds, though not necessarily in the same building). Bevan was accused of overriding other views. Richard Law, in opening the debate for the opposition, said that Bevan 'has preferred to bring to this House these proposals which are in fact feared and distrusted by the great majority of those who will be called upon to make them effective'. Nevertheless, it was not a particularly ferocious onslaught, and Sir Ralph Glyn, for example, complimented the minister on his 'great sense of responsibility'.

On Third Reading, the opposition again voted for a reasoned amendment – if anything more sharply worded than the previous one; but a backbencher – the future Chancellor of the Exchequer, Derrick Heathcoat-Amory – probably spoke for a good many Conservatives when he said:

By any test, this is a tremendous measure; there can be no question about that ... those of us who feel bound to vote for the Amendment do so with a sense of very real regret that we cannot conscientiously support the Bill as it is now. We approve of the broad principles, but it is because we feel that the Bill contains certain defects which could quite easily have been eliminated ... that we feel bound to take the action we are taking.

The vote provided the Labour Party with a stick with which they sought to beat the Conservatives for years to come.

Three years later, the Tories derived satisfaction from the National Health Service (Amendment) Bill which confirmed a pledge given by Bevan in 1948 that a full-time salaried service could not be instituted by regulation alone and that the then government had no intention of instituting such a service. This followed a good deal of tension and a plebiscite by doctors against coming into the NHS until they had such a guarantee. Walter Elliot, winding up for the Conservatives at Second Reading (24 May 1949) said: 'We feel that this is our Bill ...' Significantly, he went on to restate that because the party had voted against the original Bill on both Second and Third Reading that did not mean that it was against the NHS. But Labour continued to make much of those two votes. Conservatives might snipe at aspects of the service but they generally kept well clear of a head-on attack. Iain Macleod – the party's backroom researcher on health – argued that it was essential to give the service time to settle down and that Conservatives should make sure that they had a policy of their own before criticising that of the government. He did send to Butler in January 1949 a projection showing that the cost of health to the Exchequer would rise by at least £100 million by 1952–3, but he urged that this should be accepted.

From time to time Conservatives did of course defend what had been happening to health care under the pre-war governments – the *Campaign Guide* for the 1950 election, for example, has a full account of pre-war achievements. And as Professor John and Mrs Sylvia Jewkes showed in an important pamphlet published in 1961 (*The*

Genesis of the British National Health Service) it was certainly not the case that 1948 marked a sudden transformation from bad health care to good. As the Jewkeses put it:

> If it be true that the British people embarked upon the experiment of the National Health Service in the belief that their existing medical facilities were noticeably inferior to those found in other countries, that British medicine had failed to provide widespread service in times of sickness to the whole community and that administrative changes could of themselves produce miracles, then undoubtedly they were the victims of illusion.

With an eye to the future they continued:

> And, in turn, their rulers were in error if they supposed that people, left to their own devices, will never give high enough priority to medical advice and treatment and that, given this inherent defect in individual judgement, nothing short of central control and operation by government can put things right.[2]

A defensive case could be mounted, then, for playing down the scale of the changes in health brought about by the creation of the NHS; but by and large the public were not particularly responsive to such arguments – any more than they have sometimes seemed responsive to more recent arguments about the scale of government spending in health. But there was another significant factor which gradually dawned on Conservatives: the people who were gaining most from the new system were in fact the middle classes. The working classes (although not dependants) were broadly able to obtain 'free' health services before the war; the middle classes were not. Moreover, they often paid fees which included a hidden element of subsidy to those who did not pay. Not surprisingly, therefore, Conservatives were likely to shy off attacking a system which helped their own supporters, although they were usually sensitive to the interests of doctors.

At this stage it is desirable to say a little about how party policy making was handled in the post-war years. The Leader of the Opposition was of course Churchill, but the key figure in social policy was undoubtedly Butler. Butler was appointed by Churchill to become chairman of the Conservative Research Department, a powerful body before the war which had become moribund during it: he retained that post for eighteen years. He also became chairman of the Advisory

Committee on Policy and Political Education, to which the new Conservative Political Centre was answerable. Although the party chairman had administrative responsibility for these bodies, Butler made sure that he would deal directly with the Leader of the party, rather than going through the party chairman and the National Union set-up.

It was under Butler's aegis that there came together at the Research Department the galaxy of which the brightest stars were Iain Macleod, Reginald Maudling and Enoch Powell – all heading, of course, for the Commons. Maudling was concerned with economic rather than social policy: he was notable for his ability to come in after a good lunch, ponder for a while, cigar in mouth, and then dash off a searching piece of analysis. Powell was more obviously diligent: his romantic imagination was coupled with both a strong sense of history and a taste for argument. Macleod was not diligent: his Bridge and companionability both meant a good deal to him, but he had a broadness of view and a sense of politics which were unique, plus real eloquence and humour. And the three were surrounded by other very capable colleagues, like Michael Fraser and later Peter Goldman.

There was plenty of scope for them. Few of the Leader's Consultative Committee (i.e. the Shadow Cabinet) had any very detailed knowledge of social policy. It met erratically, often over dinner at the Savoy – and Churchill had no desire to be bogged down in minutiae. Nor were particular Shadow portfolios assigned to particular members of the committee, as in later years. Individuals were invited to speak from the front bench on a somewhat *ad hoc* basis. The regular occupants of the front bench were the privy counsellors. The continuous development of policy therefore depended a great deal on Butler's team at the Research Department.

The first, and crucial, policy initiative after the war was the Industrial Charter. After the 1945 defeat there was naturally a strong demand for policy rethinking. The young Turks of the Tory Reform Committee continued to press for it, though in fact the committee came to an end in 1946. (This was partly because it was felt that a faction of this kind was not appropriate in the much reduced parliamentary party, and partly because a number of its leaders switched their attentions to an abortive attempt to obtain some sort of merger with the Liberals). Butler not surprisingly, as chairman of the National Union, had called for a review of fundamental issues at the first post-war party conference in October 1946. The records of the Leader's Consultative Committee for this period held at the Bodleian are too patchy to give a clear idea of how much time was given to social policy. It is hard to imagine Churchill wanting much in the way of detailed discussion, though a subject like national insurance would arouse in him a sympathetic interest, not least because it would bring back to him his involvement in the pre-1914 Liberal government which launched it.

In November 1945 the LCC minutes record that Eden and Lyttelton were to arrange for a small body of industrialists to consider policy with Butler's Post War Policy Committee; then in October 1946 Churchill decided that an Industrial Committee should be set up under Butler. Its members were Butler, Oliver Stanley, Macmillan, Maxwell Fyfe, Thorneycroft, David Eccles, Colonel J. R. H. Hutchinson and Sir Peter Bennett, with David Clarke, director of the Conservative Research Department as secretary. Clarke was assisted by Maudling and Fraser. It was a powerful team, and the end-product, *The Industrial Charter*, had a powerful impact when it was published in May 1947.[3]

As its name implies, the scope of the charter is somewhat outside that of this book, but its tone was fundamental to the party's whole policy posture. Next to Butler, the strongest influence and most active member of the team was Harold Macmillan and the Charter bears some of the marks of his pre-war thinking as set out in *The Middle Way*. The aim was to reconcile free enterprise and planning, a rather pragmatic view of nationalisation was taken, and there was considerable stress on industrial partnership – all very different from the Thatcher era! The document also emphasised the need for industrial pensions and technical education.

The commitment to produce a document of this kind had been made at the 1946 Tory party conference: its endorsement followed a year later at the 1947 conference. By one means or another Churchill was lured into commending it: this followed a happily stage-managed debate at which the document was passed by the conference with only three dissentients. Anthony Eden, Churchill's heir apparent, had also endorsed the Charter in a series of speeches throughout the summer. He had already stressed at Blackpool in 1946 in particular, that 'It is essential that the worker in industry should have the status of an individual and not of a mere cog in a soulless machine'. Eden had a strong sense of the responsibilities of owners and managers, as of officers, towards their men – as, of course, did Macmillan. It was incidentally in this Blackpool speech of 1946 that Eden first used his only memorable phrase in domestic policy when he said 'Our aim is a

nation-wide property owning democracy'. That at least was a
philosophy which came to fulfilment under Mrs Thatcher.

At much the same time as the very middle-of-the-road *Industrial
Charter* was being prepared, Quintin Hogg was writing his spirited
Penguin book, *The Case for Conservatism*.[4] The chapter on social
policy begins with a fanfare:

> Conservative social policy is based upon the unity of the British
> people, upon the ultimate identity of interest between all classes. The
> aim of social policy is to create a united nation; its basis is the belief
> that such union is possible.

Much of the chapter is then taken up with an attack on the level and
system of taxation (including the particular plight of barristers!). He
then launches into an attack on the divisiveness of Labour policies –
their exclusion of friendly societies from the running of national
insurance, their antagonising of the professions in the NHS and their
obsession with council housing. As Hogg puts it:

> Conservatives believe that it is to the advantage of the occupant to
> buy his house. If he rents it at however low a figure, he never acquires
> an interest in the land to leave to his children; and he ends by spending
> on his home a figure large enough to pay for it without acquiring any
> property in it. Far different is the case of the owner-occupier; with
> every fruit tree he plants in his garden he has a greater, and more
> justifiable, pride of ownership. His furniture, his pictures, his
> gadgets, his lawn, his flowers and shrubs, his vegetable plot are
> planned with enthusiasm and joy to make the whole a home.[5]

The language may be a touch lyrical, but it anticipates a major theme in
Conservative policy a generation later.

Hogg argues – a little surprisingly – that 'badly as houses are required
in the towns they are wanted a great deal more in the country'. He goes
on to make the essential point that if houses were to be built at the
necessary rate there must be encouragement for both local authority
and private enterprise, as in the days before the war. And 'Conservatives will probably see to it that facilities be given to enable wage earners
to purchase their own homes even where these are municipally owned' –
again an interesting pointer to things to come.

The next major policy initiative was the publication of *The Right
Road for Britain*, a booklet containing the party's official statement of
policy, bearing the imprimatur of a foreword by Churchill.[6] Launched

in July 1949, it was very much a gathering together of already published policy for the election which was bound to come within the following twelve months. It just preceded the financial crisis of that summer, which culminated in Sir Stafford Cripps's drastic devaluation in September, and its tone may therefore have been less sombre than it would have had to be a few weeks later. Amazingly, by modern standards, its full and short versions between them sold 2.2 million copies within three months.

The Right Road for Britain followed the general feeling of the day when it stated: 'Housing, as one of the most important single factors in the health and happiness of the people, must have first claim upon that part of the nation's resources which can be devoted to social ends'.[7] It was able to make a strong case against the government. It argued that houses were being built less efficiently and at much greater cost than before the war – a report had shown that it took three men to build what it took two men before the war. By concentrating the housing effort on local authorities and restricting the efforts of private builders the government had prevented the latter from acting as pace-makers. The work of local authorities had anyway been repeatedly upset by changes in government policy.

The Conservative aim would be to free builders from unnecessary restrictions and liberalise the supply of building materials. There would be a drive for owner occupation, including sympathetic consideration for 'sound schemes designed to dispose of local authority houses where the local authorities have already provided an adequate pool of houses for letting'.[8]

The aim was also to encourage private enterprise to meet part of the need for houses to rent. There would be depreciation allowances for new houses to rent. Rent control would continue while shortage persisted, but it would be reviewed by a new committee of enquiry. In the public sector the attack on slums carried out between 1933 and 1939 would be resumed as soon as possible.

There was nothing particularly radical in all this, but the emphasis on getting rid of restrictions struck the right note, politically and practically, and was the prelude to the famous 300 000 pledge of the following year.

The chapter on social services was aimed to show the Conservative record in a very positive light. It starts by saying:

Mainly during the Twentieth Century a new conception of Social Services has grown up and Britain has led the world in a vast experiment in social organisation. This has been the work of the Conservative and Liberal parties, mostly in fact of Parliaments with Conservative majorities ... The Socialists in the last four years have carried out in a partisan spirit the plans prepared by the National Coalition Government with its large Conservative majority. They have no claim to any achievement of their own.

These bold words were followed by more in the same vein:

Despite the spirit of class-war with which the Minister of Health [Aneurin Bevan] in particular has sought to disrupt national unity, the Conservative Party has welcomed the new Social Services which it has done so much to create. We regard them mainly as our own handiwork.[9]

But perhaps more interesting, in the light of argument over the subsequent years, was the statement that:

The Social Services are no longer even in theory a form of poor relief. They are a co-operative system of mutual aid and self-help provided by the whole nation and designed to give to all the basic minimum of security, of housing, of opportunity, of employment and of living standards below which our duty to one another forbids us to permit anyone to fall.[10]

The first part of this statement emphasises the all-embracing nature of the welfare state – the sense of community that had been enhanced over the war years and that has been a powerful element in 'Welfarism' since the war. The second half, however, talked in terms of basic minima. Beveridge might have written it, but Richard Titmuss – the London School of Economics Professor of Social Administration who was Labour's guru in social policy – would not. The dream of the Left – however rarely fulfilled – was to see the Welfare State as an instrument for achieving equality. It was not enough to conquer absolute poverty: the target was the defeat of relative poverty, with the poverty level later defined by the Titmuss school as 140 per cent of the national assistance or supplementary benefit level – regardless of the fact that more generous benefit levels would automatically *increase* the number of those said to be living in poverty.

This passage illustrates the truth of Michael Fraser's claim that policy was not on a consensus basis – and of course the young Turks of the Conservative Research Department working on policy were not so bound up in the War-time coalition experience as were their elders and betters.

Three other points in *The Right Road for Britain* are worth noting. One is that the party had now come round to recognising the need for better technical education. First priority was to go to technical schools and colleges – a hint that people were beginning to grasp the need for social policy to respond to economic policy objectives (as opposed simply to economic pressures). At the same time there was considerable stress on the old, including easing the pensions earnings rule and retirement condition.

On the third matter, the possibility of health charges, the approach had a tactical flavour to it which one cannot but feel was the handiwork of Iain Macleod:

> The nation has been warned by the Socialist Chancellor of the Exchequer that unless there is economy in the use of the Health Service some special charge or tax may have to be imposed. Conservatives share this anxiety about the maladministration and lack of foresight displayed by the Minister of Health and any Government may find itself forced to establish priorities based on need and urgency. We shall, therefore, see that the large sums of money spent on these services yield their full value.[11]

In other words, if Labour brings in charges let them carry the can.

The general election duly came on 23 February 1950. The Tory manifesto was a very much more concise version of *The Right Road for Britain*: indeed it was called *This is the Road*. There were those who argued that after the devaluation crisis the road should be presented as winding uphill rather more of the way than had been originally projected. This spirit was not, however, allowed to infect the social policy sections. Pledges to allow free drugs to private patients and to maintain the level of university grants were dropped; but otherwise the buoyant tone of the earlier document was maintained. Housing was again prominent, with the cuts in building caused by the devaluation crisis being stressed. Rent control was to be kept under review rather than necessarily be the subject of a new enquiry. There was also a commitment to make drastic changes in the 1947 Town and Country Planning Act, in particular the arbitrary way in which it sought to distribute the anyway inadequate sum of £300 million which it offered in compensation for the loss of development gains – a wrangle which was to continue between the parties for another thirty years. The Conservative point was not that there should be no charge on development gains, but that the charge should not be at a rate which would deter owners from bringing land forward for development.

The manifesto was generally well-received, but the Labour party narrowly won the election.

Between that election and the following one on 25 October 1951 there were two events of real interest in the making of Conservative social policy: the publication of the pamphlet *One Nation*[12] and the pledge to build 300 000 houses given at the 1950 party conference.

One Nation was notable for its content and its authors alike. The authors were all men who had entered Parliament in 1950: C. J. M. Alport, Robert Carr, Richard Fort, Edward Heath, Gilbert Longden, Iain Macleod, Angus Maude, Enoch Powell and John Rodgers. It seems odd that Reginald Maudling was not among them, but there was no lack of talent without him. Published by the Conservative Political Centre the pamphlet carried a warm foreword by Butler. It was not an official statement of policy but – to quote its sub-title – 'A Tory Approach to Social Problems'; but its flavour was very much that of the party over the next two decades.

The editors of the pamphlet were Macleod and Maude, but it is said that in fact Maude and Powell did the lion's share of the work, though Macleod attracted the limelight.

The title, of course, has echoes of Disraeli and the text refers to his concern with the 'improvement in the well-being of the people' and 'the amelioration in the condition of the poor'. These were certainly the pamphlet's aims, but in a sense its tone was less obviously One Nation-like than was the tone of the older generation like Eden and Macmillan. The One Nation authors had not been through the experience of serving in a coalition government with a common cause and they were not haunted by memories of the Flanders carnage of officers and men alike. Nor did they, for the most part, have an underlying sense that conservatism was about how to carry out a graceful withdrawal with minimum losses. They were not the senators waiting for the barbarians in the well-known poem ('Waiting for the Barbarians') by C. P. Cavafy.

One Nation was certainly concerned to defend the Conservative achievement in social policy. It quoted the *Manchester Guardian*'s comment on the party's programme at the 1950 election: 'The Conservatives have never in their history produced so enlightened a statement on social policy – from full employment to education and the social services'.[13] It also quoted Churchill's speech at the 1947 party conference:

> The scheme of society for which we stand is the establishment and maintenance of a basic minimum standard of life and labour below which a man or woman of good will, however old and weak, will not be allowed to fall.

But perhaps the key quotation was: 'We believe, in Mr Eden's words, in "the strong helping the weak" rather than weakening the strong'.

The flavour of the pamphlet was strongly anti-socialist. Thus:

> We wish to speak of the social consequences of redistribution, by which we mean the effect upon the relationship between men, and between classes of men, and upon the well-being of men in all but the most narrowly economic sense. We contend that the optimum has quite certainly been passed on social grounds, and that the social well-being of the nation has already been endangered by the redistribution of wealth. We base this contention on the view that in our society the possession and transmission of property can and should produce desirable results which are not to be procured by any other means ...
>
> The first consideration which we advance is a moral one ... When the state redistributes income and property to give everyone the largest amount possible, the citizen who has paid his taxes has discharged in full his obligations to the huge benefit pool to which he belongs. The State is now the keeper of his conscience and duty; he gives and receives exactly what the State thinks right. Perhaps this is the millennium of fair shares for all. It is certainly the death of a humane society.[14]

Another passage describes how:

> Evils result from the assumption by the community of the exclusive role of Grand Almoner, which must follow from the elimination of private fortunes ... In education, in the treatment of the sick and in the care of the young and aged, it will be found that historically the course of the social services has been piloted by private initiative ... That leadership, which by its nature the state cannot exercise, depends on the existence of aggregations of wealth at the disposal of individuals.[15]

The pamphlet adds that 'Private property is an equipoise to political power'.

The pamphlet then settles down to consider the specific areas of social policy. There is a slightly muddled chapter on population policy, in which the key point seems to be that 'The future greatness and prosperity of Britain will depend on whether enough children are born, and on whether the children that are born are healthy and intelligent'. There was no sign that the baby boom was on its way, and some modest incentives to fertility were put forward. Not a hint of the Commonwealth immigration question was to be seen.

Housing was given high priority, though on familiar lines. There was one odd passage:

It would be wrong not to draw attention to the grave problem which is being created for the future by the production of large numbers of council houses at such rents that, if a fall occurs in building costs, difficulty will be experienced in letting them, despite the subsidy. It seems that when this crisis breaks, drastic policies of rent-pooling and of sale may be necessary to rescue local authorities from their financial difficulties.[16]

For one reason or another, this was not a crisis which ever broke.

Next to housing, the requirements of education ranked highest among the social services. Inevitably, the implementation of the Butler Act and building needs took priority, with schools coming before nursery education and the county colleges which the 1944 Act envisaged as providing post-school education on a wide scale. The need to improve technical schools and colleges was recognised, but the pamphlet did not really grasp the full scale of what had to be done in the fields of science and technology. The authors were not very keen on the craze for elaborate visual aids – one wonders what they would have made of the current proliferation of computers in schools.

There was nothing very radical about the chapter on health. The problem of the growing cost of meeting unlimited demand in the 'free' service was acknowledged, and the need for some charges accepted if the greatest needs were to be met. With over 50 000 beds reported closed for lack of staff, there was particular stress on the need to raise the pay and status of nurses. *Plus ça change …*

Economic realities and the need for enhanced defence inevitably tempered the desire to improve conditions for the old, whose numbers were surging, and the menace of inflation was beginning to be recognised. The authors rejected the automatic index-linking of benefits as being inflationary, and while there were a number of positive proposals for help, with a stress on voluntary effort, the pamphlet said rather bleakly that:

> The old age of a generation which (for largely material reasons) chose to have small families is likely to be somewhat comfortless. In this case, if we may mangle a metaphor, it is the absence of chickens which is coming home to roost.[17]

I have quoted from *One Nation* at some length because of the snapshot which it gives of the evolution of Conservative policy in the early 1950s.

The essence of the pamphlet was later summarised by one of its principal authors, Enoch Powell. In an article in *The Political Quarterly* he said that *One Nation* had:

> Argued that because the Labour government had sought in health, in insurance, in education, in housing to supply through the social services an average standard for all, it had thereby in practice failed to meet the requirements of those in greatest need. The health service, by attempting everything at once, had starved some of the most essential branches like dental health and mental treatment; by building council houses only, the nation had obtained fewer houses altogether; by endeavouring to eliminate differences of educational opportunity, the state was threatening the standards of the ablest; the changing age structure had been too little regarded in the planning of national insurance. The machinery of the welfare state was not helping the weak by its repression of the opportunities and independence of the strong.[18]

Powell went on to say that the expression 'welfare state' should, strictly speaking, be repudiated by the Conservative party, since the state is not a machine constructed to provide welfare but:

> an organism, which, if it is sound and healthy, will assure the well-being of its members. This sense of the relationship and proportion of the social services to the capabilities and prosperity of the nation as a whole underlies the characteristic conservative concern with the financing of the social services. The limit of what the nation can afford to redistribute through these services, though

never capable of being precisely defined, is the final expression of that due relationship and proportion.[18]

The average Conservative might have felt that Powell was being very deep about it all; but he would have taken the point that there will never be enough money to pay for everything.

One Nation came out in October 1950: the same month, at its conference in Blackpool, the Conservative Party committed itself to the target of 300 000 houses a year. The backroom researchers were nervous about stating a target, particularly given the economic climate. They knew that housing loomed large in the public perception – every single Conservative candidate in the 1950 election had made housing a main priority in his election address. But there were doubts about the ability of the housing industry to meet the target as well as the case for housing against competing claims, including defence.

The party conference delegates, however, were determined to have a 300 000 target. In a well-known passage in *The Art of the Possible* Butler described what happened:

Lord Woolton, who was sitting beside me as the figure began to be picked up by representatives with the mounting excitement one customarily associates with an auction, whispered, '*Could* we build 300 000?'. I replied, 'The question is *should* we? And the answer is that it will make it that much more difficult to restore the economy. But if you want to know if it is technically feasible, ask David Clarke'. So the Director of the Research Department was consulted behind the scenes and opined (correctly) that the thing could be done, and Lord Woolton stepped forward to the front of the platform to declare in beaming surrender: 'This is magnificent'. And so in a sense it was.[19]

The vignette tells you much about politics, much about government, much about Rab, much about Woolton. Some would say that this episode typifies what went wrong with the post-war British politics; and the pledge certainly entailed the commitment of very substantial human and material resources, as well as shipping space and foreign currency. Churchill qualified the pledge by saying that it must be subject to the needs of rearmament, and that the timing must therefore be flexible, but it was one of the most specific ingredients in the message from Churchill that constituted the Tory manifesto at the 1951 election. For the most part, both Churchill's statement and the

Butler-inspired document called *Britain Strong and Free*, which set out policy in more detail, did no more than reiterate the policies put forward the previous year. But the recipe seemed to work: the party came to power, with a majority of 17, although a smaller popular vote than Labour.

3 1951–56: Back in Government

Social policy under Churchill's 1951–5 government has about it a curiously uncomplicated flavour. Thanks particularly to R. A. Butler, the party had recovered from the disarray of 1945. Its spokesmen took every opportunity to remind people of the high proportion of social legislation over the previous century that had been enacted by Conservative governments and of the fact that the impetus for the bulk of the new legislation had come from the coalition government with its Conservative majority. The new intake in the House of Commons may have brought in some sharper questioning of the welfare state, but there was no disposition to reject it – and Macleod and Powell had anyway both been heavily involved in backroom work during the years in opposition.

The crucial factor was not ideology but resources and the state of the economy. In housing, education and health, the great need was essentially for *more* – more trained manpower, but above all more building. The 1949 financial crisis and the pressure to rearm brought about by the Korean War both meant that resources were very tight.

Ironically, it was the architect of social policy, Butler, who found himself – somewhat surprisingly – as Chancellor of the Exchequer and hence watchdog. Imports had to be cut sharply on several occasions, and bank rate went up in Butler's first budget in the spring of 1952. However, by starting to reduce food subsidies (by £160 million) the Chancellor gave himself the leeway to restore the main social security benefits to their real 1948 level: two years later benefits were raised to a rate above the more generous 1946 level.

Happily, the economy – and particularly the balance of payments – began to improve during 1952, and the 1953 budget actually contained no tax increases and some reductions – notably sixpence off income tax.

Against this background it was possible to make progress in social provision. The decision to move away from regarding food as a social service was a thoroughly wise one. It is hard to remember that before the war people like Harold Macmillan saw the provision of food as an essential social service, and indeed that it was a significant part of social policy during the war. It took an act of boldness to move away

from that view – Labour were still supporting food subsidies until well
into the 1970s; but it helped to keep social policy on the move at a
difficult time.

The most striking achievement was in housing. Macmillan had not
been involved in the 1950 commitment to 300 000 houses. In his
autobiography *Tides of Fortune*[1] he describes how he was summoned
to Chartwell on 28 October, just after the general election:

> On arrival, at 3 pm, I found (Churchill) in a most pleasant, and
> rather tearful mood. He asked me to 'build the houses for the
> people'. What an assignment!

Macmillan added:

> I was rather taken aback by this proposal. I knew nothing
> whatsoever about the housing problem except that we had pledged
> ourselves to an enormously high figure, generally regarded by the
> experts as unattainable.

He asked for, and managed to obtain, two key assistants: the civil
engineer and builder turned MP, Ernest Marples, as his parliamentary
secretary and the industrialist, Sir Percy Mills. Minister of Housing
was not the most prestigious office in government; and Macmillan was
not in the first batch of senior ministers to be announced. He took the
job reluctantly. But he himself said in his autobiography that the three
years he spent in this office proved in many ways the happiest and most
rewarding of his time as a minister.

Fortified by his chosen team – which also included the redoubtable
Evelyn Sharp as deputy secretary at the ministry – and with strong
allies at ministerial level in David Eccles, the Minister of Works who
was actually responsible for public building, and Lord Swinton, who
was in charge of materials, Macmillan set to work. Although the
Treasury was inevitably his main adversary, Macmillan pays tribute in
his autobiography to what he learned from the Chancellor:

> Faced with the need for immediate restrictions, which he imposed
> over a wide field of consumer goods, and even extended to many
> capital projects, he always kept in mind the need for a positive as
> well as a negative policy. Even in the chill refrigerating chambers of
> Great George Street, he somehow preserved his warm, expansionist
> heart.[2]

Butler and Macmillan always had a certain sort of respect for each other, in spite of all that was to happen; and of course they had worked closely together on *The Industrial Charter* – even though Macmillan had tried to jump the gun on its publication with a speech anticipating its contents before it came out.

Anyway, Macmillan threw himself into the task of meeting the target. He gradually galvanised the ministry and secured the creation of an executive arm in regional housing boards. He greatly increased the permitted proportion of new private houses, while continuing to control the maximum size. He allowed the sale of municipal houses, subject to safeguards; and he encouraged the building of smaller houses by local authorities. With the aid of a style of what he himself described as a modified 'Beaverbrookism', an increase in council housing subsidies, and a strengthening economy he was able to topple the target by the end of 1953 – the figure for that calendar year in fact reached 318 000 odd. Factory building did not keep pace. There were those, Butler among them, who continued to think that housing absorbed too great a share of resources; but Macmillan achieved a major political, as well as administrative, triumph.

At the same time Macmillan faced up to the vexed question of development. In *Tides of Fortune* he describes his first encounter with the problem:

> There was a strange piece of legislation called the 'Town and Country Planning Act'. I had paid no attention to this measure while it was passing through Parliament in 1947. Nor can I claim that I – or indeed any of my advisers – ever fully understood it. But it involved a fiscal instrument known as the 'development charge', the result of which, if not perhaps the purpose, was to hold up all development.[3]

The 1947 Act had included a scheme by which the government would buy up all the potential development value of land in Britain in exchange for £300 million compensation, to be paid to owners by 30 June 1953. It also imposed the development charge by which owners selling land would have to hand over the excess value of it above its existing use value. This scheme was, as Macmillan saw, a disincentive to bring land forward, and Macmillan abolished it. Land in future was to change hands at market prices, while compensation from the £300 million fund was to be severely limited. At the same time, however, the planning notion of development control was retained. Argument continued for years to come as to whether development gains should be taxed, but the need for planning control never became a major political issue.

There was one other major housing question which Macmillan decided to tackle: the state of the private rented sector. He wrote in 1952: 'It is all right to put up the houses. The next job is to put up the rents'. He knew the risks – he warned Churchill not to mention the word 'rent' in a speech on housing he was to make in Scotland and he prefaced his proposals to the Cabinet with the words '*Quem deus vult perdere, prius dementat ...*' (Whom the gods wish to destroy, they first make mad). Nor were his proposals all that radical. He saw that the rented housing stock was deteriorating because rent control was making landlords feel that repairs were not worthwhile, but to raise the rents of millions of houses was bound to be politically very risky. Accordingly, when he brought forward his plans to the Cabinet in the Autumn of 1953, he stressed that there would need to be two years before an election in which the scheme would have time to work.

The essence of the scheme was to allow rents to rise provided that the landlord could show that the house was in good repair and carried out any necessary works. At the same time, improvement grants were to become more easily available so that the stock of acceptable housing would increase and the slums begin to diminish. It was also decided during the passage of the Bill to free from rent control new dwellings and those created by conversion where no subsidy was involved.

The Bill was controversial, but Labour's attack was weakened by the fact that, while Bevan had been arguing that the only answer to the rented housing problem was for local authorities to take it all over, Herbert Morrison knew that this was not feasible. This gave the government something with which to tease Labour. On the other hand, Macmillan himself admitted in *Tides of Fortune* that Bevan was probably right when he argued that the new permitted rent levels would not be enough to enable landlords to make the necessary repairs; and it cannot be said that the Conservatives won the political battle of rented housing over the next decade.

Macmillan left Housing for Defence in October 1954. When he moved he could look back to an increase in the number of permanent houses built from 194 831 in 1951 to 347 605 in 1954. This was back to peak pre-war levels. Towards the end of his time Macmillan was able to plan for some switch of emphasis from subsidising council building to meet 'general needs' to a resumption of the notable pre-war slum clearance campaign.

If housing was to the forefront in Churchill's government, health was less in evidence. In a way, this was surprising: for most of the period the Minister of Health was Iain Macleod, and he was not a man to conduct politics under a bushel. But inevitably the implementation of the NHS scheme, rather than any new development, was the main task; and money was the main constraint.

For the first year of Churchill's administration the minister was Captain Harry Crookshank. Crookshank was a well-liked and witty parliamentarian whose heart lay in his other role as Leader of the House. Certainly his diaries held at the Bodleian convey no sign that he had any great interest in the problems of health: with whom he had lunch and where he went to church receive much more attention. He did not even comment on his departure from the Ministry on the day he left it, 8 May 1952.

Churchill had given Macleod the job following a parliamentary *tour de force* by Macleod on 27 March. He spoke in the Second Reading debate on the Bill bringing dental charges and charges for drugs to hospital outpatients. Crookshank's opening speech had not been a success: no doubt this made all the more impressive Macleod's ringing confidence, his clear mastery of his subject and the gusto with which he took on Aneurin Bevan. Naturally he reminded the House that it was Labour that had first brought in the power to levy prescription charges, but he also argued that the charges should be no larger than necessary to achieve some deterrent effect.

Sir Nigel Fisher has described in his life of Macleod how after a quiet beginning he soon impressed the ministry.[4] He made it clear that he wanted a period of organisational tranquillity and then to get on with the job of leading the service in a tight financial period. As we have seen, priority in resources was going to housing, and it was a battle to obtain anything significant for hospital building: Macleod anyway was outside the Cabinet. Early on, in October 1952, Macleod said he would like to be the first Minister of Health who did not pass any legislation. He was almost as good as his word – he did bequeath a Dentists' Bill to his successor. There was a lot to be said for his message:

It is about time we stopped issuing paper and made the instructions work. I want to try and recreate local interest in the hospital and above everything to get a complete partnership between voluntary effort and the State.[5]

As Fisher puts it, his main concern was to humanise the health service. He took a particular interest in mental health and set up the Royal Commission under Lord Percy which was to lead to the 1959 Act. He also issued a circular which urged hospitals to allow parents to visit their children every day, instead of the all-too-prevalent once a week.

All this was good, humane Toryism; but at the same time the financial problems of the service had to be faced. In the manner of the times, a committee of inquiry was set up in May 1953, under a Cambridge economist, C. W. Guillebaud, to review the funding of the service. It reported[6] nearly three years later that the structure was sound enough, though there were still problems to do with co-operation: the real need, however, was a period of stability.

All this probably made sense at the time, but already there was unease about how to fund the open-ended service. Education, too, was very much a matter of resources, with a rather weak minister, Florence Horsbrugh, initially in charge. The end-of-war bulge in the birthrate was causing great pressure. The number of children aged 5 and over rose from 4.8 million in 1947 to an estimated 6.4 million in 1955. School building gradually increased and more teachers were recruited; but it was becoming increasingly apparent that Britain suffered from serious shortages of maths and science teachers, and that the whole question of scientific and technological education needed to be grasped. Sir David Eccles replaced Miss Horsbrugh in 1954 and under the Eden government big advances were made.

One other major political/educational argument began to emerge. In a policy statement, *Challenge to Britain*, the Labour party committed itself to the abolition of the eleven-plus and the principle of the single comprehensive school, claiming both educational and social reasons for doing so. It was the beginning of a long battle.

Churchill's government came to an end when he resigned on 5 April 1955. He had not of course taken an immense interest in social policy, but every now and then something would spark his attention – perhaps recalling old battles about national insurance in his Liberal days; and the record of his peacetime administration was one of useful conventional progress, although with resources still hard-pressed to meet needs. In one area where a radical change was considered by Cabinet – the possibility of restrictions on Commonwealth immigration – the matter was dropped as politically controversial.

Was there any serious attempt to consider an altogether more selective approach to social policy, with concentration of resources on real need and more extensive charging, on the lines which *One Nation* had begun to adumbrate? A speech at Oxford on 9 July 1954 by Butler might suggest that there was. He certainly drew a sharp distinction between the conservative and socialist approaches.

We are confronted with the Socialist concept of the social services as a levelling instrument, a means of ensuring that everyone shall have just the same average uniform standard of life. Wherever we meet it, we can see how self-defeating this concept must be.

In education, a blind faith in the unproven virtues of the comprehensive secondary school, to which all must go, could mean denial of opportunity to the most able children.

In health, an obsession with the principle of a free service could mean and did mean, between 1948 and 1951, a denial of adequate treatment towards those in greatest need.

In housing, a concentration on council building could mean, and did mean, throughout the period of Socialist Government, a denial of homes to tens of thousands who could have been housed, and are now being housed, under methods which impose less burdens on their fellow tax-payers and rate-payers.

It is our policy to give real help to the weak. It is no part of our policy to repress the initiative and independence of the strong. Indeed, unless we allow men to rise as far as they may, and so allow our society to be served by the richness of developed differences, we shall not have the means to earn our national living, let alone to afford a welfare state.

As Butler indicated, health charges had become accepted and private house building had been successfully revived; but for the most part there had not been much change in the direction of social policy. The economic revival had made it possible to increase national insurance benefits and family allowances, but there was no move towards selectivity in this field and nearly all the tax reductions were aimed at the ordinary taxpayer rather than the better off.

The general election came on 26 May 1955; between that time and Eden's resignation on 9 January 1957, there is not a great deal to record in the field of social policy. The Tory election manifesto *United for Peace and Progress* contained no surprises. It stressed the idea of the property-owning democracy – the phrase which Eden popularised.

In education, it rejected comprehensive schools, and drew attention to the need to extend scientific and technical training. It ranked new hospital building and preventive work above 'free wigs or free aspirins', thus making it clear that charges would continue. It also introduced something of a new theme – the problems of local government finance and the proper allocation of local authority functions.

Eden himself had little experience, and no very sure touch, in social policy, but he tended to breathe down his ministers' necks. In fact, the climate soon became more difficult, for after the rising economic tide of Churchill's years there was a sharp setback in the Autumn of 1955. During the summer the economy had become overheated and there was a serious drain on Britain's gold and dollar reserves. Eden was already planning to replace Butler (who had anyway been lowered by his wife's illness and death). He did not do so, however, until after Butler had brought in an Autumn budget on 26 October 1955 which was a sad anti-climax to a very successful chancellorship.

Butler presented his measures as dealing with the problems of success:

In addressing ourselves to the cause and cure of our growing pains, we must reflect that we have not experienced the problems of a free economy for some seventeen years ... that we are sustaining, and mean to continue to sustain, a system of social services which is the envy of the world.

But we needed both incentive and restraint.

In practical terms, restraint meant reducing the general subsidy on local authority housing from £22 per house to £10, with a view ultimately to abolishing it. It also involved asking local authorities to reduce the other capital expenditure and tighter lending by the Public Works Loan Board, together with an end to the fixed contribution from rates to housing revenue accounts. All this meant that council rents would rise. Duncan Sandys, the Minister of Housing, linked this to the need to review the provisions of the existing Rent Act, which covered the private sector, foreshadowing the 1957 Rent Act.

Sandys introduced another theme when he introduced the Housing Subsidies Bill which implemented this on 17 November 1955:

Hitherto, all flats have been subsidised at the same rate regardless of the height of the building. Since construction, in practice, costs

more as you go higher, the result has been that flats in low blocks have
been more heavily subsidised in relation to costs than flats in high
blocks. Apart from being inequitable, this has unintentionally
influenced local authorities to concentrate on building blocks of
three, four and five storeys, which, I believe, many Hon Members
will agree are most monotonous.

Nobody seems to have dissented from this unhappy proposal to provide
extra subsidy for high-rise blocks which helped to produce a good deal of
misery over the years to come. The opposition spokesman, G. S.
Lindgren, rather concentrated on stressing that the Chancellor's
problems had largely risen from the strain on the economy caused by the
300 000 a year target.

Probably the most significant development in domestic policy under
Eden was the programme for the expansion of technical education
launched by Sir David Eccles in his white paper[7] published in February
1956. The plan did not require legislation and it was based on a voluntary
system: but it set out clear targets. Its impetus had come from the sudden
realisation that Britain was falling badly behind, and in particular that
we were being surpassed by the Soviet Union. Churchill in a speech in
December 1955 made the point with great force, and in 1957 the first
space flight by the Russian Sputnik was to illustrate it vividly. Indeed, it
was by using the Russian threat that Eccles was able to win Churchill's
initial support while he was still Prime Minister.

Eccles's plan was to take the form of a five-year programme. It
embraced £97 million of technical college building, to be immune from
cuts or postponements; some twelve new Colleges of Advanced
Technology; increased funding for advanced courses; an increase in the
annual output of students on advanced courses in technical colleges
from 9500 to about 15 000; and an expansion in university technology,
on top of an existing project to raise the capacity of Imperial College,
London, from 1650 to 3000 full-time students over the same period.

Eccles's programme (largely drawn up by an able civil servant,
Antony Part) was an impressive piece of government; and it was put into
effect with vigour. Later on, the so-called CATS were mostly to turn
into universities. Overall, it was one of the most serious attempts in
post-war Britain to uprate our economic performance.

The 1956 legislative programme contained a few modest but useful
measures – some social security improvements and the Clean Air Act
among them; but even if Eden had seen himself as a great social
reformer the Suez crisis would have put paid to his aspirations. It was a

dismal decline and fall; yet there is little doubt that over the period of Churchill and Eden the condition of the people had steadily improved. The houses went up, the notion of food as a social service declined and food became plentiful, education expanded and cash benefits generally moved upwards. And behind this there was a new liveliness in Conservative political thinking. The Conservative Political Centre published some worthwhile pamphlets and a group of Cambridge graduates founded the Bow Group in 1951 – among them Geoffrey Howe. Overall it was a time of promise.

4 1957–64: The Middle Ground

Harold Macmillan's years in office were marked by some lively debate on social policy: the Conservative Political Centre produced a succession of spirited pamphlets, including several from the Bow Group: the Institute of Economic Affairs was founded to restore the notion of the market, not only in economic but in social policy; the One Nation group continued to be active in Parliament; and there was generally a greater willingness to challenge the assumptions of the Coalition days.

Neither Macmillan nor Butler did anything to damp this down – they both were, and liked to feel, patrons of the young and open-minded. Nevertheless, Macmillan remained firmly where he had always stood – in the middle way. He gave a lecture to the Conservative Political Centre in March 1958 on 'The Middle Way: 20 Years After' in which he reiterated his view:

> Our Tory Party, which stressed the claims of authority (the need for the State to protect the weak) in the nineteenth century, and which champions the claims of liberty in the twentieth century, has not changed its ground; it is still occupying the same ground, the middle ground. It is only the direction of the attack which has altered. We do not stand and have never stood for collectivism or the destruction of private rights. We do not stand and have never stood for *laissez-faire* individualism or for putting the rights of the individual above his duty to his fellow men. We stand today, as we always stood, to block the way to both these extremes and to all such extremes, and to point the path towards moderate and balanced views.

And then he went on to remind his audience of the scourge of unemployment as he had seen it in his inter-war years as an MP on Tees-side: 'I am determined, as far as it lies within human power, never to allow this shadow to fall again upon our country'.[1] It was a theme he never forgot.

In fact social policy does not seem to have taken up much of his time as Prime Minister: certainly there are very few references to it in his autobiography for that period. But there was one significant incident a year after he took over – the resignation of Peter Thorneycroft as Chancellor of the Exchequer, together with his fellow Treasury ministers, Enoch Powell and Nigel Birch, in January 1958. It was this, of course, that Macmillan dismissed as 'a little local difficulty', as he set out on an overseas visit.

Thorneycroft – the old leader of the Tory Reform Committee –explained his view in the Commons on 23 January 1958 as to why public expenditure should be cut by some £50 million to offset certain increases:

> For twelve years we have been attempting to do more than our resources could manage, and in the process we have been gravely weakening ourselves. We have, in a sense, been trying to do two things at the same time. First, we have sought to be a nuclear power ... and with large ... conventional forces in the Far East, the Middle East and the Atlantic ... At the same time, we have sought to maintain a Welfare State at as high a level as – sometimes even a higher level than – that of the United States of America.

To Thorneycroft, and perhaps even more to Birch and Powell, the fight against inflation had now become fundamental; but to Macmillan and the Cabinet at large the resignations seemed unnecessary. In political terms, at least, Macmillan's judgement was right: he rode the resignations without trouble. Lord Boyd-Carpenter in his memoirs, *Way of Life*,[2] says that if the Chancellor's proposal to withdraw family allowances for the second child in each family had been accepted *he* would have resigned, while Derek Walker-Smith, new Minister of Health, argued against health cuts. Various attempts at compromise were made, but in the end Thorneycroft was not able to get the 1958–9 estimates back to 1957–8 totals, and he went. He was fighting against the mood of the times and the Prime Minister.

That is not to say that all was emollience under Macmillan.

The previous year had seen the passing of the 1957 Rent Act. Macmillan had, as we have seen, recognised the need to tackle the private rented sector – hence the 1954 legislation. But he had been guided by Churchill's admonition that legislation to amend the rent restriction acts must be so designed as to bring no financial benefits to landlords: it should simply enable them to finance repairs. The 1957 Act went very much further.

Its aim was to stimulate the private rented sector by allowing more realistic rents. All new lettings and future vacancies were removed from rent control and security of tenure provisions. So were privately rented houses with a high rateable value, although the removal of security of tenure was to be phased in gradually. In addition, the Act provided that the rents of those houses which remained controlled should move to a more realistic level. Initially, six out of seven rented houses would remain controlled, but the number would gradually fall as vacant possession occurred.

The Second Reading of the Bill was moved on 21 November 1956 by the Parliamentary Secretary, Enoch Powell. (The Minister of Housing, Duncan Sandys, wound up the debate – nowadays, with an eye to media deadlines, the senior minister will always open the debate). Powell argued that the housing shortage was ending – within twelve months or so there should be an overall balance between supply and demand. Controlled rents were leading to owners selling where they could. He said that he did not believe that people would be unwilling to pay the current value of their accommodation or want to become 'the universal tenants of the local authorities'.

Powell ended on a 'One Nation' note:

It is a caricature of our society to see it divided into antagonistic classes and sections with mutually opposing interests – employers against employees, suppliers against consumers, landlords against tenants ... if our laws are justly and reasonably framed, the profit and advantage of one section is the gain and not the loss of another section, the gain of one can contribute and should contribute to the comfort and convenience of the other and the nation can be richer and stronger by the mutual and not conflicting interests of both.

Labour attacked the Bill strongly, and James Callaghan, winding up for the opposition, took a firmly socialist line:

Landlordism is at an end in this country. This is the last attempt to shore it up, and I assure the Minister that it will fail, and housing will take its own place alongside the other social services – alongside education, the health service and the pensions Acts. We dismiss the concept that housing and homes are a commodity that can be bought and sold in the market place.

If events constitute the verdict of history, it has to be said that the 1957 Rent Act came to a sticky end; but Callaghan's statement now seems to have a very period flavour to it, although subsidies, benefits and tax relief still leave housing well short of a free market.

It was not, in fact, until the beginning of the 1960s that strong hostility to the 1957 Act really got under way – some of its decontrol provisions did not come in until 1961. In general, its impact was not particularly dramatic. Not all landlords put up their rents, but decontrol did not produce the hoped-for revival of the sector. Instead, it provided the chance for landlords to sell up to owner-occupiers, while potential investors were frightened off by political uncertainties. By the 1960s, the phenomenon of Rachmanism – the driving out of sitting tenants by the most unscrupulous methods – had become a luridly publicised scandal: the aim was either to charge a far higher rent or to sell off the property. Probably more important, however, was the fact that there was as yet no form of subsidy for the private tenant: it was not until the Heath government that the rent allowance was brought in.

Welcome pieces of social legislation in 1957 were two National Insurance Acts. The first enabled retirement and widow pensioners under age 70 for men and 65 for women to revoke their declarations of retirement and thus earn additions to their pensions when they ceased to work, as well as certain other improvements; the second provided increases in national insurance and industrial injury benefits.

The next year, 1958, brought two significant Acts. The first was a Local Government Act which was designed to give greater independence to local authorities. The particular mechanism for doing this was the general grant (or block grant) which replaced a number of specific or percentage grants. The new scheme covered education (except milk and meals), health and welfare, fire services and child care. Labour opposed this on the grounds that it would hamper the development of essential social services, particularly education and health, and also that the Bill failed fully to rerate industry; but Henry Brooke, the Minister of Housing and Local Government, had no great difficulty in passing his Bill. The education world was nervous that it might suffer from the general grant, but history does not seem to support these anxieties. For what it is worth, an answer to a parliamentary question on 11 March 1988 said that in 1958 education's share of total local authority spending in the UK was 41.4 per cent. In 1986, it was 41.8 per cent.

The second measure was the 1958 Children Act which gave local authorities greater responsibilities in relation to foster children and adoption.

This concern with the problems of family life and the individual was expressed a year later in the major 1959 Mental Health Act. The Act followed a Royal Commission, and also a well-argued Bow Group pamphlet, *Minds Matter*, written by Beryl Cooper.[3] The essence of the Act was to give as much treatment as possible on an informal and voluntary basis, but where compulsion *was* necessary to make sure that there was suitable protection for the individual, but also for the public at large. The Act ended the separate designation of mental and mental deficiency hospitals, and marked an important step towards the treatment of mental illness as another form of sickness. The categories of idiots, imbeciles, feeble minded and moral defectives were replaced by more modern definitions. A tribunal was brought in to hear challenges to compulsory admission. Psychiatric illness has continued to throw up difficult problems, but it is hard to doubt that the Act (which was unopposed in Parliament) was a real advance.

The other major piece of legislation in 1959 was John Boyd-Carpenter's National Insurance Act.

For some time there had been pressure to introduce a new pensions scheme, and the Labour party had come up with the Crossman plan, devised largely by Professor Richard Titmuss and his colleagues. There were several reasons for the pressure. The cost of retirement pensions was rising steeply, with the number of pensioners expected to rise from about 5¼ million to about 7½ million in 1980. Contribution income would not keep pace with demand – and of course the scheme still carried many pensioners who had very limited contribution records. At the same time more and more people wanted to provide in their retirement for something above the basic pension. Private occupational schemes were spreading, but it was felt that the state should offer a scheme as well.

On the Labour side, the aim was a generous state scheme with which the private sector would find it very difficult to compete. The funds raised would be available for the state to buy shares in private industry, the so-called 'back-door nationalisation'. A high rate of contributions would be required from employees, employers and government. Conservatives argued that the effect would be inflationary.

Boyd-Carpenter's approach was more modest. He provided a graduated scheme for those with earnings above £9 a week: its upper limit was £15 a week, as opposed to Labour's £40. He encouraged good occupational schemes to contract out of the graduated scheme. He also helped the lower paid by concentrating the Exchequer subsidy on them, at some cost to those better off, who did not fare proportionately so well. Overall the aim was to limit the Exchequer contribution. The scheme proved reasonably serviceable for the next few years or so, but it did not provide a long-term answer to the demand for better pensions.

The year 1959 was an election year – Macmillan's triumph marked the climax of a generally prosperous decade and a remarkable resurgence from the nadir of Suez. It is worth using it to provide a snapshot of the way in which Tory social thinking was developing at the time.

One source is the substantially revised version of *The Conservative Case* by Lord Hailsham,[4] by now the party chairman. The chapter on social provision in the new volume was more impressive than that in the 1947 book – how far this was due to the assistance of Peter Goldman, the director of the Conservative Political Centre, is not clear.

The new chapter picks up an old theme by referring to a broadcast statement by Attlee in 1948 that: 'In the building up of the great structure of our social services, all parties in the state have borne their part'.

Hailsham goes on to illustrate the point by some familiar examples, but then turns to the fundamental difference between the parties:

The Conservative theory is that despite obvious divergences of interest, rich and poor are united in a common brotherhood... and that, while a redistribution of property... may be no bad thing from time to time, the incentive of inequality, if inequality corresponds to skill and energy, is one of the main means whereby new wealth can be created, and active characters spurred on to produce of their best – to the great advantage of mankind at large.

A little later he reiterates the point:

Conservatives believe that in a free society the incentives to make oneself unequal are a necessary part of the mechanism of creating new wealth and therefore new welfare.

Hailsham goes on to argue against a state monopoly of welfare on three grounds. He favours the 'life-giving principle of voluntary action'; he believes that it is generally the individual and not the State which is the pioneer of progress; and he argues that it is an essential condition of a free society that a man may make his own provision, rather than be compelled to use state services.

The crucial point in all this is probably the argument that economic inequality and incentives will lead to greater wealth *all-round* than will a more socialist and egalitarian approach. The gap between rich and poor may widen, but in real terms the poor, as well as the rich, are gainers.

At the same time another theme was becoming of more concern to Conservatives: the to-this-day unresolved conflict between universal and selective or targeted services. The One Nation group, for example, in their 1959 pamphlet *The Responsible Society* (CPC) said of the 1959 National Insurance Act: 'Thus we move slightly, but significantly away from a flat service, regardless of needs or means, and towards giving help where it is most needed. Socially it is just. Economically it is sound'.[5] But in reality the key word in this remark was probably 'slightly'. In spite of the rhetoric, there was in practice little selectivity. The health service, family allowances and education remained effectively free for all, and the selectivity in the national insurance scheme was still very limited.

An article by Brendon Sewill in the Bow Group's journal *Crossbow* (Summer 1959) on 'Reshaping Welfare' gives another good picture of thinking at that time – the more so as Sewill was a leading member of the Conservative Research Department.[6] He admits that it is hard to find a Conservative philosophy that can be applied consistently to the social services. The concept of the net to catch those who fall off the ladder of opportunity is not easily reconciled with the health service, family allowances or wage-related pensions. He accepts the principle of compulsory insurance against unemployment and for old age, so that benefits are payable as of right and not as State charity. He makes the point that compulsion should not extend above subsistence level, yet acknowledges that in effect the government had breached this view. Perhaps more significantly he argues that the pressure to keep down public expenditure will always mean that the standard of state services will be less good than if the service were not free:

It would be a sad paradox if the system designed to improve the nation's health and education ended by stultifying progress in these fields.

Sewill asks why the State should be so concerned to run services itself, rather than simply providing the money with which citizens could purchase services, perhaps through voucher schemes. (The idea of the education voucher had recently been introduced to the British scene by the economist, Jack Wiseman.) Sewill also advocated a tax reduction equivalent to the per capita cost of the NHS to those who subscribed to health insurance schemes.

But although Sewill was adumbrating some radical ideas, he suggested that he was talking about a 25-year time scale; and indeed both the ideas in the last paragraph were still no more than ideas for discussion 25 years later – and it was about then that the Secretary for Education, Sir Keith Joseph, rejected the idea of the voucher. And whatever ideas Sewill, the Bow Group, the IEA and others may have been floating in 1959, the manifesto of that year, *The Next Five Years*, did nothing to encourage them. In education the stress was on more provision (plus a rebuttal of Labour's doctrinaire attack on the grammar schools). On housing, the emphasis was on slum clearance and the importance of both local authorities and private enterprise working to meet needs, with the idea of massive municipalisation rejected. Interestingly, there was to be no further action to decontrol rents in the next Parliament – the recent legislation needed time to increase 'house-room'. Alarm bells were beginning to be heard. For health there was to be a big programme of hospital building. Both pensioners and those on national assistance were to continue to share in the country's increasing prosperity. No significant changes were foretold.

It was emphatically not a manifesto to stir up political trouble, and it helped to do the trick. But by the beginning of the 1960s more radical ideas were spreading.

One pioneering contribution was a Hobart Paper published in 1961 by the IEA, *Health Through Choice*.[7] In it, D. S. Lees of Keele University advanced the view that medical care should increasingly be based on consumer choice and supplied through the market. He argued that under the NHS political decisions replaced personal choice, and that as a consequence of this expenditure on the NHS was probably less than it would have been in a free market. The insistence on a single standard of service and the concentration of power in the hands of the minister makes for less adaptation to change and freedom to experiment, as well as discontented professions. Hospital costs could be covered by private insurance, with subsidies where needed to hospitals and insurance institutions. There should be tax relief to those who insured themselves.

Lees made other provocative points. He backed the view that health care should not be seen as an investment but as a consumption good. He held that there was little evidence that the NHS had made a decisive contribution to improvements in health. He saw, as others had done, that it was the middle classes who were the chief beneficiaries of the scheme. He rejected the view that old people would *always* tend to be too poor to pay for their health care – 'The problem of residual poverty is one of *our* time and not for all time to come'.

This last statement may still seem utopian, but *Health Through Choice* was a brilliant essay. Right up to 1987 official Conservative party policy shied away from Lees's approach, feeling that the NHS was too popular an institution to replace or even seriously question. But Lees had caused in the pond ripples which never quite disappeared. With the third Thatcher government the whole question suddenly became very topical.

Lees's publisher, the Institute of Economic Affairs, could very reasonably claim that this showed how ideas could work their way through the entrenched wisdom of the day. In the realm of social policy, the IEA was to follow this with their own campaign for increasing choice in welfare and for ideas such as the education voucher. And although Ralph Harris and Arthur Seldon – the IEA's two intellectual entrepreneurs – always eschewed party alignment, the fact was that it was overwhelmingly Conservatives – *some* Conservatives – who found their ideas attractive. Most Liberals had long since abandoned nineteenth-century liberalism.

Another source of new ideas within the Conservative party continued to be the Bow Group, both through its pamphlets and *Crossbow*. One pamphlet, *Principles in Practice*, contained an essay of particular interest by Geoffrey Howe – the Bow Group's most active thinker on social policy at that time.[8]

Howe firmly rejected the view that social policy should be about equalising incomes:

> There is no justification for taking tax from some to meet the needs of others which they can meet themselves. Our tax structure should be as non-progressive as possible.

Nor should the social services be seen as 'a badge of citizenship' – an idea associated with the Titmuss school. But poverty and hardship should be tackled and taxes raised to meet them (but not to achieve redistribution *per se*). And 'Few Conservatives would doubt that the social services are for the most part here to stay' – though interestingly Howe adds that:

> We should hesitate to agree with Sir Keith Joseph who, while seeking 'scope for sensible men to provide additional protection or

amenity for their families and themselves *on top of* the State provision' plainly expects the State to go on making the basic provision for all of us for ever.

But that was the first Sir Keith.

Howe acknowledges that the pressure to perpetuate State provision was strong. There was pressure for higher rather than minimum standards of provision, and the 'middle classes seem increasingly anxious to surrender their independence in favour of free drugs for private patients or university scholarships for their children regardless of means'. Even Enoch Powell had concluded that 'universal provision regardless of the means of the recipient is coming to be the typical form of social service'.

But this was a long way from the tradition of individual freedom to spend wealth as one wishes on which Howe says he was brought up. Those willing to provide for the health and education of their families should be given every encouragement to do so.

The first task is the relief of primary poverty, or the removal of want, particularly through national assistance, social insurance and family allowances. All three should be subjected to means tests – including the retirement pension on the grounds that it was largely financed from general taxation. The real objection to the means test has always been that it is so mean. This should not be the case, argued Howe – and the means of implementing an effective policy was to hand in a merging of tax and benefits, an idea that was to become increasingly prominent over the next decade or more.

On health, Howe favoured an approach similar to Lees's – an insurance scheme which would help to return health to the private sector. For education Howe favoured the voucher scheme and the retention of the parental contribution to student grants (the argument in those days was about whether it should be abolished), both for economic reasons and to check dependence on the state. And support for housing should be concentrated on specific need, with rent subsidies going not to houses, but to council and private tenants alike.

This generally radical approach was designed to counter what has more recently come to be termed the 'dependency culture'. Some of the ideas have since been implemented, some have not; but the pattern of thinking was very different from that of the post-war years.

It was not likely that a Macmillan government would go very far down this path; and the party's backroom boys – perhaps intellectually disposed to be radical – nevertheless proved fairly cautious when it came to recommending what should actually be done. A Research Department group chaired by Michael Fraser reported in April 1961 on the 'Future of the Social Services'. They said that while they began with a bias in favour of radical change the general conclusion was that for most of the social services existing or planned provisions for finance were broadly on the right lines.

Some changes *were* offered. The suggestion that future pensions increases should be selective was held to be incompatible with the last manifesto, but family allowances might be increased for the fourth and subsequent children. School meals and milk subsidies might be cut back, but the savings might go to enhanced family allowances. Employers might have to pay more towards the health element in national insurance and private patients should receive free drugs and only have to pay the excess above the cost of board, accommodation and nursing in a public ward. A majority of the committee were against any direct payments for education. Little remained of the early radicalism, and what there was was not implemented.

Except at the Home Office, this was not anyway a period of striking social legislation. National insurance benefits were uprated on several occasions and other improvements made. The 1961 Housing Act gave higher subsidies to the needier councils and less to the better-off. The 1962 Education Act made student grants more generous and reduced the number of school-leaving dates; another Act in 1964 gave more freedom to vary the age of transfer between primary and secondary schools.

More significant was the 1963 London Government Act which reformed the structure of local government in the Greater London Area. For some time it had been argued that the combination of the London County Council in inner London and a proliferation of often smallish boroughs across London, together with counties in the outer areas of the conurbation, made for a lack of coherence and ability to plan in the metropolis as a whole. A Commission under Sir Edwin Herbert was set to work and came up with a two-tier pattern of the Greater London Council and 32 largish boroughs.[9] The GLC was to be a strategic planning authority, but it should also have executive powers in a number of respects – for instance over fire and ambulance services, certain parks and (shared with the boroughs) housing. The boroughs were to run the local services. The government broadly enacted the Herbert plan – with one important exception. Whereas Herbert proposed that education should go to the boroughs, the government decided that in inner London – the old LCC area – it should be run by an Inner London Education Authority: this latter was to be reviewed in 1970. The arguments that child care should also be treated in this way were rejected. In the event, the boroughs often seemed artificial and sometimes remote, but gradually they became familiar even if not always well-loved.

The extension of the top-tier body to the whole London region gave the Conservatives a chance of winning it which they scarcely had with the old LCC. For three years at the end of the sixties they actually held ILEA as well.

Apart from the creation of ILEA, the period at the end of the 1950s and the beginning of the 1960s was not one of great significance *legislatively* for education; but it was one when education rose increasingly high on the political agenda. It was an era of major reports – the Crowther Report (1959) on the 15 to 18 age group;[10] the Newsom Report (1963) on children of 13 to 16, of average and less than average ability;[11] the Robbins Report (1963) on higher education;[12] and then the Plowden Report (1967) on primary education.[13] This last was set up by Sir Edward Boyle in 1963, but reported to a Labour government.

All these were very much documents of their era – generally expansionist, optimistic, 'progressive'. They were, by and large, consensus documents, the product of long periods of evidence-taking and discussion. But there were some controversies. Robbins's belief that major expansion was possible without a fall of standards was challenged in Kingsley Amis's famous phrase 'More means worse' – and he was not alone in fearing for quality. Nor was the leaning towards comprehensive secondary education in both Newsom and Plowden to meet with universal agreement. Indeed, this was to be the major political battleground in education for the next decade.

The party had to wrestle with the fact that there was mounting dislike of the eleven-plus examination but a strong desire among Conservatives at large to keep the grammar schools. The 1959 manifesto had stated that:

> We shall defend the grammar schools against doctrinaire Socialist attack, and see that they are further developed. We shall bring the modern schools up to the same high standard.

Five years later, the 1964 manifesto had a somewhat different tone to that of 1959:

> Of the many different forms of secondary school organisation which now exist, none has established itself as exclusively right. The Socialist plan to impose the comprehensive principle, regardless of

the wish of parents, teachers and authorities, is therefore foolishly doctrinaire. Their leader may protest that grammar schools will be abolished 'over his dead body', but abolition would be the inevitable and disastrous consequence of the policy to which they are committed. Conservative policy, by contrast, is to encourage provision, in good schools of every description, of opportunities for all children to go forward to the limit of their capacity.[14]

It is clear that Sir Edward Boyle, who was Minister of Education at that time, was althogether more sympathetic to comprehensive schools than were many Conservative supporters. This is reflected in the correspondence between him and the Conservative and Unionist Teachers' Association from 1962 onwards (held in the Bodleian Library). He wanted proposals for comprehensives to be judged on their merits rather than on dogma, and felt that the party should be sympathetic to experiment in this field. The sticking point should be to resist any proposal which forced local authorities to go comprehensive – ground to which the party adhered for a long time.

Boyle was to have other differences of opinion with some Tory supporters – for instance over his defence of the right of his Principal Medical Adviser to make a speech accepting the idea of pre-marital intercourse. His relationship with his party was not always easy.

One other significant area of social policy which came alive under the Macmillan government was that of the Home Office. R. A. Butler had become Home Secretary when Macmillan formed his government in January 1957; he remained in that post until Macmillan's famous July reshuffle in 1962. It was a notable tenure of office to which I suspect justice was not quite done either in Anthony Howard's otherwise admirable biography of Butler or indeed by Butler himself in *The Art of the Possible*.

It was a long time since the Home Office had been seen as a reforming department: its ethos seemed almost to be chiselled in hard rock by equally tough permanent secretaries. But under Butler it started to take the initiative. The first measure was one that was already going through the Commons when he took over: the 1957 Homicide Act. It was a compromise measure which left the death penalty for only a limited number of types of murder: he carried it through skilfully, though it left him with what he called the 'hideous responsibility' of reviewing each case to see if the prerogative of mercy should be applied. In *The Art of the Possible* he wrote that 'By the end of my time at the Home Office I began to see that the system could not go on'.

In the penal field Butler felt that his most important work lay in the 1959 white paper, *Penal Practice in a Changing Society*.[15] This comprehensive statement led to research programmes both in the Home Office and at Cambridge; to a large prison building programme; and to more Borstal accommodation, young prisoners' centres and detention centres. The emphasis was on training and reform, and Butler rejected the demands for the reintroduction of corporal punishment. He had the usual difficulties with the Conservative party conference, but in 1961 in particular he had a considerable success in his handling of the crime and punishment debate.

But Butler was not an out-and-out liberal in the handling of Home Office affairs. He translated one half of the Wolfenden Report[16] – that on prostitution – successfully onto the Statute book but declined to tackle the other part, on homosexual practices, arguing that public opinion was not ready for it. He modernised charity law with the Charities Act of 1960. In the same year he obtained the Betting and Gaming Act, a successful balance between freedom and control. There were a Licensing Act, a Criminal Justice Act and a Betting Levy Act in 1961 – all again mildly liberalising, pragmatic measures which could certainly not be branded as permissive.

There was also the Commonwealth Immigrants Act of 1962. For a number of years there had been mounting political pressure for legislation. The issue had been considered around the time of the 1955 election campaign, but it was ignored in the manifesto. There was discussion of the possibility of controls during the drafting of the 1959 manifesto; but in the event there was no reference to it. Instead there was a statement that 'It will continue to be our policy to protect the citizen, irrespective of creed or colour, against lawlessness'. In that year there were 21 000 Commonwealth immigrants, but by 1961 the number rose to 136 000 and the government decided to legislate. Butler, like others of his older colleagues who were steeped in the old imperial traditions, did not take easily to the legislation (which introduced a system of work permits). He got the measure through but his lack of enthusiasm for it was evident. He did not like being savaged for illiberality – and drew consolation when Labour kept the measure. It was the last significant piece of legislation by the most fertile Tory social policy maker since Peel: his last two years in government were primarily concerned with overseas affairs.

Somewhat over a year later, in October 1963, Harold Macmillan resigned as Prime Minister. He had not had a great deal of time to devote to social policy in recent years – his particular grand scheme for

British recovery had been increasingly focused on entry into the European Common Market. There is no evidence that he was particularly involved in the new thinking that was beginning to bubble up: his ideas had been shaped by earlier experiences. But he liked to feel that the party was open to ideas, particularly from the young, and the Conservative party machine saw its role (particularly through the CPC) as something more than the mere dissemination of party propaganda.

Sir Alec Douglas-Home, his successor, hardly had time to make much mark on social policy, though a few useful measures were passed during his prime ministership, and it was he that accepted the Robbins report on higher education. For some time anyway the leadership in terms of policy initiative had been passing increasingly from Butler to Edward Heath. As Chief Whip he had already developed the practice of calling together gatherings of senior and junior members of the party to discuss policy at Swinton Conservative College in Yorkshire, and under Douglas-Home Heath's impact was probably increased by the absence from the government of Macleod and Powell.

If history has come to a verdict on the thirteen Conservative years, it is that while much occurred to make people's lives better, not enough was done to tackle our economic weaknesses. The social services expanded alongside consumer expenditure. Expectations were rising the whole time, without the economic strength to meet them. Right up to the 1964 election the rival parties continued to play the 'anything-you-can-do' theme. The 1964 Conservative Manifesto set out a straightforward list of achievements and aims which showed little signs of a change from the familiar post-war direction. It was said that help would be concentrated on needs, but there was little sign that that was to be translated into specific policies, beyond a review of social security and special provision for older pensioners. The area where the party was most on the defensive was probably private rented housing. The Milner-Holland report on what had happened in London was on the way, triggered off by Rachmanism.[17] As we have seen, the manifesto contained a pledge that there would be no further steps to decontrol in the next Parliament.

But it was not on social policy that the campaign was primarily fought – after all, an April 1964 Gallup poll reported that 92 per cent of the upper class and 87 per cent of the lower class was satisfied with the NHS; rather it was to do with a feeling that we should modernise our economy and institutions as a whole, as well as the sense that it was time for a change of government. In October 1964 the change of government duly took place.

5 1964–70: Heath in Opposition

Although Sir Alec Douglas-Home remained Leader of the Conservative Party after the election defeat until July 1965, Edward Heath was very much at the helm as far as policy-making was concerned. The fact that Labour's narrow majority meant that another election could not be far away, together with Heath's own energetic temperament, ensured that there was no disposition to sit back and draw a deep breath after the long years of Tory rule.

Labour had come in, at least in part, on a wave of feeling that the country needed radical change, particularly in the economic and industrial sphere, but also in areas like education; and there was a widespread stress on efficiency and the importance of institutional reform.

A spate of books had been published on what was wrong with Britain. There were plenty of Conservatives who responded to the radicalism of the day. Some were sympathetic to ideas of indicative planning and also to ideas which later came to be stamped or condemned as corporatism – the notions, in particular, of incomes policy and government embracing a kind of partnership with industry and the unions, working through such instruments as the National Economic Development Council (set up in July 1961 when Selwyn Lloyd was Chancellor of the Exchequer). There was considerable interest in the German system of co-partnership, with union representation on the top tier boards of companies. And overriding everything was a firm commitment to the possibility of more rapid growth – economically, of course, but in education and the social services as well.

This climate of change appealed to the active young men and women of the Bow Group and others of their ilk. One of them, David Howell, became Director of the Conservative Political Centre, and rapidly launched a series of short pamphlets under the heading 'New Tasks'. He himself wrote one called *Efficiency and Beyond*,[1] which was a re-examination of our long-term economic goals. I contributed one called *Conflict and Conservatism*, which caused a minor stir by its attack on consensus and willingness to accept some measure of conflict in society and 'to risk the tension that may arise from a greater readiness to root out our weaknesses, for instance in industrial relations or the pattern of our social services'.[2] I believe that Edward Heath was not best pleased with this pamphlet.

But more directly aimed at social policy were two pamphlets by Geoffrey Howe and John MacGregor. Howe's was called *In Place of Beveridge*. In a number of ways presciently, it tackled the future of our pensions systems. In essence, it argued the case for expanding private pension schemes, casting doubts on whether it had been right to introduce the state graduated pension scheme. It stressed the crucial importance of tackling inflation if pensions were to be adequate. It argued for allowing every employed or self-employed person to be given tax relief on 15 per cent of their gross remuneration if saved contractually for retirement; called for legislation to make pensions portable; and asked for a special commission to supervise and approve occupation schemes. The overall aim was 'a system of self-provision for the £40-a-week wage earners who will be typical of our society by the end of the century'.[3] The £40-a-week label has proved an under-estimate, but a fair amount of what Howe asked for has come to pass, and we are moving steadily to the point where occupational second pensions make old age very much easier for many of our people.

Howe's pamphlet came out in April 1965; MacGregor's, on *Housing Ourselves*, followed a month later.[4] Housing had proved the most difficult aspect of social policy in the latter days of the Conservative government, particularly because of the difficulties of rented housing in London and other big cities. The Milner-Holland report on London housing came out early in 1965.[5] The Shadow Cabinet decided in March to accept the essence of its recommendations and not to oppose the government's Rent Bill, which replaced the unpopular 1957 Rent Act. This Bill froze rents for the time being, but it did aim to provide machinery for fixing rents at a fair level.

MacGregor showed early on his competence and industry with a 21 point policy for homes. (What he did not show was much sign of his future watchdog role as a Chief Secretary to the Treasury!) He advocated raising the annual housing target to above 400 000; more resources for housing; more new towns; rent rebates in all local authorities; and a speeding-up of planning. He also argued for subsidies for private tenants – later implemented in Peter Walker's Housing Finance Act of 1972. He proposed that rent control should be abolished outside areas of shortage; and he fell for the fashionable nostrum of a much greater use of industrialised building systems.

(Ronan Point had not yet collapsed.) Owner occupation should be backed by grants towards deposits.

Meanwhile the Shadow Cabinet and the Conservative Research Department were actively at work in the same areas. A paper by Sir Keith Joseph and Margaret Thatcher on pensions was put to the Shadow Cabinet and discussed in February 1965. Some of it was no more than tentative. It went for the maintenance of the state basic pension scheme, but raised the possibility of some graduation of contributions according to earnings. It called for higher pensions for older pensioners. It favoured private occupational schemes as the means of adding to the basic pension, but acknowledged that a state scheme could meet inflation in a way that private schemes could not. It went back to an old Tory theme, the easing and ultimate abolition of the retirement condition and earnings rule in the state basic scheme. It raised the possibility of replacing national assistance with an income guarantee scheme for old people, but saw its complexities: a higher rate for those on long-term assistance seemed more immediately practicable. The paper also argued for a single Department of Health and Social Security.

On housing, the shadow spokesman was John Boyd-Carpenter. He acknowledged that land prices had been a difficult issue for the Conservatives at the 1964 election and that there should be perhaps a 25 or 30 per cent charge on development. In January 1966 he presented to the Shadow Cabinet a paper on housing which was a little bolder in tone that it might have been a year earlier. It recommended withholding subsidy from those councils which did not charge full rents to those who could afford them and proposed that loan sanction for new council houses should be confined to areas of real shortage. Rent control should be lifted where there was no shortage and home ownership made easier, perhaps by advancing government money to the building societies at normal government rates.

The culmination of this busy period of policy-making came first with the policy document *Putting Britain Right Ahead* in October 1965 and then with the 1966 election manifesto.

Putting Britain Right Ahead was a well-produced pamphlet designed to show that the party was full of ideas.[6] The party machine had been looking at the possibility of an Autumn policy document since earlier in the year. Plans were reasonably advanced by June, but the uncertainty about whether Sir Alec Douglas-Home would continue to lead the party complicated matters. David Howell commented that 'it would be helpful to have some idea of the Leader's thinking or what he is going to say next'.[7] In July, however, Heath was elected as Leader and his power to shape policy was still further strengthened. *Putting Britain Right Ahead* was the firstfruits. As Ramsden puts it:

> The usual horse-trading between Shadow Ministers was needed to iron out disagreements and infelicities of style, producing agreement on trades union policy, a more 'human' language for the section on the social services and tougher wording in other sections.[8]

The social services section was headed 'Transforming the Welfare State'. It stated that 'we have therefore, designed a new and coherent social policy. The aim is to help those in need effectively and, wherever possible, to set them on their own feet again'. There was a certain emphasis on administrative and institutional changes, as well as a number of improved benefits and services; but it hardly amounted to a transformation.

Another significant piece of work at this time was a pamphlet published in January 1966 by a group under the shadow spokesman for Home Affairs, Peter Thorneycroft. The pamphlet, *Crime Knows No Boundaries*,[9] included an unusually subtle piece of examination of the social causes of crime, largely the work of the sociologist, Dr Bryan Wilson, a member of the group. It talked of the breakdown of familiar forms of social control and of 'a decline in the effectiveness of the agencies of direct moral and social instruction' as well as of the way in which the emphasis on 'success' may lead to disorder among those who do not feel that they are achieving it. The fantasy heroes of the youth culture generate further discontent. On the other hand, the growth in wealth and material possessions leads to greater opportunities both for impulsive and organised crime; and crime not only becomes exciting but is also seen increasingly to pay. Moreover, 'In the impersonal society, concepts such as "the public good" and "social well-being" tend to lose their significance.'

This analysis – essentially conservative rather than neo-liberal in its approach – raised important questions which persist to this day, and are in some ways awkward for Conservatives who place competitiveness among the supreme virtues. The pamphlet argued for stabilisers to offset the strains that may be caused by ambition and opportunity. But having said that, it went on to argue for more obviously practical measures – more police, a more clear-cut responsibility on the Home Secretary for the efficiency of the police and greater central direction, a faster reduction in the number of forces, and a stress on research.

There were other practical proposals about the courts and the penal system, some of which found their way into the manifesto. It was not a blueprint for a successful party conference speech, but it was a thoughtful document.

The 1966 manifesto was very much a reflection of the busy work that had gone into policy-making since the previous campaign. Its title was *Action Not Words* – but inescapably it was through words that the policies had to be spelled out, and the words tended to be sweeping rather than particularly down-to-earth. In his foreword Heath said 'I want to see our social services recognise the overriding claims of those most in need'. The first aim of the policy was to run the country's economy efficiently and realistically so that 'we achieve steadier prices in the shops, high wages and a really decent standard of social security'.

The manifesto went on to say:

We intend to revitalise our Welfare State so that those most in need get the most help and so that our money is used sensibly and fairly ... We want to see more generous help for those who have special needs not yet met by the Welfare State.

In fact it set out a list of new or improved benefits. The party would see that everyone had a good second pension with their job, on top of the State basic pension – though it was not specified whether this was to be through the public or the private sector. Pensions could be either transferred or preserved when people changed jobs. Various groups were to receive more generous help. There was to be special help for areas of bad housing or oversized school classes. A single DHSS was to be created, with an inspectorate of welfare to improve co-ordination between local authority, hospital and voluntary services. There was to be more council house building for slum clearance. £100 million was to be taken off the rates by central government; and so on.

Against this, there were but few signs of tougher or more selective policies. Prescription charges were to be reintroduced, though with wide exceptions. Rent control was to be maintained where there was a shortage – but dropped, by implication, where there was not. Council house subsidies were to be concentrated on those who really needed them, and council building increased only specifically for slum clearance. But in general the flavour of the manifesto was to promise more, not to suggest a tightening up.

In education, the question of comprehensive secondary schools was predictably tackled by saying that proposals for reorganisation would be judged on their merits, with makeshift and hasty plans for turning good grammar schools and secondary moderns into comprehensives to be strongly opposed. Improvements for primary school accommodation would take precedence over comprehensive school building where adequate accommodation already existed. There was to be encouragement to recruit more teachers, especially for the primary schools.

A portent for the future was that crime and immigration now began to be stressed, effectively for the first time in a Conservative manifesto. There was a considerable move towards a national police force, with the Home Secretary and the Scottish Secretary very much more clearly in the lead. Criminals were to pay restitution for the injuries and damage that they caused. Many short-term sentences were to be replaced by substantial fines. Both the latter two were to become recurring themes – not so, however, the idea of a national police force.

On immigration, it was stated that all immigrants living here were to be treated in all respects as equal citizens and without discrimination; but a system of conditional entry was to be introduced, health checks were to be strengthened; and a register of potential dependant entrants to be created. Immigrants were to be helped to return to their country of origin if they wished. Stricter control of entry was to be combined with special help for areas where immigrants were concentrated.

Both these Home Office themes were moving upwards on the political agenda. The Conservative victor over Patrick Gordon-Walker at Smethwick in 1964, Peter Griffiths, had caused a stir by the strength of his line against immigration – and was denounced by Harold Wilson as a 'parliamentary leper'. Undoubtedly anxiety about immigration was mounting in a number of conurbations – and Enoch Powell's famous Birmingham speech was only two years off. But Heath and colleagues like Sir Edward Boyle were certainly reluctant to play the immigration card. As to crime, the number of indictable offences had been steadily increasing, and the clear-up rate falling, for a number of years. The elusive search for answers had to be intensified.

In spite of all the effort that went into Conservative policy-making, the Labour party came back with a handsome majority – up from the 1964 lead over the Conservatives of 13 to 110 in March 1966. By July

1966 Labour's economic policy was facing crisis – but that was too late to return the Tory party.

The 1966 election was a depressing affair for Conservatives and it is doubtful if all the work on policy made much difference. Iain Macleod's view in 1967 was that:

at the last election the Conservative Party Manifesto had contained 131 distinct specific promises. This was far too much to put across to the electorate, and the net result was that everybody thought we had no policy.[10]

Characteristically, none of this deterred Heath from his interest in policy formulation. He accepted, however, that the next phase could be conducted at a somewhat more leisurely pace – over a one to two year timescale – and he appointed Sir Edward Boyle to co-ordinate the exercise under himself.

Boyle's appointment was not an unmitigated success. This was partly because he had a great deal on his plate and he was not a man for the brisk approach. He was also very undogmatic in his attitude – becoming increasingly so with the passage of time. This was particularly true in his own area of responsibility, education, where, as we have seen, many in the party continued to feel that he was insufficiently robust on the subject of comprehensive schools. In February 1967 he set out his views in a paper to the Shadow Cabinet. He argued that a majority of public opinion, including Tory opinion, had moved steadily against 11-plus selection. The causes were the unreliability of the selective process, the disparity of provision between secondary modern and grammar schools, the 'abundant evidence' that failing the 11-plus creates adverse attitudes, and recognition that far more Tories than was always realised were actually concerned about their own children failing the 11-plus.

But if the trend was away from 11-plus selection, the party should still oppose the rapid and universal imposition of comprehensive systems. It should continue to oppose 'botched-up' systems (to use the phrase that was fashionable at the time). But the party should not oppose on principle any plan involving the reorganisation of a good existing school: Tory councils and Tory ministers had already approved schemes of this kind. In spite of Boyle's strong defence of direct grant schools – partly as a way of providing for really high flyers within the comprehensive system – the suspicion was that Boyle's heart was not in the fight, perhaps particularly in the urban areas where Tory councillors were themselves more likely to be grammar school products than in the shire counties. The minutes of the Shadow Cabinet meeting where Boyle's paper was discussed do not indicate divergence from his line, but other Tories would have shared the view of the *Daily Telegraph* which demanded that 'Sir Edward Boyle's prolonged flirtation with both selectivity and comprehensivisation must end: the two are incompatible'.[11] Shortly afterwards, however, Boyle left politics to become Vice-Chancellor of Leeds University. Mrs Thatcher became the shadow spokesman on education and then Secretary of State.

It was about this time that there appeared what with hindsight may be seen as one of the most influential pamphlets of the post-war years, the first of the *Black Papers* on education. Entitled *Fight for Education*, it was edited by two academics, C. B. Cox and A. E. Dyson.[12] Its aim was avowedly to reverse the progressive tide in education which had been flowing ever since the war. It opened with a 'Letter to Members of Parliament' which began: 'The disintegration of Ronan Point was caused by "progressive collapse"; there seems a grim humour in the phrase. How far are we witnessing the progressive collapse of education?' Two particular themes were soon apparent. First, the damage being done by the erosion of the grammar school idea; second the horrors of the anarchic disorders which had been taking place in the universities. The general target was egalitarianism. Angus Maude MP, for example, wrote on 'The Egalitarian Threat' and C. B. Cox 'In Praise of Examinations'. There was a clutch of other well-known contributors, including Kingsley Amis, John Sparrow, D. C. Watt, John Gross and Bryan Wilson.

The *Black Paper* sent a tremor through the educational world: it was not only the Labour minister Edward Short who thought it the worst thing to have hit education for a long time. But gradually, as first it and then its successors appeared over the next few years, and men like the successful comprehensive school head and later MP, Rhodes Boyson, joined the fray, the ideas began to gain ground; excellence, in many minds, replaced equality as the prime target – but not among all.

In 1971, a Penguin book on *The Politics of Education* incorporated some substantial conversations between Boyle (and Anthony Crosland) and Maurice Kogan.[13] One comment by Boyle reveals a very different view of how education policies evolved from that which might have been expressed in the late 1980s: 'I would say overwhelmingly the biggest number originated from ... the "education world"'. This was, of course, a very different approach from that which governed the Education Reform Act of 1988. So, too, were his sympathetic approach towards the local education authorities and his criticism of the *Black Paper* view that 'more means worse'. And his views on how to give access to the best in education to those in poorer areas would have been very different from the 'opting-out' provisions of the 1988 Education Reform Act.

Neither housing policy nor social security posed the same internal party difficulties as education. A Conservative Research Department paper in February 1967 discussed the sale of council houses. It came forward with arguments that were to become increasingly familiar: that the sale of council houses did not reduce the total stock, that it increased savings, that the great majority of purchasers would anyway have remained in their houses for life and then often passed them on to their families, so that the fall in the number of houses available for re-letting would be very small. You could sell 1000 houses in a year and still only need to build perhaps 15 to replace them. Nevertheless, there could still be areas where land shortage would make it difficult to build new houses. Councils therefore should neither be compelled nor forbidden to sell.

Another significant development in housing policy owed a good deal to Alderman Frank Griffin of Birmingham. Griffin's council put forward a Private Bill to Parliament permitting a rebate scheme for private tenants. The Shadow Cabinet decided in November 1967 not to take a line on this proposal; but by the time the Heath Government came in it had become official policy, and it was implemented in the Housing Finance Act of 1972. For the first time private tenants were to receive direct financial help (as opposed to rent control); this was a response to the growing belief that housing help should be attached to people rather than buildings.

Pensions policy also took up a good deal of time. Labour had for a long time promised to change the 1959 Boyd-Carpenter Act, but after many policy statements and three white papers they only finally came up with a Bill in December 1969. Labour had criticised the 1959 Act on a number of grounds – the inadequacy of many occupational pensions, the fact that they provided nothing or too little for dependents, their inability to keep pace with inflation, and the lack of transferability as an individual moved from job to job. All this had been set out by Douglas Houghton, Labour Chancellor of the Duchy of Lancaster in the Commons on 23 February 1966. He did not wish to ban occupational schemes, but argued that the essential need was for a national scheme. When it eventually emerged as a Bill, it was rather more modest than it had been at the beginning of the decade. Its essence was to replace the existing system of flat-rate contributions for a basic pension, with an additional graduated contribution on top for those earning more than £9 a week, by a system of earnings-related contributions up to a limit of one-and-a-half times average earnings for the employee, with an unlimited 7 per cent of payroll contribution from employers. Partial contracting out would be allowed, but on relatively unfavourable terms. The scheme was opposed by the Tories both on this ground and because the benefits offered for the future would, under its pay-as-you-go system, lead to high demands on future generations of wage earners and employers.

The Shadow Cabinet had a number of discussions during 1969 on how to respond to the various versions of Labour's scheme: there was some nervousness about an all-out attack. When it came to Second Reading of the Bill, however, the Conservative Party did vote against it, but in fact the Bill did not reach the Statute Book because of the 1970 general election.

The pensions issue was not the only aspect of social security to receive a good deal of attention between 1966 and 1970. The growing realisation that new categories of need were presenting themselves and the desire to concentrate resources where they were most required provided the themes for much of the work; but as always targeting and selectivity proved harder to work out in the particular than in the general. Mervyn Pike, as shadow spokesman in this field in 1967, for example presented a paper to the Shadow Cabinet on family poverty aimed to help any families below a national minimum, old people in need, the chronically sick and disabled and widows through a combination of cash and care. Although her proposals were not quite blanket provision, there was clearly nervousness about adopting them, especially as they were uncosted. The Shadow Cabinet minutes of a discussion in April 1967 of the line to be taken in a debate on family poverty said that much should be made of the proposals on care. 'As little as possible should be said on the subject of cash.'

In July 1967 a working group chaired by Brendon Sewill, Director of the Research Department, but also including Miss Pike and Maurice Macmillan MP, came up with a substantial report on 'Social Priorities'. It picked up the theme that social services should be more concentrated on need and the able-bodied stand on their own feet. It also referred to the 1966 manifesto policy of 'greater State help for those in real need', together with the implied converse of less help for those not in need. It commented that there was some evidence that Labour had been able to run an effective election scare that the Conservatives would impose a 'means-test State'. It also remarked that many leading Conservatives were convinced that there was scope for selectivity in some social services but not in others. 'But this private conviction carries little weight with the general public unless it can be explained.' The object was to clarify the arguments and see if a theme could be found valid for all the social services – and in line with policy as it was emerging from the various groups at work on it.

The conclusions were fairly cautious. The group said they were confirmed in their belief that selectivity was the right line to pursue – but

a clear distinction must be drawn between the allocation of future resources and changes in existing services. There is a grave danger that we may lose many votes at the next Election if there were a suspicion that we were going to reduce present benefits. We should state loudly and categorically that we will not impose charges for hospital treatment or for primary and secondary education and that we will maintain the real value of the basic pension.

Moreover, 'While firmly maintaining the present structure of the social services we should concentrate on talking about how to distribute the extra resources that will flow from renewed prosperity under the next Conservative Government, particularly towards the disabled, chronic sick, very old and very poor'. Prescription charges and higher council rents for the better-off should be defended as ways of increasing the resources available for children dying for lack of kidney machines or the homeless. 'We should, however, be careful before committing ourselves to imposing any further charges for existing services.'

There should be approval – but not by and large financial support – for those who look after their own needs, though there might be a scheme of tax relief for those who contracted to insure for private health, education or superannuation. This would be a form of pump primer.

The overall impression is of a desire to move towards new policies, but a great sense of caution about everything that might be seen to cut across existing public notions of the welfare state. The public had simply not yet been convinced of the case for change.

A paper from Brendon Sewill the following summer (June 1968) was not able to come up with anything very positive. It said that there was little scope for selectivity in education or health – it was against vouchers, for example. The health policy group was looking at ways of putting health on to a more genuine insurance basis and possibly some sort of tax relief for private insurance. The section on pensions was particularly inconclusive, but hinted that perhaps the right answer was to go for a bipartisan policy.

One theme that began to be developed in the second half of the 1960s was the notion that the development of computers should allow some form of combining the tax and benefit systems, the so-called tax credit or negative income tax schemes. Sewill put the idea forward in 1966. Heath's initial reaction was that it was too hot a potato, so that when Sewill wrote a pamphlet on the idea, he published it in his wife's name.[14] The idea of negative income tax nevertheless developed in 1967: the theoretical attractions of a single system for working out a person's income and then debiting or crediting him accordingly were considerable. Barney Hayhoe published a CPC pamphlet[15] in March 1968 on a new family benefit scheme to be based on a PAYE automatic means test. It was clearly difficult to work out a detailed scheme in opposition but the 1970 manifesto contained a commitment to explore a negative income tax, though nothing ultimately came of it under the Heath government.

The culmination of the opposition's lengthy policy-making was the weekend conference at Selsdon Park from 30 January to 1 February 1970. It was designed to finalise the stance at the forthcoming election. The research department had prepared papers on the major policy areas and these were duly discussed. On education, the only real altercation concerned the new independent university at Buckingham. Heath insisted on rejecting a favourable manifesto paragraph about it and was unsympathetic to Mrs Thatcher's desire to back it in a speech. Over housing, the main – and not fully resolved – argument was on whether private tenants should receive rent allowances, and also on whether all controlled rents should be converted to the so-called fair rents. There was apparently no very decisive conclusion at this stage.

On health, the meeting was presented with a Research Department paper outlining possible options for meeting the perennial problem of the NHS that 'resources are inadequate and demand is limitless', and that a good deal more money had to be spent each year merely to retain existing standards. This was due to costly new ways of treating people and the growth in the number of the old. Various small new sources of finance were considered. The idea of a charge for board and lodging for hospitals was looked at critically; the notion of taking more from national insurance contributions was raised; and the proposition that tax relief on contributions to private health insurance organisations would yield a significant net gain was treated sceptically. At the end the major question as to whether to shift from a tax based scheme to a compulsory insurance scheme (or a system of charges and refunds for GP services) was posed; but the change was described as unpopular and only likely to be acceptable in the context of severe economic circumstances or a breakdown of the service. Not surprisingly, therefore, significant changes were not endorsed.

There was a long and rather disjointed discussion on family allowances, with inconclusive consideration of the idea of dealing with family needs through the income tax system. Lord Balniel, the current spokesman on social services, stressed the extent of child poverty. Mrs Thatcher argued that family allowances tended to increase the number of the poor, which Quintin Hogg doubted. Sir Keith Joseph saw family allowances as the quickest way of tackling child poverty. By contrast, the Shadow Chancellor, Iain Macleod, said he wanted virtually to abolish family allowances, reduce taxes and increase supplementary benefit. Again, not surprisingly, the conclusion to all this was that more work needed to be done!

Some additional work was also ordered for pensions policy. The Research Department paper backed the notion of graduated contributions towards the flat-rate basic pension; above that, the emphasis was to be on private occupational schemes, though with a reserve state scheme out of which the occupational schemes were to be encouraged to contract. There were to be good benefits for short-term sickness, unemployment and widowhood and higher pensions for the over eighties. But detailed figures were felt to be needed for the mix of contributions, benefit and possible deficit in the scheme and on the problem of transferability or preservation of pension rights as a person moved from one job to another.

The Selsdon Park conference received a good deal of publicity – indeed, it was intended to. A new political figure was created – 'Selsdon Man' – who might be described as an early Thatcherite or radical right Tory. But in so far as this was an accurate image, it was in economic policy that it applied, for example through the projected purging of 'lame ducks'. Nobody could say that the social policy discussed at Selsdon Park and then endorsed in the 1970 manifesto, *A Better Tomorrow*, represented a radical change of direction.[16] The party was still not really sure whether it wanted a new stance or not.

The manifesto's housing policy, for example, promised nothing very drastic: even the proposal to bring in rent allowances for private tenants was presented tentatively. Local authorities were to be encouraged to sell houses, but then to use the proceeds to provide housing for the disabled, the aged and those on waiting lists. In education there was to be a shift of emphasis in favour of primary schools and, in socially handicapped areas especially, of nursery education. The familiar position on comprehensive schools was reaffirmed: it was stated that 'many of the most imaginative new schemes abolishing the eleven-plus have been introduced by Conservative councils'. In health, the emphasis was on improving co-ordination between hospitals, general practitioners and the local authority health services.

The social security changes *were* of some significance. There was to be more help for the over-eighties, the seriously ill and disabled (including the constant attendance allowance), and widows. The new pensions policy was to be on the lines discussed, including a reference to transferability. Family poverty was to be tackled by ensuring that adequate family allowances would go to those who needed them. The passage continued:

> A scheme based upon negative income tax would allow benefits to be related to family need; other families would benefit by reduced taxation. The Government has exaggerated the administrative problems involved, and we will make a real effort to find a practical solution.

In fact, as we shall see, this assessment proved optimistic.

Overall, Conservative policy at this stage represented a blend between the ideas of those who had worked so actively at policy-making over the previous five years and the awareness of a senior team who were virtually all ex-ministers that resources must be limited and that ideas that might seem fine in opposition still had to be proved administratively sound in government. At the same time, the penchant for institutional reform that marked the Heath government was apparent: for better or for worse the major changes in the health service, local government (on a two-tier system) and housing finance were all foreshadowed. At least it meant that there was much to get on with as soon as the party arrived in office. But as far as politics were concerned, it was not on social policy that the 1970 election was fought and won. Overwhelmingly, the decisive issue was rising prices.

The fact that the 1970 election was fought on an economic issue was not surprising: it was economic and industrial matters that had dominated the years of Harold Wilson's premiership. In striking contrast to Attlee's government, Wilson's passed relatively little important legislation in the social policy field. The 1957 Rent Act was replaced, leaseholds were enfranchised and various other measures on housing were enacted, none of them major; comprehensive secondary education was pressed, but only by circular; the Bill reforming pensions came too late to reach the Statute Book; Supplementary Benefit replaced National Assistance; and an ineffective Land Commission was set up. But none of these significantly changed the shape of social policy – and the economic situation was not strong enough to lead to spectacular advances. From the Conservative side, the Parliamentary battle had to be fought; but whereas in Attlee's days the opposition had been engrossed in the question of how to react to Labour's measures, the opposition to Wilson under Edward Heath devoted more of its energy to what it would do when it returned to office. The 18 June result gave it the chance to turn planning into practice.

6 1970–74: Heath in Government

The Heath administration, which ran from June 1970 to February 1974, was dominated by two themes. The first was the successful negotiation of Britain's entry into the European Community and its passage through Parliament; the second was the unsuccessful series of attempts to resolve the interlocking problems of trade union power, inflation and poor productivity. It was these problems, of course, aggravated by the oil price crisis of Autumn 1973, that led to the election defeat and the sense that the Heath government had ultimately failed.

But if it is for these events that the period will be remembered, it was also a busy period in the field of social policy, with several major Acts coming into the Statute Book. The economic background was for the most part expansionist. Although the government came in with the rather hardline public aura of Selsdon Park about it, and the threat to lame industrial ducks was soon issued, the control of public expenditure was fairly quickly relaxed until the oil crisis caused the brakes to be slammed on hard in late 1973.

One notable feature of social policy was an unusual degree of continuity among the ministers in charge of it. Sir Keith Joseph was Secretary of State for Social Services throughout the administration. Mrs Thatcher also ran the full course as Secretary of State for Education and Science. Peter Walker was at Environment until November 1972 when Geoffrey Rippon took over for the rest of the Parliament. Even among junior ministers, there was a good deal of continuity.

But it was not just that the Secretaries of State were left in post for long enough to have an impact: they were all energetic and competent ministers. Nor was any of them at odds with his or her Cabinet colleagues on policy. Thatcher jarred somewhat on Heath and occasionally Joseph showed flashes of the policy conversion that was to come, but broadly Thatcherism was a good way off, and Joseph in particular was still the caring paternalist seeking practical answers to social problems. At the giant Environment department, Walker was an able and ambitious young politician with an interventionist bent, determined to leave his mark both through his concern for the new environment issues and through major institutional reforms.

Over them presided Edward Heath with his commitment to modern management methods and large-scale institutions and his impatience at the inert conservatism which seemed to him to hold the country back. For all his limitations as a handler of people and as political impresario, he provided a framework in which his ministers could get on with what they wanted to do, so long as they acted competently. Political and party ideology played a relatively small part in his approach, as did the views of the parliamentary party.

The intensive work on policy which had gone on before the election included a detailed timetable for its implementation, and action was soon under way. The policy of seeking out and concentrating on pockets of unmet need was implemented in a National Insurance Act which reached the Statute Book before the end of 1970. It provided three new cash benefits. The first was a special pension (with no means test) for people too old to have qualified to enter the National Insurance scheme when it started in 1948: it benefited about 110 000 people aged 80 or over. Secondly, a pension was provided for women widowed between the ages of 40 and 50. Thirdly, an attendance allowance was introduced for very seriously disabled people who needed a good deal of attention by both day and night. (This was later extended to those needing such attention *either* by day *or* by night.) Five years later, nearly a quarter of a million people benefited from it. Indeed the recognition of disability as one of the important categories of social need was a significant theme of social policy around this time.

Shortly afterwards came the introduction of the Family Income Supplement. In his Second Reading speech on the Bill which introduced it, on 10 November 1970, Sir Keith Joseph explained why the government had changed course since the election campaign. The original intention had been to increase family allowance but to claw back a proportion of that through the income tax system. This was to be the first step in an overall campaign against family poverty (a theme brought to the political foreground to a considerable extent as a result of the campaigning of the Child Poverty Action Group, to which Joseph and other Tories had paid careful attention). Joseph gave three reasons for changing his mind. First, he recognised that family allowances gave no help for families with only one child – yet to bring in first children would take time and also add greatly to the cost of the scheme. Second, an increase in family allowance, whether or not taxed, could not be at a level which would give significant help to the particular group he set out to assist, namely the poorest of wage-earning households. And thirdly, the lowering of the standard rate income tax threshold by Labour meant that certain people who should be seen as in the category of family poverty were actually paying income tax and would therefore derive no benefit from family allowance after tax had been clawed back. The effect of the Bill would be to put some £8 million into the pockets of the poorest of the working population together with people who were not working because it was not worth their while to do so.

The Bill was not received with any great excitement, and Joseph's presentation of it was typically modest. Labour condemned its small scale, and the Tory loner and expert in this field, Sir Brandon Rhys Williams, saw Joseph and his parliamentary under-secretary, Paul Dean, as Bunyan's pilgrims labouring under difficulties.

> We shall see them ... in the Slough of Despond as they try to draft regulations which actually express what they want. We shall see them on the Hill of Difficulty as they try to wrestle with the problem of disincentives; and in the Castle of Despair as they try to wrestle with the problem of low take-up. I am sure that take-up will not be as high as Sir Keith Joseph hopes. But we can have confidence that in due course he will come to the river and that the trumpets will sound for him on the other side. Eventually he will come to the place where other blessed spirits rest, and will convince himself that the right way to have dealt with this problem all along was by a straight increase in family allowances.

This quotation is worth including to mark the part that Rhys Williams was to play over the years until his death in 1988 as the most persistent Tory advocate of family allowances and later of child benefit, as well as of a merger of the tax and benefit system. If at times he seemed Cassandra-like, he never let up in the causes he believed to be right, this particular one having been inherited from his mother, Lady Juliet Rhys Williams.

Other Tory critics said that they hoped that the Bill would have no more than a short life until a more enduring solution could be found to the problem of family poverty; but in fact it remained in useful operation until it was replaced by the Family Credit scheme in 1988.

The policy of concentrating on particular needy groups was followed by the 1971 National Insurance Act which gave a special addition to all over-eighty pensioners, providing modest additional help to about 1 250 000 people.

The year 1972 saw the publication of the proposals for a tax credit scheme, by which the full benefit of the existing personal tax allowances would be given to those who did not pay enough tax to receive all or any of these allowances. Family allowance would be swallowed up in the new tax credits. A green paper was published[1] setting out the proposals, which had been largely worked out by Arthur Cockfield. They were then referred to a Commons Select Committee. The majority of the committee supported the scheme, and in July 1973 Anthony Barber, the Chancellor of the Exchequer, said that provision for the scheme would be included in the following year's Finance Bill. The benefits would include provision for the first child and the fact that credits would come automatically, thus reducing means testing: it was also the intention, on the Select Committee's advice, that credits would be paid to the mother in cash, though this made for administrative complications. However, enthusiasm for the scheme was waning with the realisation that, if it was to be introduced with no losers, it would entail a high cost – £1300 million in the 1972 scheme: the 1973 oil crisis would almost certainly have deferred implementation.

However, 1972 did see two major pieces of social legislation reaching the Statute Book. The first was the Housing Finance Act. This Act was bitterly contested. It went through what was then the longest Standing Committee stage in parliamentary history and it led in due course to the appointment of a commissioner to take over the council housing of Clay Cross in Derbyshire, where the local council refused to implement the provisions of the Act.

In some important ways the Act in fact brought considerable help to poorer tenants living in the rented sector, whether public or private. The aim was to concentrate subsidies where they were most needed and to introduce the concept that subsidies should be linked primarily to people rather than to properties, although there was to be additional help with slum clearance. The particular feature of the new Act was the application of the notion of 'Fair Rents' to both council and private lettings and the introduction of a nationally laid down scheme of rent rebates and rent allowances for the public and private sectors respectively. The provision of council rebates had been erratic: under the Labour government 40 per cent of councils had not provided them; while there had been no help at all (other than rent control) for private tenants.

The new rebates and allowances were generally agreed to be generous (leading ultimately to the attempt to curb the successor Housing Benefit scheme in the latter 1980s); but there were other features which aroused strong opposition. The Fair Rents scheme had been applied to much of the unfurnished private rented sector by the previous Labour government, and it was expected that it would in due course be applied to the rest. The essence of the Fair Rent was that it was based on the market rent less the scarcity element. Under the Act, local authorities were to put forward fair rents for their properties; these would then be put before a Rent Scrutiny Board, whose decision would be final. In due course, furnished as well as unfurnished private tenancies would come under the Fair Rent system. Central government would then fix a notional 'needs allowance' on the basis of family circumstances: in other words, it would set the level of subsidy for each tenant. Government would fund the private sector rent allowance.

The new system had much to be said for it; but two elements aroused fierce opposition. The first was that local authorities would no longer fix rents. The loss of this power would mean in particular the loss of the ability to provide heavily subsidised rents. Secondly a great deal of anger was aroused by the provision that local authorities which accumulated a surplus in their housing revenue accounts through the introduction of the higher rents likely under the Fair Rents system would have to pay half that surplus back to the Exchequer. The argument was that the Exchequer had provided much of that money in the first place, through the housing subsidies; but the provision was probably a political mistake. Without it the Act would have had an easier passage and stood a better chance of survival under the next Labour administration – the new rent rebates and allowances *were* kept by Labour, but Fair Rents and the takeover of surpluses were scrapped. But whatever the merits of the case it is clear that the action of the Clay Cross council in resisting the Act, and the ambivalent attitude taken by the Labour party over the affair, did little good to the Labour cause.

The second major piece of social legislation passed in 1972 was the Local Government Act. This Act followed the report of the Royal Commission on Local Government in England chaired by Lord Redcliffe-Maud and published in June 1969.[2] The report did not cover London, which had by then been reorganised, nor did it deal with finance. It has often been argued that this latter decision was mistaken, although it has never been decisively demonstrated that the pattern of organisation and powers need determine the method of funding, or vice versa.

Redcliffe-Maud recommended that England should be divided into 61 new local government areas (outside London). In three of them – Birmingham, Manchester and Merseyside – there should be a two-tier system, with metropolitan county councils and districts. The remaining 58 authorities should be all-purpose unitary authorities, based primarily on the dictates of economic and social geography rather than the familiar counties and boroughs. There were also to be eight provincial councils, in place of the existing regional economic planning councils.

The Labour government, in a white paper in February 1970, broadly accepted the Redcliffe-Maud approach; but on the Conservative side opposition mounted to both the unitary authority and to the scrapping of historic county boundaries. The 1970 Conservative manifesto undertook to 'bring forward a sensible measure of local government reform which will involve a genuine devolution of power from central government and will provide for the existence of a two-tier structure'.

A white paper in February 1971[3] set out the scheme. Three further metropolitan areas were proposed (Tyne and Wear, West Yorkshire and South Yorkshire), while in the rest of the country there would be a pattern of counties and districts. As far as possible their powers were to be separated, so that there was not to be a sense of upper and lower tiers. Education, social services, transport, fire, police and some planning went to the counties; housing, local planning and various environmental services went to the districts.

Not surprisingly, there was a great deal of debate and pressure about aspects of the Bill – historical boundaries, the demise of the county boroughs, the names of the new authorities, the exact allocation of powers, particularly in planning, and the disappearance of all sorts of smaller and long established boroughs and rural and urban districts all produced fierce controversy. It cannot be held to have been a very well-loved reform – and of course a subsequent Tory government abolished the metropolitan counties. (Ironically this took place in the teeth of Labour opposition, though originally it was Labour that had most disliked the demise of the old county boroughs.) Nevertheless, the ebullient Peter Walker, and his indefatigable minister of state Graham Page, carried the Bill through on the basis that their two tiers represented the right blend of appropriate efficiency in the administration of services with as much closeness to the ground as was practicable. In certain shire counties which contained a substantial city, Nottingham and Leicester for example, there was particular suspicion of the proposals – the old city and shire areas each suspecting that they would be dominated by the other part; but the government argued vigorously for the view that the bringing together of urban and rural areas in fact made for better planning of the whole. Views still

differ on whether the government won all the arguments – but it won
the votes, and gradually the system settled down.

The year 1972 saw one other important development in social
policy, the publication of Mrs Thatcher's white paper *Education: A
Framework for Expansion*.[4] Mrs Thatcher had started her tenure of
office in a controversial atmosphere. She had moved rapidly after
taking office to withdraw the Labour circulars to local education
authorities which expected them to submit plans for reorganising
education on completely comprehensive lines. This step was inevitable, though it did not mean that she would not approve comprehensive schemes put to her if she found them educationally sound. In fact
she approved a substantial number during her term of office. More
controversial was the decision announced in October 1970 as part of a
public expenditure review that school milk would cease to be given to
all primary school children above the age of seven, though it would
continue to be provided for those with medical need for it. The
subsequent Education (Milk) Act, 1971, allowed local authorities to
sell milk where they wished to do so. The October 1970 statement also
increased the price of school meals from 9p to 12p.

The milk decision led to a considerable onslaught on Mrs Thatcher
(who was labelled 'Margaret Thatcher, milk snatcher'). Edward
Short, the opposition spokesman, described the milk Bill as the
'meanest, most unworthy Bill' that he had seen in his time in the
Commons, adding 'it is typical of the philosophy of this astounding,
pre-Disraeli Government'. But Mrs Thatcher was able to point out
that Labour had ended the milk provision in secondary schools, and
the row blew over, although it contributed to a somewhat hard line
perception of her.

The 1972 white paper, however, was very different in this regard.
The tone of the paper was thoroughly expansionist in almost every
area of public provision.

The previous April had seen the implementation of the Butler Act's
provision for raising the minimum school leaving age to sixteen. Now
Education: A Framework for Expansion followed up the recommen-
dation of the Plowden report on primary schools, published in 1967, by
proposing that within ten years part-time nursery education should be
available to all three- and four-year-olds whose parents wanted it for
them. It was to continue to be free – the minority note arguing for
charges was not endorsed. In a Commons debate on 19 February 1973,
Mrs Thatcher described this as 'an historic step forward which has
been widely welcomed'. There would be some priority in the
allocation of capital resources for the programme to areas of social

deprivation. It was assumed that 15 per cent of the provision would be for full-time education, with again a higher than average provision for deprived areas. This emphasis on extra resources for deprived areas – a form of positive discrimination – marked a significant development in social policy.

Expansion was also the keynote in the provision of teachers. By 1981 there was to be an increase of 110 000 teachers, plus 15 000 for nursery education and 20 000 more to allow for more in-service training. Between 1971 and 1981 the pupil–teacher ratio was set to drop from 22.6 : 1 to 18.5 : 1. In higher education, there were to be 750 000 places by 1981, compared with about 463 000 in 1971.

Only in the building programme was the prospect one of reductions – a fall over five years of 22 per cent, attributed largely to the decline in the rate of growth of the school population. There was to be some extra provision for nursery education and secondary school improvements. Overall, education spending was to increase at a rate of 5 per cent in real terms over the next five years, against an overall rate of increase in public expenditure of 2½ per cent. It was an ambitious programme.

The next major piece of social policy-making was the National Health Service Reorganisation Act of 1973.

The main aim of Sir Keith Joseph's Bill was to achieve greater unification of the service. The local authority health services and the school health service were transferred from local government to the NHS. The family practitioner services were also brought within the unified structure. The structure itself was recast on the basis of regions, areas and districts.

Joseph, characteristically, was concerned that, as he put it in his Commons Second Reading presentation (26 March 1973), 'the less familiar and less glamorous needs of patients tend to be neglected' – the elderly, the mentally ill, the mentally handicapped, the physically disabled and other groups. He argued that the existing fragmentation of services made it difficult to achieve the essential continuity of care across the spectrum. The system did not impose on any one authority the duty of keeping under review the changing health needs of its population and of providing the necessary services. There was no match between the existing hospital authorities and the local government authorities.

Hospital regions are too remote to tackle local needs. Hospital management committees and local authorities are just not equipped to cope with the full task that needs doing.

Joseph went on to say that:

> No doubt in a perfect world ... the answer would be to unify the
> health services within local government. That would provide what
> many of us would like to see in a perfect world, namely, one
> decision-making authority in every area. But we do not live in a
> perfect world, and that is not very practicable.

Labour, too, had rejected that approach: Bevan, indeed, had turned
his back on the ideas of local authority control which the wartime
coalition had considered favourably.

The heart of the new structure, therefore, was to be area
authorities, with boundaries matching the new shire counties and
metropolitan districts. They would have the task of identifying needs
and of organising and meeting those needs, working through districts
based on district general hospitals. They would deal directly with
their counterparts in local government who ran the personal social
services and education, though not, in the shire counties, housing or
environmental services. The community care links between health
and social services would of course be particularly important. The
social service departments had already been reorganised in a Bill
effectively handed on by the previous Labour government to the
Tory government when it came to office in 1970.

Above the areas, there were to continue to be regions, allocating
to the areas the resources provided by the Secretary of State and
responsible to him for long-term planning, certain regional services
and hospital building. The regions also employed the consultants.
Below the area level there were to be both district health planning
teams and district management teams – both multi-disciplinary in
their role and composition. There was also to be set up another
innovation – community health councils, to represent the public or
consumer element. There was to be one for each district (the number
of districts in an area varying considerably). They would have the
right to visit health establishments, to report to the area health
authority – and to receive an answer to their reports from the areas.

Three other significant changes in the Bill were the replacement of
the familiar local government medical officers of health by NHS-
based community physicians; the bringing of the teaching hospitals
into the new structure by the creation of special Area Health
Authorities (Teaching); and the creation of an ombudsman for the
NHS.

The Bill tackled one other important and difficult area – family planning. Responsibility for all public family planning programmes was brought within the health service. There was however a sharp controversy over the question of payment for it. Initially the government took the view that although advice would be free supplies would be charged for, though with exemptions. The House of Lords – which received the Bill before the Commons – responded to some outside pressure by striking out the charging power. Joseph, however, did not accept the simple view that free supplies alone would cut sharply into abortion and unwanted pregnancies. On the other hand, he did accept the case for family planning becoming 'normalised' and agreed that his original proposals would not help some people with weak motivation or marginal incomes. As a compromise solution he plumped for putting supplies on to the normal level of prescription charges, with a range of exemptions. There were some objections to the doctors being called upon to become 'social providers' rather than men exercising medical judgement, but Joseph's decision prevailed. It cannot be said, however, that a reduction in either illegitimacies or abortions followed the arrival of family planning on the health service. Illegitimate live births went up from 9 per cent of all such births in 1971 to 21 per cent in 1986, while the annual number of legal abortions carried out over the same period rose from 101 000 to 157 000.

Joseph's reform of the NHS was by any standards far-ranging and comprehensive, and he characteristically put great effort and thought into it. But it proved to be over-elaborate. An array of current ideas found their way into the Bill. Under the 'cogwheel' system, the different professional groups were to have their say in the management system. There was to be a local democratic element. The consumers were given a special outlet. A new tier was created to match local government. Yet at the end of the day, the Secretary of State was to be ultimately accountable for the whole system.

Labour attacked it on the grounds – expressed in their Second Reading amendment – that the reorganised service would be 'too managerial in aspect, unrepresentative in character, and fails to meet the need for a democratic health service'. John Silkin said that the framework was too cumbersome and could do with some slimming: 'if you have tiers, prepare to shed them now'. But the opposition's line was ambivalent: it did not go for a merger with local government or directly elected authorities. It simply argued for a higher proportion of local government and staff membership of the various bodies. And the criticism that the structure was 'too managerial' seems very hard to sustain. The failure of the Act to produce a clearcut managerial system was its greatest weakness. Under the Thatcher government, the area tier was in fact shed and a system of accountable district general managers brought in.

The principle of unification in the 1973 Act was almost certainly right, but the structure was flabby. There are still mixed views as to whether the Community Health Councils have proved worthwhile. They are not very costly, but some would argue that the health authority itself should include members specifically intended to look after patients' interests – indeed, that all their members should.

The 1972–3 session of Parliament was a particularly busy one for Sir Keith Joseph, for it also saw his Social Security Act.

This Act gave statutory backing to an annual review of pension levels. More important, it provided that the pensions and benefits under the basic national insurance scheme would be funded, up to a certain level, by a completely earnings-related scheme. The level was set at one-and-a-half times average industrial earnings. Hitherto there had been the Boyd–Carpenter hybrid system of a graduated contribution on top of a flat-rate contribution. The objective of the new scheme was to provide greater buoyancy of revenue and hence better basic pensions: low wage earners would not pay such a disproportionately high share of the cost of their benefits.

At the same time, the Act tackled the problem of second pensions above the basic level. The objective was to encourage as many people as possible to join a private occupational scheme, although there would be a reserve state scheme for those who could not receive adequate cover through an occupational scheme. In contrast to the pay-as-you-go basic scheme, both the occupational schemes and the state reserve scheme were to be funded, so that the burden would not fall on the taxpayer. To be recognised by the new Occupational Pensions Board, occupational schemes would have to meet certain important criteria, including preservation of the pension rights of early leavers. It was not, however, felt possible at that stage to provide for complete transferability of pensions from one scheme to another – it was argued that at that point this would have a discouraging effect on some employers.

In the Second Reading debate on 28 November 1972, Labour's spokesman, Brian O'Malley, accepted the idea of earnings-related contributions, although complaining that it would take too long to have an impact; but he rejected flat-rate benefits. In doing so, he rejected the redistributive element in the Tory scheme, arguing that the real redistribution needed was a bigger 'financial transference' from the working population to pensioners. But the main opposition attack was on the nature of the reserve scheme, which they claimed had been made as unattractive as possible in order to give an incentive to the occupational schemes: they pointed out that there was not only no Exchequer supplement but there was also no tax relief provided on contributions.

O'Malley argued that 'the Bill dates from the Selsdon and pre-Selsdon period of Tory thinking'. His view of Joseph seemed ambivalent – at one moment he referred to his reputation as a compassionate man, but he then said:

> I realise that the right hon Gentleman, at a time when other reputations are falling fast on his Front Bench, wishes to maintain his reputation as a Right Wing Minister who will carry through the creed and philosophy of the Tory Party.

– a useful reminder that the Joseph who emerged in 1974 was not a wholly new being.

In the event, Joseph's scheme for second pensions was never put into operation. Due to start in April 1975, it was overtaken by the Labour victory in 1974; but the changes for the financing of the basic pension and for the protection of pension rights were allowed to stand.

Joseph's two major 1973 Acts were the last substantial pieces of social reform enacted by the Heath government; and as the year wore on the oil crisis and the industrial and economic situation more and more dominated the government's actions. As far as social policy was concerned, the climax came with the Chancellor's statement on 17 December 1973 when Anthony Barber decided that the energy shortage required across the board cuts to the tune of 20 per cent in capital programmes and 10 per cent in current expenditure, except for staff costs. There was to be some relief in one or two areas, notably the NHS; but overall the impact of the cuts in the following financial year would mean reductions of some £1200 million. A projected public expenditure rise of something under 2 per cent was converted into a projected fall of 2 per cent.

It was a tough blow, not least to the programme for expansion in education. Surprisingly, following a three months moratorium on building, the under-fives building programme was still to go ahead, as was building for essential new places and special needs; but local authorities would have to look hard for other areas of savings. And in

the event the expansion of nursery education did not get off the ground in the way that had been hoped.

One way and another, the last weeks of the Heath government running up to the February 1974 election were a peculiarly sad time for the Conservative party. The verdict on what it had been able to achieve in social policy can only be mixed. The major reorganisations of housing finance, local government, the health service and pensions were all substantially revised over time – housing and pensions by Labour, health and local government by Mrs Thatcher's administrations. In part, it seems that managerially-based solutions were not enough – or perhaps they were imperfect in their own terms. There was solid achievement; but perhaps more fundamental changes were required, with maybe a new climate and confidence in which to bring them about. But one thing can certainly be said about the Heath years; if the reforms did not always succeed, it was certainly not through want of trying.

There was indeed a genuine sense of commitment about the Heath administration's social policy – nowhere demonstrated more strongly than by Joseph's approach to what he called 'the cycle of deprivation', by which certain families seemed to pass on their problems to the next generation. Although the concept was criticised by some on the Left as condescending, Joseph set up a research programme to test his hypothesis. Results of the programme were assessed in *Cycles of Disadvantage* by Michael Rutter and Nicola Madge.[5] The authors found that 'family continuity' was a moderate factor in disadvantage in intelligence, educational attainment, occupational status, crime, psychiatric disorder and 'problem family status', and a substantial factor in 'abnormalities in parenting such as child-battering'. But there are also important discontinuities – of region, for example, and indeed a reduction in continuities when the third generation is reached, so the theory should not be pressed too hard.

When it came to the February 1974 election, however, it was clear that social policy was of minor importance compared with the economic and industrial events of the day – the miners' strike, prices and incomes policy and the energy crisis. Inevitably, the Conservative social case was very much more based on what had been happening than on new promises.

There was a manifesto pledge to press on with tax credits – as soon as the economic situation allowed. *Firm Action for a Fair Britain*[6] also carried a statement that:

Subject to a right of appeal by the local authority to the Secretary of State on clearly specified grounds, we shall ensure that, in future, established Council tenants are able, as of right, to buy on reasonable terms the house or flat in which they live.

In education, the ten-year plan to make available nursery education to all three- or four-year-olds was reconfirmed, although there was to be a slow-down in the rate of expansion of further and higher education. And a firm statement was made that 'we shall continue to give the pensioner first priority in the field of social service expenditure'.

But none of this was enough to offset the feeling that the government was losing the battle with the miners – and the election was lost.

The period between the February and October elections of 1974 was a dispiriting one for the Conservative party. After Labour came to government without an overall majority (and incidentally fewer votes than the Conservatives) it was inevitable that another election would come soon: it also seemed all-but-inevitable that Labour would win. Heath's popularity was at a low ebb among many, and there was little conviction that the Tories really knew what to do about the industrial disputes that had brought about the party's fall.

None the less, the party's machine worked away at policy formation. The long and distinguished reign of Michael Fraser at the head of the Conservative Research Department came to an end. Sir Ian Gilmour became chairman of both the Conservative Research Department and of the Advisory Council on Policy, and some months later Chris Patten was appointed Director of the former.

Since there was going to be an election there had to be a manifesto, and the Shadow Cabinet was soon hard at work. One significant appointment was that of Margaret Thatcher to take over the Environment spokesmanship. She brought her energies to two areas in particular – housing and the rates.

The housing work led to a strong section in the October manifesto, *Putting Britain First*.[7] This emphasised the need to continue to bring help to areas where it was most needed with a scheme for establishing Social Priority Areas; but the particular emphasis was on help for owner-occupation. The manifesto used familiar language: 'The Conservative ideal is a property-owning democracy'.

This was to be achieved by various new subventions. One entailed varying the rate of tax payable by the building societies when interest rates generally rose, so that the government could help the societies continue to attract funds without pushing up the cost of mortgages correspondingly. Another was to provide to first-time buyers a grant of £1 for each £2 they saved (up to a certain limit). The third proposal, however, was the one that had significant long-term consequences. Council tenants who had been in their homes for three years would have the right to buy those homes at a price one-third below market value. They would have to surrender a proportion of capital gains if they resold again within five years – the first time that the party formally espoused the very successful policy of the Thatcher years.

There was a good deal of lively discussion before the policy on rates was determined. With local government expenditure growing fast, the rates had become increasingly unpopular, particularly among many reasonably well-off Tory voters. For a time Mrs Thatcher proved cautious. She believed that it would prove too costly to finance local government spending through other forms of tax such as income tax or VAT, and that therefore some form of property tax would be needed. She proposed to the Shadow Cabinet that a Select Committee should be set up on this matter, but Heath said that this was not sufficient for the manifesto. Mrs Thatcher had also come round to the view that it might be possible to shift a larger proportion of the cost of education on to the Exchequer. In the event, the manifesto committed the party to transfer to central government 'in the medium term' the cost of teachers' salaries up to a specified number. Expenditure on police and the fire service would qualify for increased central funding. Secondly there was the famous pledge on the rates:

> Within the normal lifetime of a Parliament we shall abolish the domestic rating system and replace it by taxes more broadly based and related to people's ability to pay. Local authorities must continue to have some independent source of finance.

Another active opposition spokesman was Sir Geoffrey Howe, who took on responsibility for health and social services. His probing, fertile mind was soon hard at work thinking up new plans, his sense of financial prudence barely containing his energy. A variety of ways of helping retired people were put forward, including a six-monthly review of the value of the pension – fighting inflation was still seen to be as much a matter of keeping pace with it as of striking at its roots. The second pension scheme, shelved by Labour, was to be revived and the earnings rule on the basic pension to be abolished as soon as resources allowed.

At the same time, the centre-piece of the social programme was once more to be the tax-credit scheme, starting off with a scheme of Child Credits to take the place of the existing family allowances and tax allowances – foreshadowing the child benefit which Labour actually brought in. First children would be brought into the benefit provision. There was also particular emphasis on the rights of women, including a commitment to set up an Equal Opportunities Commission. It was not hard to see the influence of Lady Howe on this.

In some ways, the trickiest area of opposition policy-making was education. A former Minister of State at the Department of Education and Science, William van Straubenzee, became spokesman, but there was soon grumbling in the party that he was too prone to seek consensus, too much in the mould of Edward Boyle to suit the current mood. By May Keith Joseph was proposing a scheme for testing standards in schools, at which van Straubenzee warned of the dangers of ministers interfering with the curriculum – the traditional view. Joseph also proposed the idea of education vouchers as a means of providing parental choice. Again van Straubenzee showed little sympathy. Before long, Heath dropped van Straubenzee and replaced him with Norman St John Stevas – not in fact a much more radical figure, but one more able to articulate the concern felt about academic standards, discipline and the drawbacks of comprehensive secondary schools. When it came to the manifesto the party said that it would set up an enquiry into the performance, size and structure of comprehensive schools. It also said that it would reopen the list of direct grant schools which Labour had closed. And one reflection of public concern about school truancy and indiscipline was to raise the possibility that the raised school age of sixteen might be modified for children seeking apprenticeships or training.

But these ingredients in a manifesto that was generally regarded as competently put together did not make any substantial difference. The October election was again lost, and the move towards a new political stance in the Conservative party began to get under way.

7 1974–9: The Coming of Thatcher

Although it was not until 11 February 1975 that Margaret Thatcher succeeded Edward Heath as Leader of the Conservative Party, 1974 was in some ways the turning point in post-war Conservative politics. Against the background of the February and October election defeats, it was the year in which the consensus really began to crack. Over the last period of the Heath government there had been rumblings, not just about the way in which Heath was handling things – for instance, his isolation from the parliamentary rank-and-file – but over the whole notion of prices and incomes policy in particular. This was seen as excessively interventionist, anti-enterprise, corporatist (with its emphasis on thrashing things out with the TUC and the CBI) and unlikely to work. Now, as they surveyed the wreck of the policy in the 1974 election, the number of dissident voices increased.

The most important of these was Sir Keith Joseph. He had had – when he had time – just occasional doubts about the policy in which he was nevertheless totally immersed; but now during the summer of 1974 he stood back, looked at the way in which Conservative policy had taken shape, and decided that the party had been in error, in effect ever since the war. As he himself puts it, it was only in April 1974 that he was converted to Conservatism. 'I had thought that I was a Conservative but now I see that I was not really one at all.'[1]

It was Joseph's speech at Preston on economic policy on 5 September 1974 that created a political sensation, but in an earlier speech at Upminster in June he announced that he was setting up the Centre for Policy Studies. He compared favourably the performance of a number of European countries – including Germany, Sweden, Holland and France – with our own, making the point that they had been governed at least part of the time by Social Democratic parties, which had nevertheless been more realistic about private enterprise than Britain had been. Interestingly he said:

> I have been entrusted by Mr Heath with drawing lessons from the relative success of these countries. To enable me to do this on the scale and depth the subject deserves, I am setting up a small policy study centre.

In a valuable interview with Anthony Seldon,[2] published in *Contemporary Record*, Joseph has described what happened. He stressed that, during all the time in government, he had never dissented from the Heath government's policies:

> Then, after the 1974 election, I said a whole load of things in criticism of the Government of which I had been a member. Now the only justification I have looking back is that while I may have been silent as a Cabinet member and did not perceive the errors we were making, I did express them fairly forcibly privately after the election and tried to persuade Ted Heath to re-examine our economic policies, particularly our attempt to overcome unemployment by means of increased spending.

He attempted to do this, not face to face, but through the Shadow Cabinet.

> Between the February 1974 general election and those Shadow Cabinets I had been persuaded by Alfred Sherman, Alan Walters and Peter Bauer, three very disenchanted old friends, very disenchanted by the errors of our policies... Now I failed to persuade Ted Heath to re-examine policies. Only then, after I failed to persuade him in Shadow Cabinet, did I go public.

It was Sherman who was the particular influence and he became the first director of the Centre for Policy Studies.

Mrs Thatcher soon became associated with the CPS, but Joseph says 'I think Margaret Thatcher had seen the light herself; I don't think I converted her... I wasn't an influence over Margaret Thatcher. We were along parallel lines'.

Joseph spoke about inflation in a speech in Leith in August 1974 but it was the Preston speech that really caught the eye with its repudiation of the counter-inflationary policies that had been pursued by both parties. Joseph's theme was that inflation was threatening to destroy our society – 'not just the relative prosperity to which most of us have become accustomed, but the savings and plans of each person and family and the working capital of each business and other organisation. The distress and unemployment that will follow unless the trend is stopped will be catastrophic'. The essential point was the old truth: when the money supply grows too quickly, inflation results. He went on to argue that we had become too dominated by the fear of unemployment and too crude in the way that we lumped all the varieties of unemployment together.

The argument was primarily economic, but of course the social significance of it was great. His next important speech, at Birmingham on 19 October 1974 (after the general election), was avowedly about social policy and caused a furore which did much to extinguish any chance that he might have had of succeeding to the leadership.

Joseph argued that the recent general election had been almost entirely about economic issues, and that the Conservatives had lost because Labour were quite uninhibited about outbidding the Conservatives 'in promising the earth'. He said 'Would it not be better to approach the public, who know that economics is not everything, as whole men rather than as economic men?' He attacked the 'permissive society', arguing that:

> The Socialist method would take away from the family and its members the responsibilities which give it cohesion. Parents are being divested of their duty to provide for their family economically, of their responsibility for education, health, upbringing, morality, advice and guidance, of saving for old age, for housing. When you take away responsibility from people you make them irresponsible.

He went on:

> Real incomes per head have risen beyond what anyone dreamed of a generation back; so have education budgets and welfare budgets, so also have delinquency, truancy, vandalism, hooliganism, illiteracy, decline in educational standards … Teenage pregnancies are rising; so are drunkenness, sexual offences, and crimes of sadism. For the first time in a century and a half, since the great Tory reformer Robert Peel set up the metropolitan police, areas of our cities are becoming unsafe for peaceful citizens by night, and even some by day.

Joseph argued that the message of socialism is that self-discipline is out of date and that the poor cannot be expected to help themselves, that they want the state to do more.

> I am not saying that we should not help the poor, far from it. But the only real lasting help we can give to the poor is helping them to

help themselves; to do the opposite, to create more dependence, is to destroy them morally, while throwing an unfair burden on society.

He went on to praise the campaigner for traditional morality, Mrs Whitehouse, and called on Tories to put over these arguments. But then he came to the passage that caused an outcry.

The balance of our population, our human stock is threatened. A recent article in *Poverty*, published by the Child Poverty Action Group, showed that a high and rising proportion of children are being born to mothers least fitted to bring children into the world and bring them up. They are born to mothers who were first pregnant in adolescence in social classes 4 and 5. Many of these girls are unmarried, many are deserted or divorced or soon will be. Some are of low intelligence, most of low educational attainment. They are unlikely to be able to give children the stable emotional background, the consistent combination of love and firmness which are more important than riches. They are producing problem children, the future unmarried mothers, delinquents, denizens of our borstals, abnormal educational establishments, prisons.

Joseph then asked what we should do about all this. Extending birth control facilities to young unmarrieds evoked understandable moral opposition – but was there an alternative 'until we are able to remoralise whole groups and classes of people'? But beyond that he simply argued that we should find a way through these moral dilemmas, primarily as individuals or 'members of all manner of bodies', but also through government.

Much of this speech foreshadowed views that would in due course be expressed increasingly strongly, and not only by Conservatives. Parliament itself turned notably less permissive than it had been in the 1960s. The theme of individual responsibility became a major theme in Conservative social policy in the late 1980s. Moreover, Joseph could claim that for the most part the statistics provided support for what he was saying, though at some points he could be held to have oversimplified the picture. But for all that there was a wide feeling that he had carried the concept of the cycle of deprivation to a point where it seemed almost to have a genetic determinism about it that gave it a shocking impact. One of the gentlest and kindest of politicians became for some people a demon.

While Joseph was thinking his thoughts, the party under Heath was, as we saw in the last chapter, producing its manifesto for the October election. The election took place on 10 October; within a few days the executive of the 1922 Committee had held its famous Milk Street meeting and before long Heath announced that there would be a leadership election to determine whether he or another should lead the party. Joseph did not stand – he himself was to say in the *Contemporary Record* interview that 'Had I become party leader, it would have been a disaster for the party, the country and for me' – and in truth he had not the temperament for the job. Perhaps he was never quite so influential again, but during these months he set out much of the essence of what came to be called Thatcherism.

For a British politician, Joseph was unusually much of an intellectual – much more so than Mrs Thatcher, whose themes have largely reflected her instincts. Joseph liked the relentless torrent of ideas that poured out from Sherman and some of the others in the manner of the old middle–European Jewish intelligentsia. Mrs Thatcher incorporated more pragmatism with her anyway instinctive rather than intellectual approach. She liked to be sent writings by Hayek and Friedman among her weekend reading, but she used them more as carapace than essence, or as sources of references and quotations rather than strict guidelines for policy.

The Centre for Policy Studies was not the only think-tank generating ideas about the directions which the Tory party might take. The Institute of Economic Affairs continued to pursue its market approach with undiminished gusto, producing a succession of publications advocating choice in welfare and such ideas as education vouchers. But its somewhat buccaneering pride in not being formally aligned with any political party – and the perhaps rather variable quality of its output – gave it a less direct political impact than the CPS, which after all was very much set up to advise Joseph and then Mrs Thatcher. The range of the CPS' subject matter was also a little wider than that of the IEA, which normally focused on economics (though certainly not in any narrow sense). Moreover, the CPS kept up a series of discussion groups on specific policy matters, often involving front bench Tories and their political advisers: it aimed to be on the inside track – and sometimes was. And both Thatcher and Joseph used the services of Sherman as a speech-writer.

But what were the themes that were to emerge in this period? Underlying them was great dissatisfaction with Britain's progress since the Second World War. This was partly a matter of our relative economic decline and the upsurge of inflation; but it straddled social as well as economic matters. Joseph talked constantly about the ratchet effect of socialism – the way that a middle ground of consensus politics had emerged where socialism was constantly able to squeeze its way to further advances and no one seemed to stand up against it. This was part and parcel of what Joseph labelled 'statism' and the denial of freedom and choice for no doubt perfectly well-intentioned reasons.

A speech at the Oxford Union in December 1975[3] sets out what Joseph felt had been happening:

> The economy is in crisis, a deeper crisis than most people realise. The unspoken consensus which makes society work is severely eroded. The rule of law is seriously attenuated from both ends by vested interests which use force and intimidation to gain their purposes; and by an ever more powerful and insolent executive. Crime and vandalism have increased to an alarming extent.
>
> We spend more than ever before on education and health, but with results that can please only the most blinkered. We spend more on welfare, without achieving well-being, while creating dangerous levels of dependency.

Mrs Thatcher agreed with Joseph's arguments, and she brought to them a strong sense of the importance of good housekeeping (and shopkeeping?). She wanted to see free market capitalism for the strong and able-bodied with compassion for the weak. To a biographer, Russell Lewis, she remarked that:

> The more people your political philosophy enables to be self-reliant and prosperous by their own efforts, the fewer you have to look after ... If we run our visions properly, there should be less and less for the social services to do, but there should be the means to enable them to do it really well.[4]

And in a speech to the Greater London Young Conservatives in July 1976 she referred as she often has done to Victorian values:

> The Victorian age, which saw the burgeoning of free enterprise, also saw the greatest expansions of voluntary philanthropic activity of all kinds: the new hospitals, new schools, technical colleges, universities, new foundations for orphans, non-profit making housing trusts, missionary societies ... We who are living largely off the

Victorians' moral and physical capital can hardly afford to denigrate them.

Earlier in the same speech she had said:

> There is not and cannot possibly be any hard and fast antithesis between self-interest and care for others, for man is a social creature, born into family, clan, community, nation, brought up in mutual dependence. The founders of our religion made this a cornerstone of morality. The admonition – love thy neighbour as thyself and do as you would be done by – expressed this. You will note that it does not denigrate self, or elevate love of others above it. On the contrary, it sees concern for self and responsibility for self as something to be expected, and asks only that this be extended to others.

Years later, on 21 May 1988, Mrs Thatcher made a speech to the Church of Scotland in which she seemed to play down the notion of society and stress individual responsibility more strongly than ever, probably provoked by a feeling that the churches more and more appeared to stress the importance of social action as opposed to individual responsibility. But there is no doubt that her instinct and preference has always been one of generosity towards those who cannot help themselves and a bracing attitude towards those who can.

Economic and social policy alike led to a determination to try to reduce the scope of the state, reduce public expenditure (for reasons monetarist, fiscal and social) and transfer more choices (and costs) to individuals. The story of social policy in the Thatcher years is to a considerable extent the story of how far these objectives have been fulfilled.

Mrs Thatcher was certainly in no position to transform the whole of Conservative social policy from the moment when she became leader. For one thing, it is doubtful if she had thought the whole area through. She had, of course, been Secretary of State for Education throughout the Heath government and she had earlier served for a spell as junior minister for pensions. She had been opposition spokesman on the environment after the February 1974 defeat and had a spell in the 1960s as transport spokesman. But she had generally been seen not as a generalist in politics but as someone who would immerse herself with great competence in her particular subject. True, by the time she became leader she had in fact covered much of the ground (apart from health), and she was always prepared to bring her knowledge to bear, but she had not evidently taken a strategic view of social policy in the way that Macleod and Powell, for example, had done in earlier years.

But there were other important factors. One was that throughout the years in opposition there were other politically more urgent areas on which to concentrate – most notably, economic and industrial policy. She had also to develop a grip of foreign and defence policy – areas in which she had had virtually no involvement. This is not to say that she neglected social policy. Not only was she far too hardworking for that, but she saw certain facets – housing in particular – as having great political scope. But the pressure of other matters tended to limit the time she could spend in this field.

At the same time, it must be remembered that she did not immediately move into an overwhelmingly commanding position within the party the moment she had defeated both Heath and Whitelaw for the leadership. The parliamentary party had been fairly narrowly divided in the election and the members of the Shadow Cabinet had predominantly support Heath. She knew very well that she had to work with people who had not voted for her, and also that the party machine was not likely to be instinctively of her way of thinking. She made one of her leading supporters, Angus Maude, chairman of the Conservative Research Department and Keith Joseph chairman of the Advisory Council on Policy, but the able young Chris Patten, who had been Director of the Research Department under Ian Gilmour's chairmanship, remained in his job. It is always worth remembering of Mrs Thatcher that she rates competence as highly as ideological commitment.

One other point is worth making. Mrs Thatcher knew well that part of the reason for Heath's downfall was his loss of contact with the rank and file of the parliamentary party: his defeat was sometimes described as the Peasants' Revolt, and she was keen to let the backbench committees and particularly their officers feel that they were part of the policy-making process.

But the main drive lay with the coalition that made up the Shadow Cabinet. There was a feeling that in the opposition years under Heath the party had become over-committed to a mass of detailed proposals, and initially at least there was more emphasis on stating themes.

The policy process was soon under way. Joseph presented to the Shadow Cabinet in April 1975 a document entitled 'Notes Towards the Definition of Policy' which set out his view of what was needed. He pointed to the errors of the past: the commitment to full employment 'in the sense of a job for everyone of the kind, location and reward he broadly considers right, regardless of wage-levels, productivity and the state of the economy and the world'; over-promising in housing, reflected in decades of rent control and expensive council building, which had only led to homelessness, costly new slums and a housing crisis; in education, the overriding of differences of talent, motivation and home background, leading to a decline in levels of education and behaviour from which the poor had suffered most; the increase in crime resulting from progressive views; mass immigration imposed against the wishes and foreboding of the overwhelming majority; the over-extension of local authorities; the subordination of the rule of law to the avoidance of conflict; the denial of rewards for talent; and the failure to resist political and moral attacks on society and its values.

Joseph offered his views as to how these problems should be approached. In social policy he particularly stressed the family. As we have seen, at the DHSS he had become concerned about the 'cycle of deprivation' – the way in which problem families pass on their problems from one generation to the next. In this paper he talked of the harm done inadvertently to the strength of families by urban redevelopment, the dependence on two incomes, too much television, easier divorce and the spread of the one-parent family. The results seemed to include hooliganism, truancy, alcoholism, child abuse and criminality generally. Ways had to be found of rebuilding family life and responsibility – perhaps by incentives to mothers to stay at home, perhaps by education vouchers which would increase choice and therefore responsibility, certainly by reducing dependence on council housing and encouraging voluntary services generally.

Joseph was given the task of chairing a Shadow Cabinet subcommittee which would examine policy proposals before they went to the full Shadow Cabinet and a network of policy study groups got under way. There was a strong emphasis on public expenditure control – there were to be no further increases in public expenditure and cuts wherever possible, with a special public sector group under John Nott given the task of working with the policy groups to see how cuts could be achieved.

During the summer of 1976 the policy groups presented their first reports to the Shadow Cabinet. The social services policy group under Patrick Jenkin reiterated the familiar difficulties of increasing demand and lack of resources which faced the National Health Service, but did not come up with any very radical response. It said that Labour's policy of closing pay beds in NHS hospitals should be reversed and the private sector encouraged; administrative costs should be reduced; preventive measures such as fluoridation encouraged; and the length of stay of patients in many hospitals reduced. Prescription charges would go up and the area health authorities might be abolished. The vexed question of whether the whole system should move towards an insurance base, on the pattern of some continental countries, was left for futher examination.

The social security review produced some proposals to ease life for the self-employed and to tackle abuse. There was a plan to discuss with employers the possibility of firms taking on responsibility for paying sick pay for the first four weeks of illness, with 5000 to 6000 civil servants being saved and employers having the national insurance contribution reduced. On the familiar question of a tax credit scheme, it was reasserted that the party was committed to the principle, but that once again more work needed to be done on its costing. At least a start might be made – and credit with women gained – by endorsing the child benefit scheme which Labour had postponed. On pensions, the party had already affirmed its readiness to keep Labour's 1975 Social Security Pensions Act. The party was willing to take the question of the second pension out of the political cockpit – not least because the pensions industry and employers were anxious for stability.

The interim report on education, from a group under Norman St John Stevas, gave in some ways the most interesting foretaste of what was to come. The emphasis was on quality. National minimum standards for reading, writing and arithmetic were to be set and assessed as part of a scheme for the national monitoring of schools. The idea of a common examination at sixteen was to be opposed, at least in the form put forward by the Schools Council, and that body was probably to be abolished. There was to be an experiment with vouchers, play groups were to be encouraged (Mrs Thatcher's scheme for universal nursery provision would be dropped), the ILEA was to be reviewed and early school leaving allowed for those going into valid apprenticeships. There was also to be parental choice of schools unless local education authorities could show that this entailed unreasonable expenditure.

A policy group under David Lane on urban deprivation came up with a report urging additional funding for up to ten areas, although William Whitelaw, through whom the group reported, did not endorse the plea for additional funding. Michael Heseltine, in a report on regional policy, proposed the creation of regional development councils for England on the pattern of the Scottish and Welsh development agencies.

The policy group under Keith Speed tackled one of the knottiest of questions – local government finance. Mrs Thatcher's commitment in the October 1974 election to abolish domestic rates was very much in people's minds, but the question of how exactly this was to be done was not yet ready for answer. Government would however provide the bulk of the cost of education and social services. The Shadow Cabinet accepted this, but it did not agree to the proposal that central government should be empowered to fix an absolute limit or cap on local authority spending. More work clearly needed to be done.

The housing report was produced in June 1976. I was chief environment spokesman at the time and Hugh Rossi was the housing spokesman: together with a good team we worked to produce a policy document that laid the foundations for housing policy after 1979. The aims were to 'maximise choice and the provision of housing appropriate to people's needs, desires and resources, with particular emphasis on the opportunity of owner occupation'; to effect a significant reduction in public expenditure on housing; and to stress the positive attractions of the new approach and handle it in a way which would minimise the kind of opposition which had been shown to the 1972 Housing Finance Act.

The paper did not endorse the idea being pressed by Peter Walker that council houses should be given to their occupants but it favoured the right of tenants to buy the freeholds of their houses after three years of occupancy. The normal conditions would include a 30 per cent discount on market value plus 1 per cent a year up to a 50 per cent maximum. Local authorities would have the right to buy back the houses if the first purchasers wished to sell them within five years; and the sale price was not to fall below the cost of the house.

In the private rented sector, the plans envisaged the gradual restoration of a climate in which private renting would once more be seen as acceptable. Security of tenure could not be generally abolished, but some decontrol would be brought in and a 'shorthold' system of fixed-term lettings which did not confer security would be introduced.

In the public sector, the aim was firm limits on new building and a significant reduction in public expenditure, to be achieved primarily by a reduction of central government grant, which would push up council rents, and by the support for home ownership. The possibility of restricting rate fund contributions to housing revenue accounts was mooted. Public sector provision generally was to be concentrated on particular categories of need, such as sheltered dwellings. The somewhat generous Parker Morris space standards for council housing would be reviewed, but a tenants' charter would be put forward.

Overall, it was suggested very tentatively that on a housing budget of a little over £4 billion, some £700 million might be saved in the first year and £1500 million after three. The paper was prepared very close to the time of the Labour Government's recourse to the International Monetary Fund – a climate in which the control of public expenditure seemed more than ever important; and housing was seen as a major contributor in this regard – though the right-to-buy proposals (which included shared purchase schemes) were intended to provide a strong positive balance.

Perhaps I might add that these proposals were warmly received by the leadership – but the paper's author rather less so: I was replaced as environment spokesman in the Autumn by Michael Heseltine – on the not unreasonable grounds that he would be better at selling the package.

Parallel with the housing paper a paper on land policy accepted that some form of tax on development gain or betterment was necessary, but undertook to repeal the Labour Government's Community Land Act.

One other significant paper in the field of social policy was put forward by William Whitelaw – that on immigration policy. Keith Joseph (prodded no doubt by the strongly anti-immigrant Sherman) had on several occasions put forward public concern on this issue, notably in his Birmingham speech, and found a not entirely unsympathetic ear in Mrs Thatcher. Both in opposition and in government, she *normally* refrained from treading on Whitelaw's territory. But Whitelaw was ready to argue for a tightening up of the control, with the aim that the British people be given the prospect of an end to immigration. There should be a register of all dependents eligible to come, with a cut-off date to their entitlement. The entry of dependants should be subject to an annual quota, only one wife should be admitted and the annual quota for United Kingdom passport holders from East Africa should be reduced from 5000 to 3500.

All this energetic policy work was designed to enable a major statement to be published in the autumn of 1976, and in due course *The Right Approach*[5] appeared on the eve of the October party conference. It was a well-presented booklet, seen as an 'approach' or strategy rather than a detailed document. The emphasis naturally was on economic and industrial policy, but the sections on social policy by and large reflected the policy work of the previous year.

Not everything put forward in that policy exercise, however, found its way into *The Right Approach*. The immigration proposals were in some ways less specific. There was nothing about a cut-off date for dependants or a lowered quota for the UK passport holders. There was however a pledge to bring in a new Nationality Act 'to allay fears of unending immigration and to establish a rational basis for British citizenship'.

The section on local government finance is also worth noting. Indeed it was focused on local authority spending. There was no mention of the pledge to abolish the domestic rate. Instead, the booklet said that:

> The tensions between the government and the authorities in the summer of this year over the Rate Support Grant probably herald the death throes of the present system. The need for substantial changes has in any case been made clear by the analysis of the Layfield Committee.

The section then seems to go back to the idea of some kind of national controls on the *total* of local authority spending, coupled with much greater freedom as to how that money should be spent.

The Right Approach was not a radical document, but it played a significant part in showing that the Conservative party had moved on from the agonies of the last part of the Heath era and was confidently rebuilding its policies. A year later came *The Right Approach to the Economy*[6] setting out an economic strategy. Significantly, its four authors were Geoffrey Howe, Keith Joseph, James Prior and David Howell – a quartet designed to show that the 'wets' and 'dries' were in harmony. Its policies were largely outside the scope of this book, though of course the commitment to firm management of public expenditure was important. The Labour government's recourse to the IMF in 1976 was still fresh in everyone's minds, as was Anthony Crosland's famous admonition to local government that 'the party's over'.

In many ways, the financial crisis of summer 1976 was the turning point in Labour's years of office between 1974 and 1978. Harold Wilson had resigned earlier in the year, to be replaced by James Callaghan. The Callaghan period was dominated more and more by economic and industrial problems, by the long-running wrangle about devolution for Scotland and Wales and by the fact that in its latter period the government was only kept in power by the Lib-Lab pact, with the result that its ability to produce controversial legislation was severely limited. Certainly in social policy it was the 1974–5 and 1975–6 Sessions of Parliament that proved most active.

The least controversial major measure was the 1975 Social Security Pensions Bill. As Barbara Castle said when she commended the Bill on Second Reading on 18 March 1975, this was the third attempt in five years to tackle the problem. The previous Labour government's Bill came too late to reach the Statute Book in 1969. Sir Keith Joseph's Act had been passed, but not put into operation. Now she was coming forward with an attempt to provide a measure which would endure.

It was based on five aims. Pensions must be adequate – which meant that the scheme had an element of redistribution to help the low paid. It must have a shorter period of maturity than the existing scheme. It must allow women at work equal responsibilities and rights with men. It must end discrimination against manual workers – and it set about doing this by basing benefits on the recipient's best 20 years of earnings, rather than his final salary. And it must be inflation-proofed, both in the public and the private sector.

The Opposition thought carefully about how it should respond, and the spokesman, Norman Fowler, took extensive soundings of the pensions industry in particular, as well as of business in general. He found a strong desire for certainty and stability. Accordingly, at Second Reading, he expressed considerable doubts about the problems of inflation proofing, in the private sector in particular, but nevertheless came to the view that the Conservative Party should not vote against the Bill. It duly became an Act, and at the time was thought likely to endure.

Two other measures in 1975 proved much more controversial. One was the Housing Finance (Special Provisions) Act, by which Anthony Crosland rather shamefacedly exempted the Clay Cross councillors from the surcharges they had incurred by their defiance of the 1972 Housing Finance Act. A provision exempting them from disqualification was defeated during the passage of the Bill.

The other measure was the 1975 Community Land Act, by which John Silkin took up the mantle of his father Lewis Silkin – a minister under Attlee – in tackling the question of land development. Its aims were:

to enable the community to control the development of land in accordance with its needs and priorities and to restore to the community the increase in the value of land arising from its efforts.[7]

But this time, instead of a national Land Commission the decision was taken to give local government the control of land development and a substantial slice of the profits accruing from it – though the Treasury would take a share. Initially there would be a development land tax of 80 per cent; in due course 100 per cent of the development gain would be taken, and local government would dispose of all but small parcels of land.

The opposition, with Hugh Rossi as the land spokesman, attacked the Bill flamboyantly, concentrating particularly on the grounds that it would lead to the complete stagnation of development and housebuilding. There was a fairly general feeling that the government had not got it right, but with its majority it carried the day in Parliament.

The next session saw two more controversial measures. One was the 1976 Education Act, brought in by Fred Mulley but completed by his successor as Secretary of State, Shirley Williams. Its aim was to convert all secondary schools to comprehensives. The previous Labour government had used a circular issued in 1965 to try to bring this about; and in fact between 1965 and 1970 almost 1000 new comprehensive schools were established. This circular was withdrawn by Mrs Thatcher, but another 1000 comprehensives were established between 1970 and 1974. But in spite of attempts by the new Labour government to speed up the process, seven local authorities had made it clear that they would retain some measure of selection.

The new measure gave the Secretary of State power to call for proposals for secondary reorganisation, but it did not set any time limit on the operation, in recognition of varying local circumstances. Some local authorities, like Buckinghamshire, were accordingly able to spin things out until the Thatcher government repealed the Act. Moreover, in 1976 an important court case concerning the Conservative Tameside Council's plans for retaining selective schools provided a brake on government action by ruling in effect that ministers must not themselves act unreasonably in ruling that a local authority had acted unreasonably. It was a decision that had implications that went wider than the field of education.

The other controversial measure was the 1976 Health Services Act. It will be recalled that Aneurin Bevan had agreed to allow private practice and paybeds to continue in the hospitals of the National Health Service, but for a long time socialists had pressed for either the complete abolition of private practice or at least its removal from the

NHS. The government now decided to bring about the latter. There was a period of protracted wrangling with the medical profession, during which the lawyer, Lord Goodman, was brought in to try to negotiate an agreed solution. The government made concessions, allowing a gradual run-down of paybeds, but the fact remained that they were to go and also that the private sector was to be regulated. There were some in the private sector who felt that separation might make for an easier solution, but the opposition, led by Patrick Jenkin, argued vigorously that the government's plan would lose the NHS useful revenue – some £30 to £40 million a year – and that doctors would be tempted to withdraw from the NHS, and perhaps from the country. They pointed with relish to Bevan's words in the Standing Committee on the NHS Bill (21 May 1946) that the more the consultant spends his time in the hospital, the better for everyone concerned. Again, the government won its measure, but it was rapidly overturned in 1979.

The combination of parliamentary opposition with longer-term research meant that, in the field of social policy at least, the first half of the opposition years between 1974 and 1979 saw the breaking of the back of the task of reformulating the party's position. The *Campaign Guide* for the next election appeared unusually early in the cycle, in 1977,[8] with a supplement a year later. This early publication was partly a reflection of the fact that a minority government, which in due course became dependent on the Lib-Lab pact, might have to go to the country at any time; but it probably also reflected the progress that had been made on the policy front. Anyway, the latter years of Callaghan's government were more and more dominated by the political scene – the devolution battle but above all the long saga of industrial and economic affairs and union power which culminated in the Winter of Discontent of 1978–9.

Although it was by no means foreordained that the Conservatives would win the next election – many felt that Callaghan might have won if he had gone to the country in September 1978, as he so nearly did – it was nevertheless a period when the tide of ideas seemed to be flowing in the Tory direction. The long work of the Institute of Economic Affairs, and more recently of the Centre for Policy Studies, was beginning to make headway. There was increasing dissatisfaction with the corporatism implicit in the so-called Social Contract between the Labour government and the unions. Callaghan himself had responded in October 1976 to what had been very much a Tory theme when he called at Ruskin College for a 'great debate' on standards in education.

And in the universities Conservative thinkers were beginning to make the running.

An example of this was a book called *The Conservative Opportunity*.[9] Edited by two Oxford dons, Lord Blake and John Patten, it was a collection of essays by mostly academic contributors from Oxford. Blake in his opening chapter was very critical of the Heath administration, not least over such measures as the reforms of local government and the health service. He went on to question whether increasing public expenditure on social services should continue to be seen as the hallmark of progress and described the surge of feeling against bureaucracy which had recently swelled up.

Patten's essay on housing was particularly knowledgeable and interesting. (He was to become Minister of Housing some years later.) He did not advocate a crude market solution on IEA lines. He was prepared to accept the value of council housing in terms that would be rather unfashionable today. But he also saw its limitations, not least its paternalism, quoting the well-known description by Frank Field, then director of the Child Poverty Action Group, of council tenants being treated like serfs. To meet this, Patten supported the idea of a Tenants' Charter, incorporated in *The Right Approach*. At the same time, he accepted the need for rents to rise and also for energetic measures to promote home ownership, including of course the sale of council houses. (He was lukewarm about Peter Walker's idea that they should be given away.) He argued that it was cheaper for society to support home ownership through tax relief than council housing through subsidies, but that the proceeds of council sales could be used to build new council houses where necessary – not a view that was to be supported by, say, Nicholas Ridley a decade later.

An essay by Vernon Bogdanor exposed some of the arguments that were to feature in Conservative education policy over the next decade. Bogdanor saw the aims as the creation of an enlightened citizenry and the pursuit of quality. He argued that the consensus created by the 1944 Education Act had been replaced by an attempt to create a new progressive consensus rooted in institutional changes designed to create a more egalitarian society and in the belief that educational advance could be measured by the resources devoted to education. Bogdanor wrote:

> The role of the Conservative Party during this period was a passive one; it found itself unable to combat the new consensus; some Conservatives, dazzled by contemporary fashions, were happy to

accept it: but most Conservatives remained obstinately attached to the *status quo*. The sad result was that the Conservative Party became defensive and apologetic about education; its policies became concessionary and not creative.

Bogdanor put forward proposals that were later to be broadly implemented by the Thatcher government: the setting up of attainment standards for the ages of seven, nine, eleven and fourteen and some means of monitoring them, and the introduction of greater parental choice of school. He rejected the idea of the education voucher on the grounds that it would shift resources into more favoured schools from those in areas of deprivation, creating a kind of educational apartheid. 'Anything militating more strongly against a true Conservative philosophy it is difficult to imagine.' The One Nation view should prevail over the market argument. Beyond that, Bogdanor argues that the age of selection should finally shift from eleven to fourteen. He also argued that the true Conservative approach was that power should shift from central to local government – the reverse of the 1988 Education Reform Act. Indeed, at that stage Conservative thinking was generally more sympathetic to local government than it later became: the phenomenon of the 'loony left' in local government had not yet surfaced, apart from the defiance of the 1972 Housing Finance Act in Clay Cross, Derbyshire.

As the general election drew nearer, so a number of Conservative policies received greater definition – the idea of an assisted places scheme in secondary schools, for example. And one quietly receded – the pledge to abolish domestic rates was not formally dropped, but it was emphasised that the reduction of income tax and the restoration of the economy must take priority. Keith Speed said of the abolition proposal at Gloucester in September 1977, 'It would be wrong to pretend that the task could be accomplished easily within the lifetime of a Parliament'.

Eventually in May 1979 the election took place. The Conservative Manifesto[10] inevitably concentrated once again on industrial relations and sound money, together with denationalisation, cuts in income tax and steps towards a property-owning democracy. But the rule of law received a strong emphasis – crime was a mounting concern. The question of capital punishment was to be left to a free vote of the Commons, but a short, sharp shock system for certain young criminals was to be tried out. The recommendations of the Edmund-Davies review body on police pay were to be implemented in full. There was also a relatively detailed section on immigration, which stressed the argument that effective control was essential if racial harmony was to be achieved.

It was not long since Mrs Thatcher had talked in a television interview of people's fears of being 'swamped' by immigration, and the proposals were designed to relieve this fear. But William Whitelaw, as Shadow Home Secretary, really wanted to see the whole question taken off the political agenda, using a register of those entitled to come in conjunction with a quota system to hold out the prospect of an end to substantial immigration. A number of other restrictions were to be introduced, and the whole system was to be buttressed by a new, and overdue, British Nationality Act, which would replace the outdated citizenship of the United Kingdom and Colonies.

Social policy generally was treated in a chapter of the manifesto headed 'Helping the Family'. The proposals on housing were broadly similar to those in the policy paper, though there was not much indication of the plan to secure substantial reductions in housing expenditure. In education, there was naturally a pledge to end those sections of Labour's 1976 Education Act which required all secondary schools to be comprehensive. There was a statement that the Government's Assessment of Performance Unit would set national standards in reading, writing and arithmetic, to be monitored by tests worked out with teachers and others and applied locally by education authorities – a pledge that was not redeemed until the 1988 Education Reform Act. There was also emphasis on greater parental choice, a requirement for schools to issue prospectuses, including examination results, and the plan to revive the old direct grant principle, abolished by Labour, with a scheme for assisted places at certain designated schools.

The health service section did not say much. Paybeds would continue to be provided and tax relief restored on health insurance schemes at work. The possibility of more radical changes – such as greater reliance on insurance for NHS funding – was no more than hinted at. And on social security it was made clear that progress towards the goal of a tax credit scheme would be slow, for reasons both of cost and technical problems to do with computers. However, child benefits were welcomed as a step in the right direction.

Overall, the manifesto was probably well-judged – it certainly avoided a mass of potentially awkward detail. Anyway on 3 May the election was duly won, by a majority over Labour of 70, and a watershed in British politics reached.

8 1979–83: Thatcher in Government

Chris Patten once said of Mrs Thatcher: 'She's the only party leader I can think of, certainly in the post-war period, who's been more radical in government than in opposition'.[1] Over time, in social policy this remark has certainly been proved true. Education, local government, housing and to some extent social security have all seen major changes – not just of organisation but also of philosophy: only in health, prior to 1989, did the radical spirit make little headway. Indeed, some of the changes – for instance in the powers of local government or the control of education – were probably not even contemplated by Mrs Thatcher when she came to office in 1979.

The initial emphasis after the May victory was very largely on the control of public expenditure. The debate on the Address following the Queen's speech on 15 May 1979 did, however, see the setting of certain important themes. The Prime Minister herself tackled the question of 'How is society to be improved?'. Her answer was characteristic:

By millions of people resolving that they will give their own children a better life than they had themselves ... For too long individuals have been unable to benefit their families sufficiently from the fruits of their efforts.

Her second theme was that of restoring choice to individuals.

Many, many people wish to see choice return, whether it is choice over how people spend their own money or more choice in housing and education, and some choice in health.

These simple statements were in many ways to be at the heart of social policy over the next decade.

Sir Geoffrey Howe's first Budget followed a month later, on 12 June 1979. The main feature was a significant reduction in income tax, together with an increase in VAT. But Howe stressed strongly the need to get a grip on public expenditure and borrowing as part of his monetary policy, though he was limited in what he could do by the fact that it was already two and a half months into the financial year.

107

His policy was that 'Finance must determine expenditure, not expenditure finance'. He would not automatically raise cash limits to accommodate public sector price increases, although pay commitments to universities and health authorities would be honoured. As far as local government was concerned, some account would be taken in rate support grant increase orders of pay settlements, but there would be a significant reduction from the level needed for full funding. The reduction totalled £350 million (against total rate support grant of about £9 billion). Health service spending would not be reduced, but prescription and dental charges would go up.

There was an important development in social security. The government increased the retirement pension by £6.10p for couples and £3.80p for single pensioners, which took account of an under-estimate made by the previous government of the likely rise in earnings between November 1977 and November 1978. (Eventually the government sensibly reverted to the system of basing increases on actual or historic increases, rather than projections.) Other social security benefits were also raised, though not child benefit which had gone up only two months before. But what looked in general quite a generous package was accompanied by the significant decision that from then on social security benefits would be protected against increases in prices but not, as had been the case, against whichever was higher of rises in prices and earnings. It was a clear sign that the costs of social security must be contained. The decision naturally gave Labour a certain amount of ammunition over the years and led to pensioners feeling that they were falling behind (perhaps particularly at the 1987 election), but it never proved a real political embarrassment.

✳ Overall, the impact of Howe's Budget was probably to introduce the notion that the country was entering an era of 'cuts' in the public services: the underlying assumption of continuous expansion which had lasted for 30 years since the Second World War had come to an end. In fact this had already been heralded in the Callaghan, Healey, Crosland era after 1976. Crosland had proclaimed that the local government party was over, Healey had turned to the IMF, Callaghan had started to stress that you could not spend what you had not got. But with Labour the assumption was that all this was being done very reluctantly: under Mrs Thatcher the argument was that people were entitled to keep more of their own earnings.

Although the objective was to bring about cuts – and cuts in real terms were made, at least as against earlier expectations – in fact the combination of demography and unemployment caused a considerable increase in social security spending. There was an increase of about half a million in the number of retirement pensioners between 1978–9 and 1982–3. The number receiving unemployment benefit more than doubled over that time, while the number of people receiving rate rebates shot up from just over three million to just under five million. By and large 'cutting' public expenditure meant no more than holding down its rate of increase.

Apart from the budget and public expenditure changes, 1979 saw little more than an Act making provision for the regular payment of the £10 Christmas bonus to pensioners and another one restoring to local authorities their freedom to decide whether or not they wanted their secondary schools to be comprehensive. Naturally enough, the following year was legislatively busier.

One significant Act was the Local Government, Planning and Land Act which launched the series of local government Acts which have marked the Thatcher years. Mrs Thatcher had never served in local government, and her time at the Department of Education and Science does not seem to have given her any particular sympathy for it. Nor was her first Environment Secretary, Michael Heseltine, very different in his approach, although generally speaking he was a more avowed interventionist than she was.

Anyway the 1980 Act, although reducing or relaxing a large number of lesser controls, gave central government a tighter grip over local spending than it had previously possessed. The existing system was widely recognised as having faults: it was very hard to understand and was largely based on a system of rewarding high spending, which was much resented by the lower spenders. But the new system was not less complex and the attempt to put rate support grant on to an objective basis was not really achieved. Indeed, a renewed attempt was to be one of the objectives of Nicholas Ridley's 1988 Local Government Finance Act.

The essence of the 1980 Act was the introduction of expenditure targets based on an assessment of expenditure needs. This was the so-called GREA (grant related expenditure assessment). But these targets had the drawback from the government's point of view that in some cases they would be higher than existing expenditure levels, so that authorities would be tempted to increase their spending – while the high spending authorities would not necessarily come down to their GREA levels. An additional system of government-determined spending targets was therefore introduced. Authorities which overspent on these targets were to lose grant accordingly. Conservative as well as Labour local authorities found the new system not only confusing but, in many cases, objectionable in principle. Local government had always had to accept that central government could determine how much support it gave, but the idea of intervening to influence the amount raised by the rate was regarded by some as unconstitutional and by many as unnecessary.

But the government had its arguments. First of all, it held that the amount of local spending had a real impact on the economy of the country, and was anyway part of public expenditure, which it was pledged to contain. Moreover, it had long been accepted that the government was entitled to control the amount of capital, as opposed to current, spending. Next, the government argued that excessive rate demands were driving industry away from areas where it was often particularly needed; and overall it held that a party that was trying to reduce government and its powers and costs could not leave local government out of the operation. But whatever the merits of the case, the 1980 Act did not suffice to achieve what was wanted. Local authorities found ways round it, by raiding their reserves, devising schemes of 'creative accountancy' such as capitalising expenditure, and by levying supplementary rates. The government had to bring in a further Bill two years later.

The Michael Heseltine–John Stanley 1980 Housing Act proved much more popular, for it introduced the right to buy council housing. Council and new town corporation tenants who had been tenants for at least three years were enabled to buy their homes with the aid of generous discounts, and a small social revolution got under way. Between the 1979 and the 1983 general elections something like half a million council house sales took place: the number was later to pass the million mark. It was far and away the most dramatic boost to home ownership since the Second World War. Across the land one could see the results as the new owners set to work to distinguish their properties from the old council houses in ways that may not always have pleased the aesthetes but which clearly gladdened the hearts of the new owners.

Labour naturally opposed the policy, and it was not only Labour authorities that had doubts about the absolute right to buy. In some rural areas, for example, councils felt that former council houses would be 'gentrified' and lost over time to the less well-off villagers. Housing specially designed for the old and disabled was exempted; but the policy by which local authorities were only able to spend a limited proportion of the receipts from council house sales on new building was also to concern those who had originally supported the right to buy on the ground that it would help to fund new council building. But the fact remains that the right to buy was a triumphant success for the Conservatives, as it brought home ownership to many who would otherwise have no hope of achieving it. It represented the old notion of the property-owning democracy in vigorous action (and was to be matched, of course, by the massive increase in share-ownership brought about by privatisation). Anyway, in due course Labour gave up the struggle to oppose the right to buy and its repeal disappeared from their programme.

The Housing Act also introduced two other measures. One was a tenants' charter for local authority housing, which gave a number of useful rights. The other affected the private rented sector. The new system of 'shorthold' tenancies, propagated by Sir Brandon Rhys Williams, was adopted. This allowed landlords to let for fixed terms of between one and five years, subject to certain safeguards. The Act also brought in 'assured tenancies' by which approved landlords could build for rent at freely negotiated rents, outside the Rent Acts. Assured tenants would have security of tenure. Both these measures seemed sensible enough, but neither achieved the hoped-for revival of the private rented sector.

The third important Act of 1980 was the Education Act, brought in by Mark Carlisle. Its first aim was to widen parental choice of schools. Within certain limits on numbers parents were to be able to send their children to the school of their choice, even if the school were in another education authority's area. Secondly, the statutory requirements to provide milk and meals were withdrawn; the proposal that this should also apply to transport was defeated in the House of Lords and not reinstated. Thirdly, schools were normally to have their own governing bodies, with parent and teacher representation. Fourthly, the Act made clear that education authorities were not compelled to provide nursery education – something that had not been clear since the 1944 Act. Lastly, the Act set up the Assisted Places Scheme, under which independent secondary schools could offer places to the fees of which government contributes on the basis of the parents' means. This was a replacement for the old direct grant school system, abolished by Labour.

The Education Act was a significant piece of legislation, implementing ideas which Mrs Thatcher had not attempted to promote when she was Secretary of State a decade earlier. It demonstrated that the arguments of the new radicals in the field of education – the *Black*

Paper group, the Centre for Policy Studies, the Institute of Economic Affairs and others – were beginning to have some impact against a background of growing doubt about the effectiveness of the mono-lithic-seeming local authority system in delivering quality. The demand for choice was mounting: the advocates of the voucher system, for example, were still vociferous.

There was also pressure at this time for another change: the abolition of the Inner London Education Authority and the transfer of its powers to the boroughs. But here, as with vouchers, change was not adopted – for the time being. A careful enquiry was carried out by a ministerial committee under Lady Young, the Minister of State for Education. It was not persuaded that all the boroughs would be capable of operating effective systems; it was concerned about the difficulties of managing further education at a time when provision for over 16-year-olds was increasingly seen as involving both schools and further education colleges; it was also aware that there was a good deal of respect for such ILEA services as adult education and special education. Nor was there yet the concern about the hard left that grew up later.

The other area where there was significant legislation in 1980 was social security. In the course of two Acts a number of changes were made. In the supplementary benefit system, the Supplementary Benefits Commission was abolished and their work taken over directly by the Department of Health and Social Security, with a Social Security Advisory Committee. At the same time, the range of discretionary payments was reduced and entitlements were to be more clear-cut. In the second Act, a long-standing grievance among Conservatives was tackled; families of those on strike were deemed to be receiving a certain level of strike pay, resulting in a reduction of benefit. There was also a tightening up of certain rules with a view to fighting abuse of social security, together with a move towards making short-term benefits liable to income tax, as retirement and widows' pensions were already. The government was gradually trying to bring a greater tightness into the social security system, both for political reasons and, fundamentally, because of the daunting prospect of ever-increasing demands, from the mounting number of retired people in particular.

In legislative terms, 1981 was a quieter year in social policy. The Budget saw an increase in child benefit, but the most important Act was a well-received measure implementing recommendations of the Warnock Committee on special education which had reported in 1978.

The definition of handicapped children was widened and local authorities were required to make a full assessment of the needs of any handicapped child. Parents were also given the right to appeal against LEA decisions as to which school a handicapped child should be sent.

The main arguments in educational policy at this time concerned not legislation but public expenditure. The school population fell by something like a tenth between 1978–9 and 1982–3, and the March 1980 white paper on expenditure[2] had projected a 6.9 per cent fall in expenditure in real terms over that period. The government's view was that this fall would still allow an improvement in the pupil–teacher ratio: it saw significant cut-backs as coming in school meals and milk. But in reality nothing like the planned public expenditure cuts were achieved, because the local authorities used their freedom to spend well above the level on education which the government had postulated. The drop over the period stated was only about 1.2 per cent in real terms. Nevertheless, it was a period of some contraction. Several hundred schools were closed, spending on books fell and the rise in nursery education which Mrs Thatcher had originally planned was halted, but the pupil–teacher ratio in English schools fell from 19.5 in 1978 to 18.1 in 1983. The steady decline which had taken place since the mid-1950s was maintained.

Public expenditure was also inevitably the dominant factor in health policy during the first Thatcher government. But where in education there was at least the fall in pupil numbers, all the factors in health seemed to push towards higher costs. The old idea that a better health service would reduce the amount of treatment required had long since vanished: in particular, as people lived longer so their demands on the service increased. At the same time, the constant progress in medical technology and drugs has pushed up most costs relentlessly. Moreover, health is labour intensive. The throughput of hospitals has increased rapidly as new methods of treatment have made shorter stays feasible and managers have become more aware that productivity can be produced by greater bed occupancy; but the flow of patients awaiting to occupy those beds has normally been ceaseless, and they have all required care and treatment.

In the period between 1978 and 1982 the number of nurses in the NHS in England rose by some 45 000 – from 351 000 to 396 000; doctors and dentists increased from 36 000 to 40 000. The total staff increase over this time was 66 000. A particularly important development was that nurses had their working week reduced from 40 to 37½ hours, which in itself triggered off the need for a substantial increase in their numbers. Moreover, their pay between 1978–9 and 1981–2 rose on average by 61 per cent, against a rise in prices of about 52 per cent.

These factors inevitably had considerable public expenditure implications. The government achieved a growth rate in health spending of 3 per cent in real terms, but even with higher charges the combination of these factors (not least the growth in the number of the very old) meant that a substantial proportion of that growth rate was swallowed up in the process of simply maintaining existing levels of service. Administrative savings and contracting out might do something to help, but the open-ended nature of the service made people feel that crisis was almost endemic to it.

Health was always liable to create political problems; but the greater drama came elsewhere. During the spring and summer of 1981 social concern was dominated by a series of events which sent something of a tremor through the country – the riots which took place in Brixton, Toxteth (Liverpool), Moss Side (Manchester), the West Midlands, Southall (West London) and other urban areas. They were not – it was generally agreed – race riots, in the sense of black and white communities fighting each other, but the rioters were predominantly black. In Southall, the Asian youth responded violently to racialist provocation from outside – but it was the police who bore the brunt of their onslaught. In the other areas, the rioters were primarily youths of West Indian origin who came into fierce conflict with police and the Establishment. (In Toxteth, the black community had roots which went back further than the post-war West Indian migration, and the proportion of those of direct African descent was much higher.) In the extraordinary rampaging and looting which took place plenty of whites also joined in.

In fact, the first foretaste of violence had come the previous year, in Bristol. There, just before Easter, in the largely black St Paul's area, a police search for drugs in a club had triggered off a violent reaction. For a while, the police were badly outnumbered, and they were withdrawn for a time by the Chief Constable until reinforcements were mobilised. The rioting had started in the early evening; it was over by midnight. During its course, considerable damage to police cars, shops and other premises was inflicted, but the greatest concern was caused by the fact of the police having to withdraw for a while.

The event came as a particular shock because it was generally thought that race relations in Bristol were good. There may have been some complacency in this respect and the extent of cannabis use in black areas was always liable to cause friction between young blacks and the police. Moreover, the high unemployment among young blacks was prone to make things worse. It was accepted by most of those concerned, including both government and (on the whole) local government, that close attention had to be given to conditions in the area. Nevertheless, it is probably fair to say that there was a good deal of the fortuitous about the St Paul's disturbance. Lessons had to be learned, not least about effective police handling of disorder, but in my own assessment at least the mood in Bristol was nothing like that which was later seen in other areas.

In the months that followed there was some argument about the whole situation. The Commission for Racial Equality – under its chairman, the former Tory minister David Lane – took the view that there was a serious risk of trouble. As the Home Office minister responsible for race relations, I was not very happy with their thesis that we faced 'the fire next time'. However, early in 1981 I ran a conference in Birmingham attended by a number of youngish black leaders as well as others at which some very frank speaking took place. Meanwhile thought was being given as to how the position of the ethnic minorities could be improved, against a background of tightened immigration control and the British Nationality Act of 1981.

Then came the great shock of the April 1981 riots in Brixton, which lasted over three days. About 150 police officers and nearly sixty members of the public were injured and very considerable damage was done – and of course the events received very wide television coverage.

William Whitelaw, the Home Secretary, visited the scene on the third day, the Sunday, and the following day announced to the House of Commons that he had invited Lord Scarman to report on the disorder and make recommendations. The Opposition, in the form of Roy Hattersley, wanted a wider inquiry which would explore housing and employment problems. Enoch Powell predictably asked the Home Secretary and Government to 'bear in mind, in view of the prospective increase in the relevant population, that they have seen nothing yet'.

Scarman duly reported in November,[3] but in the meanwhile there had been further riots across the country in July, the most ferocious of them being at Toxteth. This led to the decision to send Michael Heseltine, then Secretary of State for the Environment, to Merseyside to see what could be done to resolve the problems of the area. Heseltine's programme, and more particularly the Scarman report and the government's response to it, constituted the major part of the

government's plans to see that the riots, and their causes, were effectively tackled.

The Heseltine foray had about it a personalised aura that seemed more characteristic of American than of British politics. No doubt there were plenty of cynics, and not all the Merseyside establishment took to this colourful outsider with a touch of iconoclasm about him. But ordinary Liverpudlians, black and white, seem to respond to style and panache. In this case, they liked the fact that they could see Heseltine on the ground, that he would listen to them and seemed affected by their arguments. They liked the sense of dynamism and urgency that he brought with him.

Heseltine responded energetically. He circulated a report within government called *It Took A Riot* to argue that the deprivation and disadvantage that he found *must* be tackled. He set up a Merseyside Task Force under a lively civil servant to promote and coordinate greater efforts from both public and private sectors. Following a much publicised tour of the area by a party of business leaders, a financial institutions group was set up to harness investment. A new urban development grants scheme was announced and Liverpool's own housing investment allocation was stepped up. The peculiar degradation and demoralisation of some of the housing estates which ringed Liverpool had had an unforgettable impact on Heseltine. And to raise the quality of life there were to be a garden festival and a Tate gallery of the North.

None of this transformed Merseyside overnight – its economic and social problems were deepseated – but nobody could accuse the government of inertia. At the same time, William Whitelaw, as Home Secretary, was concerned to soften the hard atmosphere that seemed to characterise policy–community relations in a city with a tough tradition, without undermining the authority of the police. It was a difficult task, but some progress was made.

Meanwhile the national picture after the riots was dominated by the Scarman report. The thoroughness of Scarman's investigations, and his willingness to listen with a sympathetic ear to the blacks in particular, may have upset some people understandably concerned with the rights and wrongs of law and order but it showed the ethnic minorities that their voice was being heard. And though Scarman focused on Brixton, providing a detailed analysis of events there, his conclusions were of general relevance, covering both policing and wider social policy.

All this was sensitive territory in a variety of respects, but Whitelaw decided to make as positive an approach to Scarman's recommendations as possible. He endorsed the fundamental need for effective two-way communication between police and public, with both sides having a duty to make it work. He denied that there was any question of the police being told to 'go easy' on crime or to permit 'no-go areas', or that the law should not be the same for all; but he did not quarrel with Scarman's stress on the need for sensitivity. Conflicting lifestyles and habits (and the wide use of soft drugs) do indeed make this a very tricky balance to get right.

Whitelaw accepted the need to find new ways of increasing ethnic minority membership of the police and also the importance of high quality race relations and other training in the police service. The need for a new police complaints procedure was also accepted, and in due course enacted.

Scarman also laid a great deal of stress on police–community consultation. Scarman said that consultation should be backed by legislation, but Whitelaw took the view that no law could compel people to talk to each other. On the other hand, full encouragement was given to consultative mechanisms. I myself had the somewhat delicate task of initiating the process in Lambeth (where Brixton is situated). After some difficult moments, it got off the ground – thanks fundamentally to people of goodwill in Lambeth who insisted that it must, in spite of some obstruction from the local council.

The government also responded to Scarman's argument for a strengthened social policy commitment. The government strengthened the so-called Section 11 provision which provided grants for areas of high immigration and increased significantly the money made available to inner city areas under the Urban Programme. The £270 million made available in 1983 represented an increase of £60 million. The government also carried out a sample survey of civil servants in Leeds to test their ethnic origins – though the history of ethnic monitoring has proved controversial and chequered, just as the introduction of a code of race relations at work proved a protracted business.

All in all, while positive or reverse discrimination were rejected – and Scarman did not favour this approach – the case for positive action was endorsed; and at the same time the government was making clear its abhorrence of the racial attacks which were disfiguring society. Nobody could claim that the whole problem of racial disadvantage – or of law and order in places like Brixton and Toxteth – was solved overnight: it was not. The problems still persist. But while the government may have been rather slow to get to grips with the problems, the response when it came was significant.

Although the response to Scarman entailed some increase in resources, the start of 1982 saw another attempt by the government to tackle what it saw as local government over-spending. Local authorities had increasingly responded to the 1980 Act by levying supplementary rates or precepts – more than 30 had done so in 1981–2. To block this development, Michael Heseltine originally brought in a Bill in late 1981 which would subject any supplementary rate to a local referendum. There was also to be a fixed maximum rate for every local authority in the country. These proposals had however aroused a storm of objections from local government in particular, including some opposition in the Conservative party, so the new Bill simply abolished the power to levy supplementary rates at all – although in cases of real difficulty local authorities would be able to obtain the Secretary of State's permission to make temporary borrowings. At the same time, authorities that spent within the government's limits were given protection against loss of grant.

Heseltine justified the government's new restrictions on local government's freedom to spend by arguing on the second reading of his Bill on 18 January 1982 that:

> parts of local government are determined to scrap the traditional relationship between central government and local government whereby local government recognised and accepted the right of central Government to set the level of local government expenditure.

He said that Labour authorities were using their position to challenge the mandate of the national government. Some defendants of local government argued that central government has every right to decide how much it intends to give local government, but that local government then has the freedom, which should be regarded as constitutional, to raise what it likes from its electors. But in terms of hard political fact local government is subordinate to Parliament, or a creature of it, and Heseltine secured his Act. This Act also set up an independent Audit Commission which would secure the audit of local authorities and provide studies of local government efficiency. Scotland already had a similar scheme, and most people would probably judge that the commission has been a success.

Other measures during 1982 transferred the responsibility for meeting housing needs from the supplementary benefit system to the housing authorities and strengthened the safeguards for compulsorily detained psychiatric patients. Probably most significant, however, was an attempt to fulfill the manifesto and get to grips with the mounting problem of crime, especially among the young, through the Criminal Justice Act 1982.

The riots of 1981 had of course highlighted an aspect of the problem, and the growing number of young blacks in the penal institutions and the extent of mugging and similar offences was giving concern; but of course crime, among the young especially, went far wider than that. The call for action was persistent, normally reaching a crescendo at Conservative party conferences. But William Whitelaw was faced with other considerable problems, notably the pressure of numbers in the prison system – not to mention the mounting belief that prisons might contain, only sometimes deterred, but hardly ever reformed.

Whitelaw had in fact in the previous session obtained the Criminal Attempts Act which had ended the so-called 'sus' provision which it was claimed allowed the police to arrest people on mere suspicion: it was felt that it was particularly directed against young blacks. The 1982 Criminal Justice Act was altogether more substantial. It replaced imprisonment and borstal for young offenders with a new determinate sentence of 'youth custody' for 15- to 20-year-olds: these offenders were not to be housed in ordinary prisons. Detention centre sentences were to be reduced (the emphasis was on the 'short, sharp, shock'); day attendance sentences were to be more widely used; curfews were introduced; parents could be fined for the offences of children and young persons; and partially suspended sentences were brought in. There was also introduced a controversial power for the Home Secretary to introduce early release for prisoners who were not convicted of a serious crime, where circumstances warranted it. Critics argued that this would undermine the authority of the courts, and was a soft measure, but the pressure on the prisons was so great that the government felt it was right.

Overall, Whitelaw's Criminal Justice Act was a characteristically skilful blend of the forward-looking, the realistic and the popular. The short, sharp shock regime has not proved very successful and the quality of youth custody has suffered from the excessive pressure on the system, the difficulties with prison officers and other factors; but the Act still had much to be said for it. Coupled with the substantially greater resources for the police, including good pay, and the significant increase in their numbers, the Home Secretary could not be accused of inertia. But popular demand for tougher action was coupled with increasing concern about police conduct, and in particular demands for an independent prosecuting system. The Police and Criminal Evidence Bill, brought in by Whitelaw in November 1982, did not propose such a system. It did propose an independent assessor of complaints against the police. It also proposed stronger powers to stop and search suspects, balanced by safeguards concerning their treatment. The Act went through a protracted and contentious committee stage, only to fall when Parliament was dissolved for the June 1983 general election. For all the effort put into tackling crime during Whitelaw's period at the Home Office, the recorded figures rose steadily. It was a reminder, if one were needed, of the limits to what the Home Office and the police can do.

The early months of 1983 – the last period of the first Thatcher administration – did not see much important social legislation. One Act did provide that the yearly increases in pensions and other social security and housing benefits should be based on the historic increase over a twelve-month period, rather than on a basis which entailed forecasting price increases, which had palpably proved unsatisfactory. Another measure encouraged community care, one of the themes of social policy throughout the 1980s, though sometimes a difficult one to implement. But with an election clearly imminent, it was the Budget which probably mattered most. Child benefit reached its highest value ever in real terms; one-parent benefit was also substantially raised; and other steps included new tax help for charities – again a regular feature of Tory policy in the 1980s.

During all this period, the party's 'think-tanks' had been active – active, but often frustrated. In their different ways, the Centre for Policy Studies, the Institute of Economic Affairs, the Adam Smith Institute (founded in 1977), all continued to throw out ideas of the kind that Joseph has articulated since his 'conversion'. The evils of high public spending, the over-taxation of the less well-off in particular, the lack of choice, the failure to bring about a voucher system in education, the dominance of providers over consumers (e.g. in the NHS), the elevation of equality at the expense of standards (notably in education) – all these were recurring themes, explored in a variety of different publications and seminars.

Inside government, the policy unit at Number Ten was there to match them and there was a good deal of interchange. The Central

Policy Review Staff was less favoured by Mrs Thatcher than Edward Heath because its approach was less committed, and it was disbanded just after the 1983 general election. The leaders of the policy unit – Sir John Hoskyns and then Ferdinand Mount during this period – were clearly in line with the Thatcher approach.

But all this did not mean that the traditional Whitehall, department-based machine had gone out of business. One area where the new thinking made virtually no progress between 1979 and 1983 was health. In spite of some stimulating writing about the failures of the NHS and the possibility of alternative approaches, together with study groups which entailed fairly regular contact with ministers, the CPS made no headway in their attempts to persuade first Patrick Jenkin and then Norman Fowler and Kenneth Clarke to espouse moves towards greater use of insurance or a pattern of health maintenance organisations modelled on the American pattern. The popularity of the NHS seemed too great, and it was a long time before Mrs Thatcher herself was willing to think of challenging it.

In education, too, progress was slow. Indeed, the greatest irony was that it was Keith Joseph himself, after he became Secretary of State for Education in September 1981, who abandoned the idea of the voucher scheme and failed to introduce student loans. The ideas appealed, but somehow the practicalities seemed too daunting.

So there were frustrations for the thinkers of the New Right. The idea that sinister *éminences grises* like Sherman and Hoskyns really shaped policy was certainly overstated – they themselves have both made clear the sharp limits on what they felt that they were able to achieve. Of course, personality factors were sometimes important, perhaps particularly in the case of Sherman; anyway some Tory politicians still shared the old feeling that too many ideas were indigestible and that while they wanted intelligent advisers they did not want a European-style intelligentsia confusing them with a torrent of opinions with which they found it tedious to try to keep up. And being politicians they sensed the risk of going too far ahead of their electorate – particularly over health, but also to some extent in education, housing and social security. At the CPS, Sherman's influence first declined and then he left in not very happy circumstances: the organisation went through something of a doldrum period before it picked up again.

There was one attempt to consider radical changes in social policy within the ministerial machine itself. Peter Riddell in *The Thatcher Government*[4] describes the creation of the Family Policy group of senior ministers. The Central Policy Review Staff is quoted as saying in a note to ministers that:

> The objective of the Family Policy Group is to identify, and to seek ways of counteracting, those factors which tend to undermine, or even prohibit, the exercise of personal responsibility and a sense of individual self-respect.

The group considered ideas to do with strengthening the voluntary sector, private provision of welfare needs, business involvement in the community and the possibility of defining a minimum safety-net for welfare needs. But there is no evidence of any significant impact on the 1983 manifesto, or indeed of much impact on social policy in the next two or three years.

Anyway, once again the 1983 general election was not about social policy: it was about the economy, nuclear weapons, Europe and leadership, and took place against the backdrop of the Falklands. Labour failed even to make headway on unemployment. The Conservative manifesto stressed the old themes of encouraging people to take responsibility for their own decisions and giving more choice to individuals and their families but it was keen to rebut 'the totally unfounded charge that we want to "dismantle the welfare state"'. The success of the right to buy in housing was naturally stressed and to be further developed; there was nothing new in social security; and with health the emphasis was on what had been achieved rather than plans for change – although contracting out of services and the pruning of administrative costs were emphasised. The most radical proposal was the abolition of the Greater London Council and the Metropolitan Counties.

In education, too, the primary emphasis was on the record, but there were plans for the future. They included better teacher training, publication of reports by HM Inspectors, stress on school attendance, help for refresher courses and play groups, encouragement to schools to keep records, buy computers and carry out tests, and the promotion of 14 pilot projects to bring better technical education to teenagers.

Joseph felt particularly that the tripartite system envisaged at the time of the Butler Act had failed to provide adequate technical training for the less academic. But there was no suggestion of radical change. But, again, these were not the things that the election was about. Anyway, the result on 9 June 1983 was triumph.

9 1983–7: The Tempo Mounts

The 1983 Conservative manifesto may have been a mild document as far as social policy was concerned, but in fact the pace of change intensified during the years of Mrs Thatcher's second administration. A major – though not profoundly radical – reform of social security was enacted in 1986. The Greater London and Metropolitan County Councils were abolished. The powers of local government – particularly over their spending – continued to be clipped, and a drastic recasting of local government finance was put forward, although it was not enacted until the next Parliament. The school examination system at sixteen was recast. The Burnham system of paying teachers was abolished. The way was paved for the major changes of the 1988 Education Reform Act. An independent prosecution service was created. In the health service a system of accountable general managers was introduced, and a stir was caused by the decision in 1985 to limit somewhat doctors' freedom to prescribe what drugs they chose, when cheaper alternatives were available.

Why did the pace of change step up? In part, it was a continuation of the drive to hold down public expenditure, as for instance in the Social Security Act of 1986. In part, it was the feeling that standards were too low, notably in education. In part, it was strongly political – the desire to attack those Labour local authorities which were seen as profligate, often in crazy causes, incompetent and interfering. In part, it reflected the readiness to challenge the trade unions, as shown in the ending of Burnham. In part, it reflected the growing confidence of the government and the Conservative party – the willingness to do things which in earlier years would have been thought too difficult or too likely to be reversed by a succeeding Labour government. By the mid-1980s, Conservatives – and Mrs Thatcher in particular – had a strong feeling that history was on their side.

Who were the influences and articulators in all this? Clearly, Mrs Thatcher's impact was important – perhaps more so in education and local government than in Home Office affairs. She had intervened very little in the Home Office in Whitelaw's day, and did not do so much more under his successors, Leon Brittan and then, from 1985, Douglas Hurd. She was instinctively interested in health, and appreciated its political significance, but she was cautious about jeopardising what she saw as the popularity of the NHS with the public at large. She applied to social security her own experience as a one-time junior minister of pensions – but probably did not have time to immerse herself in all the intricacies of modern social security. On the other hand, she naturally saw the continued spread of home ownership as one of the jewels in her government's crown. She was eager to press on with the reform of local government; and she was often actively involved in pressing for educational changes.

But of course the various ministers were important. At education, Keith Joseph – in a sense, the father figure of the radical right – was in practice a less determined reformer than his successor, Kenneth Baker, who was generally seen as coming from a different wing of the party; but he laid much of the groundwork of change, even though his own self-deprecatory style led him to play down his successes and concentrate on his failures. This was not a fault to which the ebullient, politically skilful (and genial) Baker was prone. At the DHSS, Norman Fowler did not have about him any special charisma, but he had a competence and attention to political detail, in particular, that generally kept his department out of trouble and enabled the Social Security Act 1986 to pass through Parliament relatively peacefully. (The row came later, when it was implemented and he had moved on.) He also shared Mrs Thatcher's reluctance to be dragged into any drastic change in the NHS, concentrating instead on improved efficiency.

At the Home Office Leon Brittan's grasp and lucidity were assets, and he showed a willingness to tackle some matters that Whitelaw had put on one side as hornets' nests; but a not-very-happy handling of a Commons debate on capital punishment and a feeling that he had not yet quite the stature and appeal that were necessary to handle the extraordinarily difficult task of embodying the government's approach to law and order led to his replacement by Douglas Hurd. Hurd was not a radical either – he was very much one of the party's moderates; but while not one to win standing ovations easily at party conference, he brought a wisdom and integrity to his role that were valuable.

For much of the time, however, it was the Department of the Environment that was at the forefront of the political battle. Patrick Jenkin, who moved there in June 1983, brought an unusual ability to grasp complexity, as well as basic good sense, to the department, and was a willing implementer of government policy; but there was a stiffness and lack of deftness in his presentation that led to unfavourable comparisons with his opponent in the dismantling of the GLC, its Leader the witty and articulate Ken Livingstone. Kenneth Baker took over the job for a short while, and was then in due course followed by Nicholas Ridley – perhaps the most 'Thatcherite' and anti-public sector minister of all, with a very clear brain and sense of direction, though no great flair in presenting a seductive case or carrying the House of Commons along with him.

Behind the ministers were think-tanks. The policy unit at No 10 Downing Street was clearly important, as a place to which fresh thoughts could be brought and the received wisdom of the government departments challenged. It was led by men of intellectual quality like John Redwood and Brian Griffiths. Increasingly ideas about how to escape from the dependency culture and the all-pervasive state were being discussed, and Griffiths particularly brought a moral force to the market arguments that obviously struck a responsive chord with Mrs Thatcher.

Among the outside bodies, the Centre for Policy Studies began to take on a new lease of life. Alfred Sherman had left, but under the chairmanship of Hugh Thomas and with better managed publishing useful work was produced. Thus its search for new solutions to the problems of the NHS went on. A CPS paper in 1983 put forward the proposal that after the GLC was abolished the Inner London Education Authority should be directly elected. This was what happened – though subsequently, of course, the paper's view that ILEA should be kept was to be up-ended in the 1988 Education Reform Act.

Another CPS paper in April 1985 (*Bringing Accountability Back to Local Government*)[1] by Cyril Taylor suggested that one possible contribution to the funding of local government might be a resident's tax on all adults, though excluding pensioners – a partial foretaste of the community charge. (Even within government, a poll tax was still regarded as heretical.) Another 1985 CPS paper (*Trust the Tenant: Devolving Municipal Housing*)[2] by Alex Henney set out a range of ideas for altering the management and ownership of municipal housing that almost certainly influenced subsequent developments, particularly in the 1988 Housing Act. The CPS was also keen to promote the idea that pensions should be both personal and portable – again an idea that made headway.

The Institute for Economic Affairs also continued to press its familiar themes, fundamentally to do with the need for choice in welfare to be achieved through markets. Ralph Harris and Arthur

Seldon formally retired from the day-to-day directorship of the Institute, but their guiding presence continued to be felt. The education voucher; the belief that surveys of consumer preference established clearly the case for market-based welfare; the need for choice in pensions as in health – all these continued to be pressed with gusto. And the picture drawn from United States experience of the failure of welfare programmes to do anything more than increase dependence (notably in Charles Murray's *Losing Ground*)[3] attracted increasing attention, not just at the IEA but elsewhere on the radical right.

One way or another, the pressure for change began to mount. What would once have seemed unthinkable began not only to be thought but even sometimes enacted – though there were plenty of opponents and pitfalls on the way.

But what was happening in government itself?

There were a number of significant pieces of legislation in the first session of the new Parliament. The Finance Act (No. 2), which was brought in immediately after the election, raised the limit for tax relief on mortgage interest from £25 000 to £30 000. It was a reflection of the Tory party's commitment to home-ownership; but perhaps what is of more interest is that there was no subsequent increase in the limit, and indeed in 1988 it was to be confined to one beneficiary per residence. The new Chancellor, Nigel Lawson, clearly began to fret at both this tax relief and that on pensions (particularly the tax-free lump sum on retirement): the one merely seemed to push up house prices, the other to put excessive power in the hands of the big institutions. Both reliefs, however, have proved too deeply embedded to be easily tackled, although in the 1984 Finance Act the life assurance premium tax relief scheme, which favoured institutional as against personal savings, was abolished for new policies. That Finance Act also scrapped the Employers' National Insurance Surcharge which Labour had introduced and which served as something of a tax on jobs.

Nineteen eighty-four – that long-awaited year – saw one measure to do with citizens' rights which would, I think, on balance have met with George Orwell's approval. The Police and Criminal Evidence Act was the successor to the Bill which had fallen at the general election. It provided the police throughout the country with a power to stop and search for stolen goods and offensive weapons and a new power to search under warrant for evidence of any serious arrestable offence. But at the same time it provided new safeguards for the individual whom is stopped, a statutory right to legal advice for those detained without charge and the introduction of tape-recording of interviews with suspects to avoid mispresentation by the police of what had actually been said. It seems fair to say that the Act had the kind of balance between the attack on crime and respect for individual rights that the Home Office generally seeks and sometimes finds.

Most of the other significant legislation in 1984 came once again from the Department of the Environment. The Local Government (Interim Provisions) Act paved the way for the abolition of the GLC and the metropolitan counties, which had been promised in the 1983 election, by extending the life of the existing councils for one year, but restricting their freedom to act in ways which would make life more difficult for their successor authorities. The Rates Act 1984 brought into being the system of rate-capping under which 18 councils in 1985–6 and 12 in 1986–7 had their rates limited. The saving to rate-payers in the former year was estimated at £300 million, in the second year at above that. The Act also required that industry and commerce should be consulted before rate levels were fixed – an attempt to restrain councils who were held to drive away employment by exorbitantly high non-domestic rates, which was welcomed by business.

The Housing and Building Control Act made the right to buy public housing still more favourable, with still more generous discounts; it included provision for shared-ownership. The Housing Defects Act provided a somewhat unfortunate footnote to post-war local authority house-building in that it provided compensation for houses bought from councils and originally built by non-traditional methods in a way which subsequently caused defects in them which left them virtually unsaleable.

In health, the very tight monopoly held by opticians over the supply of spectacles was curtailed by the Health and Social Security Act 1984. It continued to provide for free professionally-administered sight tests, but spectacles could be bought by adults against a prescription from non-opticians. Advertising was also to be permitted. There was predictable opposition but before long the government was able to claim that the benefits of greater competition had been felt. More important, perhaps, the review of NHS management by a team under Sir Roy Griffiths had by then reported, leading to a system of general managers at district level and a management board in the centre. One other significant piece of legislation in 1984, though of a non-party nature, was the Matrimonial and Family Proceedings Act. Its aim was to give greater protection to children in divorce proceedings and to bring about fairer financial arrangements when a marriage ends. The essential point was that the welfare of children should be the first consideration, but it also marked a change by trying to encourage the divorced parties to become as far as possible financially self-sufficient. The 'clean break' or division of assets was preferred where possible to maintenance of former spouses. There was more recognition that women could be expected to work (though not necessarily when they were looking after young children). In place of a *normal* rule that divorce petitions could not be presented for three years after marriage, there was introduced an absolute rule that they could not be presented for one year. In this sense, divorce could be said to be made easier. Overall, the reform was a response to changing social conditions, and a reminder that not all social policy is party political.

Another interesting development in 1984 came with the Education (Grants and Awards) Act. This gave the Secretary of State the power to make grants to local education authorities to finance specific improvements. These Education Support Grants could not amount to more than 1 per cent of the education element in the rate support grant. Nevertheless, they represented a break in the principle of the general or block grant which had financed education for a generation. They were initially used to fund projects in micro-technology and the avoidance of drug abuse, as well as midday supervision; but their existence clearly opened up the possibility of an important weapon in the armoury of any Secretary of State looking for more direct power over the system. It is likely that others had shared the frustration that Kenneth Baker described to the Conservative party conference at Bournemouth on 7 October 1986:

> Many people have no idea how decentralised the education system is. I get just as frustrated as parents when I read that this or that school is short of textbooks or needs a coat of paint. I think it is important to realise that I am not directly responsible for that ... My privilege is largely restricted to picking up the bills which other people run up.

This may have underplayed his role as paymaster, but the point is one which holders of his office felt increasingly.

The hardest fought legislation of 1985 was the Local Government Act which abolished the Greater London Council and the six metropolitan county councils. The fact that bodies such as these had been set up by earlier Conservative administrations did not inhibit the

Thatcher government from abolishing them (any more than it had been inhibited in abolishing the area health authorities in 1980).

Although the Labour party opposed the abolition of the metropolitan counties as well as that of the GLC, it was around the latter that the fight raged most fiercely. Labour controlled all the metropolitan counties at the time and not surprisingly made much of the argument that the Tories were scrapping them out of political vindictiveness. But it did not require a very long memory to recall how many socialists had strongly opposed the creation of those counties and argued in favour of the old single-tier county borough to which abolition meant a substantial return (although certain important functions like policing and transport continued to be run on a metropolitan basis).

The GLC, on the other hand, was a rather different case. The government argued that – as with the metropolitan counties – its strategic role was nebulous and that many functions could be better performed by the boroughs. (Housing had been moving increasingly to the boroughs.) The GLC was seen as an expensive bureaucratic monstrosity; but it was also seen as a political monstrosity. Under Ken Livingstone and his friends, it had become more and more concerned with support for sexual and racial minority groups, often of a seemingly bizarre nature. It was also responsible for a policy of very low fares for London Transport which entailed substantial subsidies, although this was eventually curtailed in a court case brought by the Bromley Borough Council. It was argued that business was being driven away from London by both the rate levels and the antics of the local authorities. The Inner London Education Authority was naturally regarded as the GLC's partner in all this. Two thirds of its members came from the GLC and one third from the inner London boroughs.

The government was able to claim that since its foundation the GLC had not only lost much of its housing role to the boroughs, but its ambulance service to the NHS and its water and sewage to the water authorities. Moreover, transport had been taken away from the GLC by the London Regional Transport Act of 1984.

All these were relevant points; but the GLC mounted a strong and often witty campaign against abolition. Livingstone was not afraid to use advertising and public relations men and tactics in a way which seemed far removed from the old-fashioned socialist style. But the GLC was also able to draw some support from many who would not normally have dreamed of being in the same camp as the left-wingers. A number of people who had been closely associated with the GLC as councillors and in other ways simply did not want to see it go – they did not believe that all their work had been misplaced. Others felt that London must have some kind of overall local government authority, whether for planning or for ceremonial and representational purposes. There was also considerable support for the work the GLC (and ILEA) had been doing in a number of different spheres – for example the arts, historic buildings, parks and (in ILEA's case) adult and special education. Nor was the GLC's support for voluntary groups confined to the more way-out.

The result of all this was that when the Local Government Bill abolishing the GLC and the metropolitan authorities came before Parliament it did not have an easy time. The second reading debate took place on 3 and 4 December 1984. Patrick Jenkin's opening speech was repeatedly interrupted, notably from his own side. A number of Tories made questioning or sceptical speeches; the former Environment Secretary, Geoffrey Rippon, was particularly critical and Edward Heath was downright hostile. In spite of a typically adroit winding-up speech by Kenneth Baker, who had been brought in as Minister for Local Government to undertake the detailed passage of the Bill through Parliament, several Tories refused to support the government, but the Bill still received its second reading by 354 votes to 219.

One important aspect of the government's plans concerned the future of the Inner London Education Authority. Many Conservatives had argued for some time that ILEA should simply be abolished and its powers be handed over to the boroughs. This had been rejected by the government because, as Joseph put it in the second reading debate on 3 December 1984:

> There is so much movement across London boundaries by London children and students that to break up ILEA would mean a very big departure indeed from current practice.

The original plan, as expressed in the white paper *Streamlining the Cities*,[4] had been to maintain a single authority with its members made up of councillors appointed by the inner London boroughs and the Common Council of the City. However there was pressure coming from different parts of the political spectrum for a directly elected body, and on 5 April 1984 Joseph announced that the government had decided that the forthcoming Bill should in fact provide for this. Interestingly, this move was welcomed by the Labour spokesman, Andrew Bennet, as well as by most Conservatives, though there was some fear that a directly elected body would prove to be a strong engine of pressure for higher spending. Anyway, it was decided in due course that the new directly elected ILEA should come into operation in April 1986.

The conversion of ILEA into a directly elected body was only one of a number of significant moves in education policy during Mrs Thatcher's second term of office. Keith Joseph's period as Secretary of State was not marked by one major event like Kenneth Baker's Education Reform Act in the next Parliament, nor did Joseph have his successor's flair for presentation; but new developments were introduced and new directions taken, a number of which pointed to the ingredients of the 1988 Act.

Joseph's strategy was set out in the white paper entitled *Better Schools*[5] which came out in March 1985. It was the most important Conservative statement of education policy since Mrs Thatcher's white paper in 1972. Its premise was that, although there is much to admire in our schools, standards had to rise to meet the needs of the modern world. This required action in four areas. First, there should be greater clarity and agreement about the objectives and content of the curriculum. Second, the examination system should be reformed and assessment and the recording of the achievements of pupils improved. Third, the professional effectiveness of teachers and the management of the teaching force should be strengthened. Fourth, school government should be reformed and parents and employers particularly should be more heavily involved in it.

How was all this to be brought about? The white paper brought together a substantial package of both recent and new initiatives.

For a start, it tackled the question of the curriculum – always a sensitive area in British educational politics. The essential vehicle for this was to be a system of policy statements on specific areas (one had already been issued on science), together with publications by Her Majesty's Inspectors intended to inform and stimulate discussion. The government would therefore in a sense set the objectives, but the different functions of the Secretary of State, the local education authority and the school would mean that those objectives would be pursued in a variety of routes in accordance with local judgement.

For example, it would not in the view of the Government be right for the Secretaries of State's policy for the range and pattern of the 5–16 curriculum to amount to the determination of national syllabuses for that period.

And the 'Government does not propose to introduce legislation affecting the powers of the Secretaries of State in relation to the curriculum'.

In this respect, the Baker Reform Act was still some way off. Nor did Joseph accept the principle of a system of testing all pupils, which had been advocated by some Conservatives for a number of years. Instead, he decided to publish the results of surveys carried out by the Assessment of Performance Unit of his department, and to commission more such surveys in subsequent years, so as to provide a yardstick of progress. On top of this, the new General Certificate of Secondary Education, which had been announced the previous year, would also serve to provide a national picture of performance. This was to replace the existing GCE and CSE: it came into operation in time for the 1988 examinations. When it came, there were fears about its impact on knowledge (facts to some extent replaced by 'empathy' in history, for example) and about the speed with which it was introduced; but overall it seemed to be welcome as getting more out of pupils.

GCSE was not the government's only new initiative in this regard. The technical and vocational education initiative (TVEI) had been launched in 1983, with the specific aim of linking schools more closely with industrial and commercial needs. In 1984 Joseph had also decided to introduce an alternative to A levels in the Advanced Supplementary (AS) levels. The white paper now confirmed the way in which this would develop. The essence was that the AS level course would provide about half the study time of an A level course – with the corollary that more subjects could be taken. A course could combine both A and AS levels. Fears were naturally expressed that this would represent a dilution of standards, but it was held that shorter courses need not be of lower quality. Planning for the scheme went ahead and it was confirmed in the white paper.

A number of proposals were made in the white paper to do with teachers and their training. Not surprisingly, there was emphasis on the regular and formal appraisal of the performance of teachers. There was also a decision to introduce a new specific grant from government to support the LEAs in their spending on the in-service training of teachers – a step that was interesting both for its emphasis on continuing training and for the evidence of the desire to whittle away at the block or general grant system of local government finance which had held sway for a generation.

The other principal area for reform was to be in the management of schools. The 1980 Education Act had introduced some changes in governing bodies; but now the government had decided to go further.

No single group – LEA, parents' or teachers' representatives – would have a majority on governing bodies; co-opted governors were to be included as a way of strengthening the influence of business; and all schools should normally have their own governing bodies. The relationships between the various elements in the system were set out carefully. Overall, the aim was to give more power to parents, on the one hand, and employers, on the other – all very much in line with the philosophy implemented in the 1986 Education Act.

Sir Keith Joseph's manifest concern for education, and his willingness to discuss matters, won him many friends in the education system – but somehow it was not until he had left office that this respect for him really surfaced. To his fellow politicians he seemed as ready to talk about his failures and difficulties as his successes, and not to be quite the man to carry through the reform programme or deal with the worsening industrial relations and pay disputes with the teachers. A little over a year after his white paper was published, he stepped down, to be succeeded by the ebullient Kenneth Baker. But once again Joseph could be seen to have paved the way for someone else.

Meanwhile, the Home Office was busy legislating. The field of law and order saw three new Acts in 1985. One, the Prosecution of Offences Act, actually set up the new independent prosecution system under the Director of Public Prosecutions – a wise step though the new service has had problems in building up its staff. The second was a response to a wave of public concern about rape and the sentences given for it. The Sexual Offences Act 1985 raised the maximum sentence for attempted rape from seven years to life imprisonment and for indecent assault on a girl from two to ten years. Thirdly, the Sporting Events (Control of Alcohol, etc.) Act brought in strict controls on alcohol at football matches – a response to the mounting problem of football violence and hooliganism.

The other main feature of 1985 was the publication of first the green and then the white paper that led to the 1986 Social Security Act. Under Norman Fowler a substantial review exercise had been carried out over eighteen months. There had been 19 public sessions at which oral evidence was presented and nearly 4500 pieces of written evidence were submitted. Over 40 000 consultation documents were issued.

The green paper, *Reform of Social Security*,[6] published in June 1985, set out the reasons for change. It started with the words 'To be blunt the British social security system has lost its way'. The system had helped to raise the living standards of the poorest, provided a safety net against urgent need, and improved the position of such vulnerable groups as the retired, poor families with children and sick and disabled people. But the cost had soared. It had reached £40 billion a year by 1985 – having grown since the Second World War five times faster than prices and twice as fast as the economy as a whole. Moreover it was set to rise steeply over the next forty years.

But the problem was not just cost. The system had developed piecemeal, resulting in a

multitude of benefits with overlapping purposes and different entitlement conditions. The complexity in benefit rules has meant that social security is difficult to administer and at times impossible for the public to understand. While the gap between social security and income tax means that significant numbers of people are paying income tax and receiving means-tested benefits at the same time.

A new approach was needed.

This approach

should respect the ability of the individual to make his own choices and to take responsibility for his own life. But at the same time it must recognise the responsibility of government to establish an underlying basis of provision on which we as individuals can build and on which we can rely at times of need.

The green paper continued:

Such an approach does not lead ... to a system based on a single concept: whether it be universality or means testing ... State provision has an important role in supporting and sustaining the individual; but it should not discourage self-reliance or stand in the way of individual provision and responsibility.

The green paper then quoted the Beveridge report, when it said:

The State in organising security should not stifle incentive, opportunity, responsibility; in establishing a national minimum, it should leave room and encouragement for voluntary action by each individual to provide more than that minimum for himself and his family.

The spread of home ownership illustrated the point well.

But Beveridge's ideas had not all been followed.

> The decision at the outset of national insurance to pay pensions at
> once rather than after a build-up of entitlement substantially
> changed Beveridge's concept. The later development of earnings-
> related benefits and contributions was a further step away from the
> 1942 report.

Moreover, national insurance was not a normal insurance scheme: it
was a pay-as-you-go scheme, with today's contributors meeting the
cost of today's benefits. Even the State Earnings-Related Pension
Scheme was doing no more than pay the cost of current pensions.

But the green paper acknowledged that there was no chance of
going back to the insurance principle in the state scheme: the need was
to define its limits and leave the rest to individuals and their
employers. Overall, there should be three main objectives of social
security: meeting genuine need; consistency with the government's
economic objectives (including not only the control of public
expenditure but also the avoidance of barriers to employment and
occupational mobility); and greater simplicity in understanding and
administration. But at times choices have to be made between these
objectives. Thus a scheme could be constructed by which *all* benefits –
including pensions – were means-tested. But

> It is an entirely proper function of government to provide a basis on
> which individual provision can rest. In particular, such support can
> come at a time when expenses are high (as when raising children) or
> when income is limited (as in retirement). Here government is
> underpinning individual effort: encouraging it, not replacing it.

The green paper explained in more detail why the Beveridge approach
had not fully worked out. Beveridge had envisaged that social
insurance would cover most needs, anyway after the build-up of
contributions had taken place. But in fact within three years around 15
per cent of pensioners and unemployed people were receiving national
assistance and by 1985 30 per cent were receiving its successor,
supplementary benefit. Another change concerned family benefits.
Beveridge had envisaged family allowances to be paid alongside
the existing system of child tax allowances. For those out of
work, allowances would be paid for all children, while for those in work
there would be no allowance for the first child. In either case, the

allowance would be paid at the same rate so as to maintain a sufficient gap between incomes in and out of work. But family support payments were never introduced at the same level for people in and out of work. Family income supplement and child benefit (going to all children) had done something to offset this; but some working families were still worse off than they would be unemployed.

The green paper showed how the social security budget had grown. Part of the growth was due to changes in definition, particularly the introduction of child benefit in place of tax allowances and the amalgamation of support from rent and rate rebates to form housing benefit in 1982/3. Of the total cost of £40 billion plus, £20 billion came from contributions, the rest from tax. Nearly half of all this spending went on the elderly; 20 per cent to families with children; 17 per cent on unemployment; 13 per cent on sickness and disablement. Over 100 000 staff were involved in administering the various benefits.

Obviously the increase in the cost of social security over the years owed much to usually more generous benefits, to longer lives and in more recent years to the rise in unemployment. But there were other factors. One was a doubling over fifteen years of the number of one-parent families who received a special supplement. Over time, significant new benefits had come in for the disabled. Of particular concern was the way in which housing benefit had seemed to grow from a scheme designed to help those most in need to cover a much wider area of the population. Its share of social security expenditure had risen from 1.5 per cent in 1979/80 to 7.7 per cent in 1984/5, although this partly reflected the change in the system. But perhaps the most striking fact of all was the demography of old age. In 1985 there were 9.3 million pensioners and 2.3 state pension contributions for each of them. By 2035 there would be 13.2 million passengers and only 1.6 contributors for each of them – a substantial burden for an essentially pay-as-you-go scheme.

These, briefly, were the factors that underlay the government's approach. How did it plan to translate them into new policies? Clearly it did not intend to reverse the whole pragmatic philosophy that had marked social security: contributory and non-contributory benefits would continue to co-exist; so would universal and selective benefits. What there was was a desire to rein in both public expenditure and what came to be termed the dependency culture, as well as to provide a leaner, simpler, more effective service, increasingly based on computerisation. There was also at this stage the wish to move towards the merger of tax and benefits in a tax credit scheme by providing the new family credit through the pay packet; but this was subsequently lost during the passage of the Bill when the new benefit reverted to being paid direct to the 'caring parent'.

The first major change put forward was a reduction in, and gradual running down of, the State Earnings-Related Pension Scheme (SERPS), coupled with encouragement of contracting out into personal or occupational pension schemes.

The primary reason for this was financial. According to the *Conservative Campaign Guide 1987*, the costs of SERPS in 1985 was running at less than £200 million a year, but that cost would have risen to £25½ billion by 2033 (at 1985 prices). The government viewed this as unacceptable. But it was also anxious to encourage the private sector – to get as much of the burden of pensions as possible (apart from the basic scheme) off the state. This meant encouragement for the occupational schemes, but also particular encouragement for personal private schemes which were not tied to particular jobs. This would give greater freedom to individuals, particularly those who might move from job to job. It would also do something to reduce what many felt was the excessive hold of the big pension funds, though of course private schemes would also go through pension funds.

The initial green paper idea was to get rid of SERPS altogether except for those within 15 years of retirement. When a white paper later in the year came out this was changed: SERPS was not to be abolished but its costs and benefits would be substantially reduced.[7] The pensions paid would be based (for those retiring after this century) on a lifetime's average earnings instead of on the best 20 years, and on 20 per cent of earnings rather than 25 per cent. Widows and older widowers would be able only to inherit up to half their partner's pension entitlements rather than the existing full entitlement – again this would only apply to those widowed in the next century. There was also to be a reduction in the level of government support for the inflation-proofing in occupational schemes.

At the same time, the personal schemes were encouraged not only by receiving the same tax advantages as the occupational schemes already possessed, together with full portability, but also by a rebate for five years on national insurance contributions for those contracting out of SERPS. As a result of all this, it was hoped that the cost of SERPS in the year 2033 would be halved, to £13 billion, and that a substantial reduction in dependence on the state would have been brought about.

The next major element in the Fowler scheme was a restructuring of the principal means-tested or income-related benefits to bring them into line with each other; this covered supplementary benefit, housing benefit and family income supplement. The green paper said of this that the government was looking for major reductions not only on SERPS, but on administration and housing benefit. The change from supplementary benefit to income support was not, however, designed overall to reduce spending, and support for low paid families with children was intended to increase through the new family credit scheme. This was to have an appreciably wider coverage (and cost) than the existing family income supplement.

The objective of bringing benefits in line with each other was to be achieved in a number of different ways. The basis of assessment was to be net income, that is after any tax and national insurance contributions had been paid. This was designed to help the low paid who were in work, who often received a worse deal than those out of work. There was also to be standardisation of the amount of disposable capital that could be possessed by those seeking benefits. The supplementary benefit (to become income support) maximum was raised from £3000 to £6000: a maximum for those on housing benefit was introduced for the first time at the same level. There was to be a simplification in the rate of taper for housing benefit (with different rates for rent and rates), and it was decided that every household should make some contribution (20 per cent) towards local rates, though there were to be ways of offsetting this. In the income support scheme those under 25 received reduced benefits, while pensioners, lone parents and long-term sick and disabled received special additional premiums.

The search for greater consistency and simplicity clearly had a good deal to be said for it: the crux of the arguments when the new measures were actually implemented was more to do with actual levels of benefit and taper than to do with the broad system. One change, however, aroused a great deal of argument on the principle involved. This was the decision to convert the existing supplementary benefit single payments into a new 'social fund' which would run alongside the new income support scheme, which in turn was to replace supplementary benefit. The existing single payments and urgent needs payments were considered to have become cumbersome, as well as expensive: it was said that 'help is often more dependent on intricacies of interpretation than on a genuine assessment of need'. The new scheme would be discretionary (as indeed its predecessor had been in earlier days).

There was one particularly important change. Whereas payments for community care needs, such as helping to re-establish themselves after coming out of institutional care, would be on a grant basis, payment for sudden needs and debts would be on the basis of loans, to be repaid through reductions from future benefits. And the whole sum available to the social fund was to be cash limited.

Fowler also decided to replace the existing small death and maternity grants by a system under which more substantial payments would be available from the Social Fund, but only for those in need. Other changes affected widows. Payments to them after bereavement would be speeded, with a £1000 lump sum replacing the existing weekly allowance paid weekly for the first six months of widowhood. This was coupled with raising the ages at which widows' pensions were paid by five years – a reflection of the fact that among younger women at least it was becoming increasingly normal to work and that there was therefore less need for benefit for them. For mothers, the entitlement to maternity allowance was to be related more closely to a test of recent employment than it had been, but there was to be greater flexibility for mothers in deciding how far to take the allowance in the period before, and how far after, their baby was born.

Such, in summary, were the main changes to be brought in under the new system; but in one respect in particular there was to be no change. Child benefit – a universal, untaxed benefit which went to the mother for every child – was an obvious target for anyone seeking to introduce greater 'selectivity' into the system; but in fact the government decided that it should continue as it was. The idea of doubling it, as a way of bringing help without causing unemployment or poverty traps, was rejected on the grounds of expense; but so too was the notion that child benefit should be increased but made subject to means test or tax. As the green paper put it:

> To do so would result in an unacceptable degree of 'churning' (where the same people receive money through the benefit system and pay it back through the tax system). It would also go against the Government's belief that the responsibilities of all families with children should be recognised.

It was a view that the third Thatcher administration was increasingly to question.

By any standards, the Fowler review and the subsequent 1986 Social Security Act represented a very substantial undertaking, and it is too early to assess its overall impact. (I shall come back to its actual implementation in 1988.) Some of it looked tough, and the old view that nobody should actually be worse off as a result of social reforms was clearly eroded. Savings were to be made in SERPS (though not retrospectively), in housing benefit, in the special payments under supplementary benefit, in the benefit to younger widows and in the reduced level of income support to the under-25s. Other changes might lead to marginal disadvantages. But against this there were clear gains to many poorer families with children, including one-parent families (except for some at work with significant work expenses). There was a greater coherence in the system in some respects: there was a valuable stimulus to second pensions in the private sector; and it was probably inevitable that the soaring cost of the SERPS scheme and of housing benefit should be tackled. Those who yearned for the tax credit system or pure selectivity were inevitably disappointed, and there was no sweeping transfer of new needs on to an insurance basis – nor for that matter dismantling of the welfare state. But it was the biggest upheaval since the Beveridge era.

The Social Security Act was clearly the major piece of social policy law-making in 1986, but there were a number of other measures. They included an Education Act which was focused particularly on the management of schools. There was to be an equal number of elected parent and local education authority nominated governors of schools, and the co-option of additional governors, including business representatives, would mean that LEAs lost their dominance over governing bodies. The powers of governors were strengthened in a variety of ways, including general oversight of discipline and the right to modify an LEA's curriculum policy, together with an effective veto over the appointment of headteachers and greater powers over the appointment of other staff. They were also to approve the way in which sex education was provided – and it was enacted that sex education had to be set within a moral framework. The propagation of partisan political views was forbidden. And, as a result of a decision in the European Court of Human Rights, corporal punishment was banned in state schools. Overall, the Act marked a loss of local authority powers, an increase in those of parents, as expressed through governors, and – except on corporal punishment – a check to what was seen as permissive or leftist infiltration.

The Social Security Act also affected schools, in that it restricted the duty of local education authorities to provide free school meals to those children whose families receive income support. Other low-income families would receive a cash allowance in lieu through the new family credit.

As usual, the Department of the Environment was active in the legislative programme. The Housing and Planning Act 1986 set out to bring home ownership to large numbers of council tenants living in flats, particularly by a more generous system of discounts to buyers. It also made it possible for local authorities to delegate the management of flats and houses to other bodies such as housing associations. Indeed, once the Act was passed estates could be either owned or managed not only by housing associations but also by pension funds, building societies or tenants' co-operatives, with particular emphasis placed by the Minister for Housing, John Patten, on the latter. It was a considerable move from the post-war ethos of housing policy, with its unquestioning acceptance of the role of municipal housing.

The Department of the Environment obtained another Local Government Act in 1986 affecting the powers of local government. This required local authorities to fix a rate by 1 April each year, and it debarred councils from publishing material designed to benefit a particular political party. This followed an interim report from the Widdicombe Committee on the Conduct of Local Authority Business.[8] In fact the House of Lords weakened the government's initial provisions, and the government said it would come back to the matter after the general election, but the Act showed the government's determination to root out what it saw as left-wing abuse of the system.

One other important piece of legislation in 1986 was the Public Order Act. It had been a long time in gestation and covered a sensitive area, seeking as it did to balance the rights to protest, march and picket peacefully with the need to preserve order and the rights of others. The problem had been brought to a head by a variety of factors – political demonstrations of a violent nature, aggressive picketing (as in the miners' strike of 1985), ugly examples of racial incitement and harassment and football hooliganism – not to mention a hippy 'peace convoy' which moved on to some farmland in 1986. Considerations of order were entwined with considerations of freedom.

Successive Home Secretaries had given much thought to the matter and it seems fair to say that the Bill when it came provided a delicate balance between the different considerations. By now, Douglas Hurd was Home Secretary, though his predecessor Leon Brittan had shaped the white paper on which it was largely based. The Second Reading took place on 12 January 1986.

Much of the Act falls rather outside the scope of this book, but the new offence of disorderly conduct was designed to deal with the growth in racial harassment and threatening hooliganism, while the offence of incitement to racial hatred was widened in scope to include certain media. Hurd described the problem clearly in the Second Reading debate on 10 January 1986.

> The new offence is aimed at protecting those in our communities who are most vulnerable to loutish and abusive behaviour – particularly the elderly and people from the ethnic minorities. Many hon Members will be only too familiar with the type of behaviour to which I refer. It casts a blight upon an area, whether it be a shopping precinct or a city housing estate, and makes the lives of people living there fearful and miserable. People are frightened to open their own front doors. They are kept awake by rowdy behaviour late at night. Ethnic minority families are victimised with racialist slogans and abuse. Gangs of hooligans make some pedestrian and shopping areas places where ordinary people fear to go. There cannot be many right hon and hon Members who do not have examples in their postbags and at their surgeries.

The Act also gave certain powers to deal with football hooliganism. The previous year legislation had been passed to control alcohol at football matches. The Public Order Act gave the police power to limit attendance and impose conditions when disorder was expected. It was a reminder that violence among young males was one of the most intractable problems in society.

As the next election drew nearer so the tempo of legislation slowed down. There was however one significant piece of legislation in the Teachers' Pay and Conditions Act of 1987. From 1984 onwards the schools had seen sporadic industrial action over pay disputes. The situation got worse in 1986 with a series of unsuccessful negotiations. Education was beginning to suffer, in some areas at least, and the climate became increasingly bitter. Teachers felt that they were undervalued and militancy spread. The unions found it impossible to agree a position amongst themselves. The government meanwhile was anxious to couple additional pay with a reform in the teaching structure so as to improve the long-term prospects of teachers and to do more for those with special responsibilities. It also wanted a clear definition of the professional duties of teachers. On 30 October 1986, Kenneth Baker, by now Secretary of State, tried to break the negotiating deadlock with an offer of a 16.4 per cent pay rise by the following October, provided his structural changes were met. This would mean that overall teachers' pay would go up by 25 per cent between 1985 and 1987.

The Burnham Committee, which had long negotiated teachers' pay, failed to come to any agreement on this proposal, and Baker stepped in to abolish it with his new Act. For three years at least, pay would be determined by the Secretary of State, following advice from an independent review body. Naturally there were strong protests at the loss of negotiating rights, but the Burnham system had been increasingly criticised. This was not least because the Secretary of State – the paymaster of much of education – was not effectively represented in what was essentially a negotiating body between local authorities and unions, even though he did have a power of ultimate veto. The new Act provided a three-year span in which to work out a new system (though this could be prolonged by parliamentary order). With the aid of the improved pay, the schools gradually settled down – though to a period that could not be described as serene as the pace of other reforms intensified.

Nor was reform confined to the schools. In February 1987 a *Review of the University Grants Committee* by a committee under Lord Croham's chairmanship was published.[9] Then in April the government produced a white paper, *Higher Education: Meeting the Challenge*.[10] The aims and purposes of the government's policies were clearly defined: higher education should serve the economy more effectively, pursue basic scientific research and scholarship in the arts and humanities, have close links with industry and commerce and promote enterprise. The tone was frankly utilitarian, and this was reinforced by the stated objectives in terms of quality and efficiency. Research was to be funded with an eye for commercial exploitation and efficiency increased by an approach more in line with modern management methods than had been the tradition in the past. At the same time, the need for highly qualified manpower led the government to seek an increase in student numbers, particularly among young women and mature entrants, and to press on with the development of continuing education, particularly professional updating.

These objectives were to be accompanied by institutional changes. The polytechnics and major colleges undertaking higher education were to be transferred from the control of the local authorities to a new status as corporate bodies working under contract with a new Polytechnics and Colleges Funding Council. This council would in effect be responsible not only for funding but for planning the higher education sector outside the universities. Local authorities, who felt with some reason that they had done a useful job with the polytechnics, tended to resent the change, but it had been long anticipated and the polytechnics themselves welcomed it. There was some argument that the binary system – the division between universities, and polytechnics and other colleges – should be ended and the two sections placed under one body; but when the time came to enact the new system there was no great opposition to it.

The universities themselves were to have a new Universities Funding Council in place of the old University Grants Committee. Again, the notion of contracts between the universities and the new UFC was to be at the heart of the system. The government would provide funding and general guidelines for the UFC, and the UFC would then distribute those funds and make sure they were spent on specific purposes. The government would, in particular, 'be concerned to see that the UFC's arrangements for making funds available to the universities properly reward success in developing co-operation with and meeting the needs of industry and commerce'. In a sense, the new UFC was to have more freedom than the UGC, in that it was to be a statutorily incorporated body, as opposed to the advisory UGC; on the other hand, it was argued that the UGC's advice had always been taken and that the new contractual relationship would give government a much more effective power to shape university expenditure to its own strategy.

The policy clearly flowed out of a mounting feeling in government that the universities were neither as efficient nor as well-targeted at serving their country's interests as they should be. Together with threats to academic tenure in universities, and the tightness in funding which stirred the scientists in particular, the white paper probably contributed to a worsening political climate in the universities (Oxford had already turned down a proposal to give Mrs Thatcher an honorary degree). But only a few weeks after the white paper came out, the general election was called, and the controversy was left to be resolved by the Education Reform Bill.

Increasingly during the second Thatcher term of office the prospect of radical reforms aroused suspicion, particularly among professional and other workers in the services concerned, not least where they felt their own pay was being left behind. Teachers, doctors, housing managers, social workers, local government finance officers, hospital manual workers and so on resented the upset in their familiar ways of working and argued variously that both their client groups and they themselves were under attack. As far as the white-collar workers at least were concerned it seemed likely that this feeling might damage the Conservative party and help the Alliance in particular. On top of this, there was opposition at the elected level of local government to much of what happened – most obviously among the militants and, of course, the authorities that were abolished, but also among a good many traditionalist moderates. Relations between ministers and some of the Conservative local authority chieftains became uneasy. But the government was not often deterred. With the help of the considerable curtailment of the power and authority of the trade unions, it was able to carry out its programme without too much difficulty, both in this and the first year of the next Parliament. Even Liverpool, the most militant of city councils, had eventually to face the facts and call off its rebellion. As for the public at large, the government's specific actions were not always popular; but by the test of the 1987 general election result at least all was well.

10 1987–8: The Flagships Launched

As the likely time for the next general election drew nearer, a considerable policy effort was mounted to prepare for the next Conservative manifesto. A range of policy groups were set up in the latter part of 1986, normally chaired by the appropriate minister: they were to report to a steering group of senior members of the government, nicknamed 'the A-team'. Although there were some Conservatives, like the Leader of the House John Biffen, who argued that the need was for a period of consolidation rather than radical change, both the Prime Minister's temperament and the belief that a policy of consolidation would make it look as though the party had run out of steam led to the party fighting the June 1987 election on what seemed to some a high risk social policy.

When Mrs Thatcher presented the manifesto to the party in May she emphasised its three 'flagships': Bills to reform education, local government finance and housing. And these were indeed to form the legislative basis of the hectic first session of the new Parliament.

The manifesto in fact came in two separate booklets.[1] One, *Our First Eight Years*, was a record of what had been achieved since 1979. In social policy, the stress was on the increase in home ownership by two-and-a-half million families and a million council house sales; increased spending on the National Health Service of 31 per cent above the rate of inflation; 'special help, better targeted, for those who need it, like elderly and disabled people'; and a substantial increase in real terms in spending per school pupil (19.7 per cent for secondary and 16.8 for primary pupils), together with a fall in the teacher–pupil ratio from just under 19.1 in 1979 to 17.6 in 1986.

The second booklet, *The Next Moves Forward*, set out the plans for the future. Many of them were contained in the second chapter, headed 'Wider Ownership and Greater Opportunity'. Home ownership continued to be stressed, and there was a firm pledge to keep the present system of mortgage tax relief. The particular emphasis, however, was on the private rented sector. Once again the party committed itself to its revival and to the proposals for encouragement of new private investment in this sector.

There were also to be important developments in council housing, described in a section headed 'Rights for Council Tenants'. Their essence was that 'municipal monopoly must be replaced by choice in renting'. Groups of tenants were to have the right to form co-operatives, owning and running their own estates, or alternatively asking other institutions to take over their housing.

In education the manifesto talked of four major school reforms. The first was to be a national core curriculum for all pupils between 5 and 16, with attainment assessment at 7, 11 and 14. Secondly, all secondary schools and most primary schools were to have control of their own budgets. Thirdly, parental choice would be extended by requiring schools to accept pupils up to the limit of their agreed physical capacity. At the same time, there would be more assisted places and a pilot network of the already announced City Technology Colleges. Fourthly – and probably most controversially – state schools would have the possibility of opting out of local education authority control. At the higher education level the changes which had already been put forward in the white paper discussed in the last chapter would now be put into effect.

It was however the third of the manifesto flagships that was to have the stormiest passage: the proposals for local government finance. The section on local government first of all denounced the 'abuses of left-wing Labour councils' and set out the steps taken to protect ratepayers' interests through rate limitation and the abolition of the metropolitan counties. Then it announced the intention of reforming local government finance to strengthen local democracy and accountability. 'We will legislate in the first session of the new Parliament to abolish the unfair domestic rating system and replace rates with a fairer Community Charge'. Business ratepayers were to have to pay a Unified Business Rate at a standard rate pegged to inflation.

The flat-rate community charge was no surprise. It had already been set out in a green paper and legislation had been passed to bring it in in Scotland a year ahead of England and Wales. But the notion of a poll tax produced intense controversy. There was to be much argument as to whether or how much it contributed to the very poor Conservative election results in Scotland. But at least the famous 1974 pledge to abolish the domestic rate was to be fulfilled – even if not everybody agreed that the new scheme was 'related to people's ability to pay'.

The community charge, the opting-out scheme for schools and the likelihood of increased private sector rents gave the Conservatives' opponents ammunition with which to attack the Tory flagships, and Labour worked hard at it. Their campaign was thought to be effective, and there was a moment a week before polling day when a degree of alarm seemed to blow up on the Conservative side. In the North of England as well as in Scotland the party did indeed do badly, and it may be that the broadside against the flagships had something to do with this. But the fact was that once again the Conservatives had a very large overall majority, and the government could claim that the manifesto had been endorsed. The first Queen's Speech of the new Parliament, delivered on 25 June 1987, stated that all three measures would be brought forward in the long session which was just beginning.

The first of the Bills to receive a second reading (and the last to receive Royal Assent) was the Housing Bill. It followed a white paper, *Housing: the Government's Proposals*[2] which had appeared in September 1987. The Bill received its second reading on 30 November 1987. The Secretary of State for the Environment, Nicholas Ridley, opened the debate by describing the Bill's objectives.

The main purpose was 'to make a cautious move towards evolving a new policy for rented housing'. Unusually for Ridley, he laid stress on finding an agreed way forward. He recalled how rent restrictions on unfurnished lettings had started in the days of the First World War, back in 1915. In 1937 and 1945 interdepartmental committees chaired by his father, Viscount Ridley, had made recommendations, the second of them leading to a system by which rents were registered with local authorities and rent tribunals determined fair rents; but the first major change came with the 1957 Rent Act. That in turn had been replaced by Labour in 1965, with security of tenure for tenants of unfurnished lettings and again a system of fair rents: in 1974 this was extended to furnished lettings. The consequences of all this, said Ridley, were plain to see: 'private renting has declined from 30 per cent of the housing stock in 1914 to just under 8 per cent today'. At this point, a Labour MP, David Winnick, argued that the 1957 Rent Act had led to a substantial reduction of rented accommodation and the scandal of Rachmanism, by which tenants were intimidated into leaving their accommodation so that it would be decontrolled and sold off.

Ridley acknowledged that there was force in this, but said that the new bill was designed to avoid the mistakes of 1957. It would not apply to existing lettings; it would not remove all statutory controls over new lettings; it would tighten up the laws against harassment; and there was now in existence the housing benefit system to provide help towards the higher rents that would ensue from decontrol.

Ridley made one other general point in introducing the Bill. He pointed to the rise in the public sector housing stock from 1.1 million homes in the 1930s to 5.5 million council and new town homes by 1979:

> To manage that number of houses is a massive undertaking, and that is precisely what went wrong... Much post-war local authority housing, built in a hurry, is in enormous estates, either in the inner city or on the periphery of the conurbations. Those places are often monotonous, soulless places in which few would choose to live – if they had a choice. The worst such estates suffer from poor design and layout: bad repair; a poor environment with vandalism, graffiti and rubbish-strewn streets and open spaces; and high levels of crime. No one responds to the tenants' cry for help.

Ridley did not blame all local authorities for this:

> Some authorities have proved appallingly inefficient in managing their estates and disgracefully unresponsive to the wishes of their tenants, but many others have done their best to act as good landlords.

He rejected the suggestion that the government wanted to end the role of local authorities in housing:

> With some 4.5 million homes on their books, it is inconceivable that they will not remain major providers of rented housing for the foreseeable future.

But a variation of the role was in prospect:

> We are trying to shift the future emphasis of their role from direct provision to securing the provision of housing by other agencies and organisations.

It was clear that these would include housing associations, co-operatives, building societies – and private landlords.

So the two aspects of the rented sector – public and private – came together in a Bill. But what, specifically, were the proposals?

The essence of the first part of the Bill was that new lettings in the private sector should take one of two forms. The normal method would be an assured tenancy, by which market rents would be freely negotiated between landlord and tenant. (The first version of the assured tenancy had been brought in the Housing Act 1980.) But though rents would be fixed initially through free negotiation, tenants would have a degree of security based on the fact that when the agreed period came to an end a tenant would broadly be entitled to remain. If a new rent could not be agreed it would be determined by a rent assessment committee at a market level. The existing provisions by which landlords of assured tenancies had to be companies or partnerships and approved by the Secretary of State, and by which assured tenancies were limited to new or improved dwellings, were all scrapped.

Assured tenancy was seen as the main instrument for long-term commercial letting; but there was also to be a revised version of the shorthold tenancy introduced in the 1980 Housing Act. The aim here was to attract landlords who wished to let their properties for short, fixed periods, of not less than six months, and then be able to regain possession if they so wished. The rent would be negotiated between landlord and tenant, but the tenant would be able to apply to the rent committee for a rent to be 'registered' at any time once the tenancy had started. The committee would compare the rent with other shorthold rents in the area, and if it was excessive have the power to reduce it.

These two provisions represented the essence of Ridley's plans for reviving the private rented sector. Together with tightened provisions against eviction and harassment, they provided an ingenious basis for a new drive to attract landlords back into the market. But, as always, success in the attempt to revive the sector would depend on a number of factors. First, and crucially, would be confidence that housing benefit would be available to meet the higher rents that would result from the Bill – and it was clear from the 1986 Social Security Act that the Treasury was becoming restless about the soaring cost of housing benefit. Next there were the counter-attractions of normally lower local authority rents, largely due to subsidies, and of the heavy support for owner occupation through mortgage tax relief and heavy council house sale discounts. There was still also a fear of landlords to be overcome among potential tenants and of the return of a Labour government among potential landlords. But housing benefit was probably the most important of these factors, with the government – reasonably enough – taking steps to limit payments where rents were exorbitant or the housing inappropriately large or luxurious.

These new provisions would also apply to housing associations. They would provide both assured and shorthold tenancies at generally higher levels than their present normal fair rents; but since government grants would continue to be available through the Housing Corporation to housing associations their rents would be expected to be below the full market level. The new flexibility was intended to enable housing associations to attract private finance, as part of what Ridley saw as an enhanced role for them. The housing associations themselves had mixed reactions to all this. Some welcomed the new opportunities: others feared that they would be part of a system which would make it harder for them to house their usually poorer clients – not to mention an influx of traditional local authority tenants.

The third part of the Bill embodied another important theme: an attempt to tackle the worst areas of poor, large-scale municipal housing through Housing Action Trusts. These trusts would be broadly based on the urban development corporations which had come into being to revive substantial areas like the docklands in London and Liverpool. The HATs would take over whole areas of run-down council housing, of up to 5000 to 6000 homes, refurbish and improve them and then, at the end of a short-life operation, hand them over to new forms of ownership and management, normally housing associations or private sector landlords.

Ridley showed in his second reading speech that he was aware that HATs might meet with strong local authority opposition – the authorities tended to argue that they could do the job perfectly well if only they had the resources. He asked for their co-operation, but made it clear that he might establish HATs even if the local authorities rejected them. And he laid particular stress on the rights of tenants to be consulted about the plans of the HATs.

The last part of the Bill was in some ways the most radical of all. It introduced a new right for council tenants, as well as tenants in new towns and in HATs, to transfer to a new landlord, while retaining the right to buy their homes. The landlords would have to be approved by the Housing Corporation, but they could be housing associations, tenants' co-operatives or private firms. In formal terms the application for transfer would come from an approved landlord: in the case of blocks of flats the application would go ahead unless more than half of *all* tenants (not just of those voting) were opposed to it. This decision was strongly criticised by both opposition and local authorities (and in due course peers): they were not assuaged by the fact that any tenant who stated that he wished to remain a tenant of the local authority would be able to do so.

The Labour front-bench spokesman on housing, Clive Soley, pointed in the second reading debate to the failure of previous

Conservative attempts to revitalise the private rented sector, and claimed that the Bill did nothing about homelessness. He argued strongly that the government could not be relied on to raise housing benefit in line with the higher rents, and he tried to pour scorn on the Housing Action Trusts. He particularly attacked the right of council tenants to choose their landlord – and the lack of a right for private tenants to do likewise; and he objected vigorously to the voting arrangements. Yet somehow, neither at second reading nor in the Standing Committee, did the Bill turn into the major party battle that had been expected. That this was so owed an enormous amount in committee to the skill and good temper of the Minister for Housing, William Waldegrave – who even managed to take the Bill through its committee stage without recourse to a guillotine motion. Some limited concessions and the offer of a 'Social Landlords' Charter' eased its passage.

Perhaps the most significant concession – almost a year after the Bill started its Parliamentary passage – was one given in response to pressure in the Lords: it established that there should be a ballot of tenants before a HAT was set up, with a majority of those voting determining the issue.

It is, of course, far too soon to consider the consequences of this or the other major Acts passed in the first session of the new Parliament; but of its radicalism there can be no doubt. This was not so much true of the new system of tenure in the private sector, where the emphasis is on building on forms of tenure which had already been developed, the assured tenancy and shorthold. The real significance is the attempt to shift social housing, or housing for the less well-off, away from the domain of local authority control into other forms, which it is hoped will be more flexible and responsive to the desires of tenants. Of course, for a mixture of social and political reasons, the right to buy council properties had already made big inroads into the local authority fiefdoms; but whether or not council tenants will wish to switch to other landlords remains to be seen. The devil they know may have its attractions as against private landlords in particular – and the switch to other landlords would mean the loss of the right to buy. Much depends on two factors – the expected level of council rents, as against other rent levels, and the extent to which housing benefit keeps pace with the rent increases expected in both public and private rented sectors.

If the passage of the Housing Act 1988 was relatively serene, the same could certainly not be said of Nicholas Ridley's other measure, the Local Government Finance Act 1988. Ever since 1974, the Conservative party had been seeking a solution to the problem of the rates. The October 1974 pledge to abolish domestic rates lingered in the political consciousness, but the matter had never really been resolved during the years in opposition. The Layfield report, with its preference for a local income tax, had come and gone. Policy groups had studied and restudied the matter. Other priorities had been found to allow the matter to be left pending for a while; but eventually the government decided that it must act. And so in January 1986 there appeared the green paper *Paying for Local Government.*[3]

The paper was signed by three ministers – the then Secretary of State for the Environment, Kenneth Baker, the Secretary of State for Wales, Nicholas Edwards, and the Secretary of State for Scotland, Malcolm Rifkind. It was not until the summer of that year that Baker moved to Education and Ridley took over the Environment.

The essence of the government's critique was that the existing system of local government finance did not strengthen local accountability. The three main sources of local authority income – non-domestic rates, domestic rates and Exchequer grant – were all unsatisfactory.

Non-domestic rates are paid by businesses and public institutions to whom local authorities are not directly answerable.

Domestic rates are paid by a minority of local electors, and vary in a way that now has little or no regard to the use made of local authority services. The burden of rates is carried on too few shoulders.

Central Government grants are calculated in a very complicated way that conceals the real cost of local services from the local electorate.

The conclusion was that in almost every respect the system made it almost impossible for local electors to relate what they paid to the services provided.

The government made it clear that as far as individuals were concerned the emphasis was on paying for services, rather than redistribution of income. More spending on services would mean residents paying more and vice versa. Local taxpayers would have a direct incentive to see that their local authorities spent less. But this could only be meaningful if virtually *everybody* had to contribute. Otherwise voters who did not have to pay local taxes (who in some areas constituted a large proportion of the electorate) had every reason to vote for councillors who stood for high spending.

The means through which this change was to be brought about was a local poll tax, to be known as the community charge. It would be a flat-rate charge which virtually everybody would pay, regardless of income. There would, however, continue to be a system of rebates for the less well-off. Everybody would have to pay at least 20 per cent of the charge but benefits would be raised in line with the *average* cost of this 20 per cent minimum figure. Where local authorities spent above average, those on the minimum level would have to pay their share of the increased spending. In low spending authorities they would gain.

It was the introduction of the community charge which caused the major furore which was to surround the Bill. A poll tax had been considered on previous occasions, but always rejected. A 1981 green paper, *Alternatives to Domestic Rates*[4] had said of a flat-rate charge payable by all adults that although it was technically feasible:

> the tax would be hard to enforce. If the electoral register were used as the basis for liability it would be seen as a tax on the right to vote. A new register would therefore be needed but this would make the tax expensive to run and therefore complicated, particularly if it incorporated a rebate scheme.

However, the 1986 green paper said that these problems were not insuperable, and that the overriding importance of local accountability meant that they must now be tackled. But it was not primarily the administrative problems, real though they were, that led to the unpopularity of the Bill with many. It was the fact that – above the rebate level anyway – it bore no relation to the ability to pay which had hitherto been one of the Conservative criteria for a new system.

The second element in the scheme – its treatment of the non-domestic or business rate – was also controversial. In essence, although it retained the system of rating property, it took the power of fixing and distributing the rate away from local authorities and handed it over to central government. The government would set a uniform rate in the pound. The proceeds would be pooled and redistributed to all authorities as a common amount per adult. The amount of the rate would not rise above inflation, and before the system could start there would have to be a wholesale revaluation of non-domestic property.

The rationale of this unified business rate was that it would block those local authorities that were imposing heavy and capricious charges on business in a way that was sometimes frightening employment away from exactly those areas which most needed it.

Business rates would come under national control and would be pegged to inflation. But the system would also in fact be sharply redistributive between local authorities in its effects, and a transitional period was seen as necessary.

The redistributive effect would essentially flow from the revaluation with which it was to be accompanied. Rateable values had become out of date and revaluation was clearly essential; but in a national scheme those areas where rents had risen disproportionately would also see their rateable values rise disproportionately following revaluation. In broad terms, this would hit the more prosperous parts of the country and help the less prosperous. It would also tend to hit retail property and many offices and favour manufacturing, where rents had not as a whole gone up by so much. In inner cities and hard-hit areas, the scheme would tend to help: the more buoyant – and politically Conservative – parts of the country would very often suffer.

The overall balance sheet of the government's scheme would, however, depend on the third element: the replacement of the existing Rate Support Grant by a new form of revenue support grant. Its essence would be two forms of grant. One would be a needs grant, which would compensate for what different authorities would need to spend to achieve a comparable standard of service. The other would be a grant paid to all authorities as a standard amount per adult. The needs grant would offset the special burdens of authorities with large problems, a high proportion of old or young, and so on. The other existing mechanism of redistribution, the resources element in the Rate Support Grant, would disappear along with the valuation of domestic property on which (together with business property) it was based.

In very rough and ready terms it might be argued that the new revenue support grant would tend to channel money towards the more prosperous areas, while the new business rate would tend to help the poorer. But it would all ultimately hinge on the level of grant set by the Secretary of State. With his responsibility for setting some three-quarters of the total level of local government finance, and the local authorities through the community charge only accounting for one quarter, it was clear where the strongest hold on the purse-strings would lie.

Such in essence was the scheme for which the green paper provided the basis. It was followed by the decision to make a start by bringing in the legislation for Scotland ahead of England and Wales and before the expected date of the next general election. The reason for this was clearly the strong political upset that had been aroused in Scotland by a rating revaluation in 1985, which had been highly unpopular in Conservative areas especially. Scotland anyway would expect to have separate legislation on a matter of this kind.

Accordingly, the Queen's Speech in the Autumn of 1986 announced Scottish legislation for that session, and the battle accordingly began. Some Conservative doubts on the wisdom or fairness of the community charge were expressed in the debate on the Address, but the Bill was duly brought in and enacted in time for the general election the following summer. Labour naturally tried hard to fight it in Parliament, but in fact it had a somewhat smoother run there than had been expected. This was due partly to the skill and normally emollient approach of the Scottish Office ministers, Malcolm Rifkind and Michael Ancram, and partly to the sheer difficulty that an opposition has in making a splash on Scottish matters in the Westminster Parliament. In Scotland itself, however, the campaign against the poll tax ran strongly, and the Labour party certainly believed that it contributed significantly to the substantial Labour gains in Scotland at the expense of the Conservatives when the general election came. Some Conservatives challenged this view, but it was difficult to argue that the community charge represented the political asset that had been envisaged when it was first adopted.

By the time that the Local Government Bill for England and Wales was presented to Parliament in December 1987, the climate was rather different. It is fair to say that the local government world for the most part disliked the Bill. Party leanings no doubt influenced the intensity with which this dislike was expressed, but neither the community charge nor the unified business rate found many friends in the councils. The community charge was seen as difficult and expensive to administer, as well as unfair in its impact, and the new unified business rate was resented as a straight transfer of power from local to central government. Over the years, the rates had been perceived as the symbol of the (relative) independence of local government, even though that independence was recently diminished by rate-capping and penalties; but they had also had the attraction that they were easy to determine and collect. And naturally enough the new element of accountability entailed in the universal community charge was particularly unappealing to those authorities that had thriven in its absence.

The second reading of the Bill, on 16 and 17 December 1987, saw the beginning of the long parliamentary battle. Before it began an attempt had been made by over 40 Conservatives who were unhappy with the community charge to obtain a debate on an instruction to the standing committee on the Bill that it should examine the desirability of linking the charge to the ability to pay. This was ruled out of order. It was the flat-rate nature of the scheme that worried these Conservatives. A scheme had been evolved in conjunction with staff of the Chartered Institute of Public Finance and Accountancy by which the community charge should be levied at different rates for different bands of income. As Ridley was able to argue, this had practical difficulties – the step from one income band to another could mean an increase in the charge which outweighed the increase in the person concerned's income, and the link with the Inland Revenue system would add a whole new administrative dimension to the scheme; but this was not enough to dissuade a significant number of the Tory rebels.

Ridley's speech at the start of the debate was subjected to a barrage of interruptions, and indeed he seemed to end it prematurely. He demonstrated effectively one aspect of the existing system in showing how payments based on rental values bore little relationship to the services provided. To take the extremes, the average rate bill per adult in South Buckinghamshire district was £400, with spending per adult at £650. In Pendle, the rate per adult was £130, but spending was £700. A ratepayer would accordingly pay three times as much for less in the way of services in South Buckinghamshire as in Pendle. But it would be the change in the Rate Support Grant system that would be fundamentally expected to alter this; while the two-day debate for the most part focused on the community charge. One after another Conservatives came out against it: Michael Heseltine, Timothy Raison, Edward Heath, Sir Ian Gilmour, Sir George Young, Sir Philip Goodhart, Robin Squire and Patrick Cormack all in turn declared their opposition to it, and David Howell was a very reluctant supporter.

The essence of their objections to the Bill was quite simply the flat-rate nature of the community charge. There were differing views as to the question whether it was right to try to bring everyone within the tax's net in the interest of greater accountability; but it was the fact that the richest in the land would pay no more than those only just above the rebate level that caused both political and moral anxiety. Heseltine, for example, spoke of the 'platform of crude regression which seeks to make equal in the eyes of the tax collector the rich and the poor, the slum dweller and the landed aristocrat, the elderly pensioners living on their limited savings and the most successful of today's entrepreneurs'. After describing how the 1981 review of local government finance, in his days as Secretary of State, had seen the Cabinet dismiss the idea of a poll tax 'with hardly a backward glance', he went on to say that:

> The most significant change that the poll tax will produce is that we shall be held totally responsible for it ... That tax will be known as a Tory tax.

On the second day, Sir George Young, who had played a crucial part in organising Conservative opposition and in the formulation of the alternative scheme of a banded charge, stressed the dislike of the scheme among Conservatives in the country and in local government, as well as in public opinion at large. He concluded: 'The Bill is inconsistent with our principles, irrelevant to our programme and inimical to our prospects ...'.

Other Conservatives spoke of the risk of disorder that could flow in certain parts of the country from the compilation of the register and the collection of the tax; but it was the impact on the nearly poor that was the greatest concern.

Some Conservative doubts were also expressed on another aspect of the Bill – the impact of the new business rate on some of the Tory heartlands, but it was the community charge that was the heart of the objections. Some Conservatives, mostly young Members, did support the scheme, and the government was able to stress the practical drawbacks of the 'banded' alternative, but it was not a happy experience for the government. Seventeen Conservatives voted against the government and a number more abstained.

The Bill, however, duly made its way into Standing Committee – where the Minister of State, Michael Howard, proved a skilful minister – and then in due course back to the floor of the House for Report stage. There, on 18 April 1988, another battle took place. A backbencher, Michael Mates, who had not originally been much involved in the argument and was not on the standing committee, had nevertheless been upset by what he considered were misleading undertakings made to him by the government before he voted for the Bill. He now put down an amendment on Report which presented a new version of the banded scheme, made possible by the recent Budget. For those who did not pay income tax, the rate of community charge would be half the normal level (they would still also be eligible for rebates). Those on the standard rate of tax would pay the standard rate of community charge, and those on the higher rate of tax would pay 50 per cent above the standard rate of community charge. This fitted neatly with the three levels of tax set out in the Budget, but of course it still remained the case that local authorities would have to acquire information about people's tax position from the Inland Revenue, and that in some cases the final determination of individuals' taxable income would not come until long after the point when the individual began to pay his community charge for the year in question.

Ridley was able to play on these points in his response to Mates's speech, and again a number of newer Members on the Conservative side supported the government, particularly stressing that the flat-rate community charge had been in the 1987 Conservative manifesto. The government was, however, clearly worried. Only a few days before the debate Ridley had announced that the rebates were to be more generous. In the debate itself, he said that rebates would reach nine million people – a blow to the Treasury in its attempts to reduce housing benefit, but clearly an alleviation in the impact of the scheme on poorer people. Heseltine and Young spoke in favour of the Mates amendment, but the government received more support from its own side on the floor of the House than it had done at second reading. But whereas it had obtained a second reading by 341 votes to 269, it only defeated the Mates amendment by 320 to 295. Thirty-six Tories voted for the amendment – but in spite of considerable difficulties in the Lords (and a massive whipping effort there to secure the community charge) the government duly obtained its Bill in pretty much the form it wanted. The thought remains that it is just possible that if a technically satisfactory way of relating the community charge to ability to pay had been found, the government would have adopted it.

Important though Nicholas Ridley's Bills to reform housing and local government finance undoubtedly were, the most significant of the three flagships was almost certainly Kenneth Baker's Education Reform Bill. Its origins could be found in a variety of different sources. The concern over standards enunciated by James Callaghan in his Ruskin College speech a decade earlier; the 1985 white paper of Sir Keith Joseph; the more recent white paper on higher education; the pressure from parents for greater access to the more popular schools; the belief among some that schools should be more active in promoting moral standards through religious education; the decision announced at the 1986 Conservative Party conference that there was to be a pilot network of 20 City Technology Colleges funded directly by government and industrial contributions – these were some of the elements that went into the Bill.

As we have seen, the 1987 manifesto set out proposals for four major school reforms. The election was followed by a hectic consultation process. During July a series of papers were issued, covering the national curriculum and assessment, admissions to maintained schools, financial delegation to schools, grant-maintained schools, collective worship and the organisation of education in Inner London. In every case, responses had to be sent in within a matter of weeks, so that the long Bill could be brought in before Christmas. Since this period ran over the holiday months, there was a good deal of complaint about the haste with which the process was being carried out; but the government was understandably determined to obtain its three major Bills in the first session of the new Parliament. In due course, the Education Reform Bill was laid before Parliament, and it received its second reading on 1 December.

The heart of the Bill was the introduction of the national curriculum for schools. There were to be three core subjects – English, maths and science – and seven other foundation subjects – history, geography, technology, a foreign language in secondary schools, music, art and physical education. In Wales, Welsh would be included, and religious education would continue to be required under the 1944 Act. It was expected, though not stated in the Bill, that the compulsory subjects would occupy 70 to 80 per cent of the school time. The exact distinction between the core and the foundation subjects was not clear, but it would presumably influence the bodies that were going to work out the details of the curriculum. The curriculum was to be backed by a system of testing or assessment at the ages of 7, 11, 14 and 16.

The second element of the Bill was concerned with school admissions. Under the 1980 Education Act, parental choice had been strengthened by allowing parents to claim places at schools which fell below a certain level based on a standard number based on the intake in September 1979. Schools were free to set a limit up to 20 per cent below that standard number (or lower still with the agreement of the Secretary of State). The object of this was to allow a more even spread of children between schools particularly in the era of falling rolls. The new Bill gave the right to a place as long as there was *any* room in a school.

The Bill next set out a scheme for delegating to schools (except for primary schools with less than 200 pupils) responsibility for a good deal of their financial management and the appointment of staff.

Then came what was probably the Bill's most controversial element – the so-called 'opt-out' provision by which schools would have the right to opt out of local authority control and be funded directly by central government. These grant-maintained schools were to receive funds equivalent to what they would have received from local authorities, and the places were to continue to be free. The emphasis in putting forward the idea was on lifting the opportunities for children in run down areas with poor local authorities; but critics argued that the most likely applicants would be schools trying to escape closure because of falling rolls or successful schools working their way towards independence.

Another contentious ingredient concerned the City Technology Colleges. As we have seen, the decision to create them had already been taken, but the Bill set up a long-term scheme for their funding.

Higher education was to see changes of very great importance, following the pattern discussed in the previous chapter of this book. Two funding councils were to be set up – one for universities and one for polytechnics, and the relation between the government, the councils and the universities and colleges was defined. Another part of the Bill effectively ended academic tenure.

As Butler had found, a Bill of this magnitude in education touches on many different educational interests. Butler had the time to negotiate at length with the churches and other interested parties. Baker was in much more of a hurry – to some extent the negotiations took place while the Bill was working its way through the two Houses of Parliament, notably those with the churches and the universities.

Although the Bill had its critics over certain specific provisions in the Commons, its passage was not unduly difficult. There was anxiety among some that the assessment or testing system should be primarily diagnostic (rather than unduly competitive) in its purpose. The opting-out provisions (including the voting process) aroused some concern – Edward Heath attacked it (and other aspects) ferociously in the Commons. There was considerable pressure to strengthen, and make more specific, the position of religious education – and the government in fact made concessions which met this concern. There was also, in the later stages of the Bill, some concern to meet the anxieties in the universities about excessive central control and a possible threat to academic freedom, in the tenure provisions specifically. Again, there were some concessions.

The most significant change to the Bill, however, was to the provisions for Inner London – and the change owed a good deal to the pressure of two front-benchers-turned-backbenchers, Norman Tebbit and Michael Heseltine. They both spoke on second reading to argue that instead of the original provision that inner London boroughs should have the right to opt out of ILEA, ILEA should be scrapped and all the boroughs should become education authorities (as had been envisaged years before by the Herbert Commission which led to the creation of ILEA and the GLC). Feeling was mounting that, whatever its rights and wrongs, the opting out provision would emasculate ILEA, and the proposal was quickly accepted by the government. Only one or two lone Conservative voices, notably Gerald Bowden from Dulwich, argued in Parliament that the break-up would mean handing over London education to boroughs that were felt to be incapable of handling it effectively. Naturally enough, repeated Conservative criticism of boroughs like Lambeth and Islington was sometimes a little difficult to reconcile with the notion that they should take on major new powers.

But Tory concerns, such as they were, were not focused on one major area, and there was widespread acceptance – going well beyond the party – of the idea of the national curriculum. Moreover, although there were some in the education world happy to accuse Baker of haste and superficiality, his handling of the Bill was a parliamentary *tour de force*. Extremely assiduous in his attendance at committee and other stages, he imported a genial atmosphere into the proceedings which blunted the edge of the opposition's attack. And by a willingness to make some concessions, not least in the Lords, he managed first to win round the churches and then to deflect a fair proportion of the concern in the universities – although suspicion lingered there that despite Baker's protestations the Bill was in essence a centralising measure as far as they were concerned.

Although it was Baker and Ridley who had the task of steering the three Conservative flagship Bills through Parliament, the minister who in some ways seemed most under pressure during the 1987–8 session was the Secretary of State for Social Services, John Moore. Moore had succeeded Norman Fowler after the general election, and for a time was discussed as a rising star within the party. On 26 September 1987 he made a speech to a Conservative Political Centre conference in London in which he set out his thinking on the future of the welfare state. His theme was that 'the next step forward in the long evolutionary march of the welfare state in Britain is away from dependence towards independence'.

To bring this about, two things needed to be done. First, the climate of opinion must be changed. People must stop being encouraged to see themselves as victims of circumstance and categorised by labels – unemployed, single-parent, handicapped. There must be an end to the belief that only government action could affect their lives. Moore commented on the way that voluntary organisations had shifted their emphasis from being service groups to pressure groups. The depressing climate of dependence must be reversed.

The second task was to change the policies which had largely created the attitudes. The Social Security Act of 1986 was a recognition that change was possible. Moore added that 'in a fast-moving modern society social policies should probably remain under continuous review'.

In this and other speeches Moore gave the impression that he was determined to intensify the pace of change in social policy, and that he did not see his role as merely that of implementing the Act which Fowler had passed. The first significant step came in the Chancellor of the Exchequer's Autumn Statement, when it was revealed that the government had decided not to uprate child benefit in line with inflation. The 1987 manifesto had said: 'Child benefit will continue to be paid as now, and to the mother'. The government was able to claim that child benefit had not always been uprated, but a number of Conservatives felt that this decision went against the spirit of the manifesto, particularly since the revenue was buoyant.

The advocates of child benefit were able to point to the support given to it by the Fowler review only two years before. It was seen as part of an historic commitment to help all those with children, for long achieved through tax allowances as well as since the Second World War by family allowances. It brought special help to mothers, who did not always share in their husband's prosperity. It went to those just above the benefit level – the 'not-quite-poor' about whom again a fair number of Conservatives were concerned, both for social and electoral reasons; and as a universal benefit it did not lead to the poverty trap – the disincentive caused when an increase in earnings is offset by loss of benefits. It also achieved virtually complete take-up. Against this, the government argued that it was absurd to give ever-higher universal benefits to plenty of people who palpably did not need them, while an increase in child benefit automatically led to a matching reduction in the selective help available for children through the new Family Credit and Income Support. The freeze in child benefit saved £120 million in the coming year; against this Moore was able to argue that he would be spending an additional £320 million on the two means-tested benefits.

The argument rumbled on through the following weeks and came to a climax at the Report stage of a new Social Security Bill on 12 January 1988. Sir Brandon Rhys Williams, who had long been a leading protagonist of child benefit and sadly died only a few months later, put down a new clause designed to secure uprating. There had been much discussion about the likely extent of a Conservative revolt. The government's majority in defeating the new clause was 47, as against the 85 it had secured on the immediately preceding vote. Sixteen Conservatives voted against the government or were tellers, and a number of others abstained. The Tory supporters of child benefit continued to put their arguments actively through the year, but the level was again pegged for the following year in the Autumn Statement of 1 November 1988.

It was not, however, child benefit but the implementation of the 1986 Social Security Act that probably caused most difficulty to the government at this time. John Moore gave a series of faltering performances at the Dispatch Box on this and health matters and indeed was put out of action by an attack of pneumonia. The actual levels of benefit under the Act had to be determined by a series of measures in Parliament, and some of them proved very controversial.

Labour mounted a heavy attack on the Social Fund: their spokesman, Robin Cook, proved adept at instancing distressing cases of possible hardship. But it was the changes in housing benefit that caused most concern among Conservatives. Two factors combined to mean that recipients would receive less or no benefit. One was the steeper rate of taper or withdrawal of benefit; the other the application of the new capital limit, so that those with capital of over £6000 would be disqualified from housing benefit and those with between £3000 and £6000 would receive only a reduced amount.

Gradually more and more Conservatives began to be aware as a result of representations from their own, frequently elderly, constituents that they actually stood to see incomes of well under £100 a week reduced by perhaps £10 a week, or more. It was said that the Prime Minister herself became aware of the hardship among her own constituents. In April, just after the new benefit levels came in, changes were made to stop housing benefit recipients from losing more than £2.50 a week and raising the capital limit for them (though not for those on income support) from £6000 to £8000. A threatened rebellion was averted at the last minute, but the episode was an uneasy reminder of the problems of reducing dependency.

It was not only social security that caused the government difficulties: health was even more prominent on the public agenda. The problems concerned both the general funding of the NHS and the recurring question of nurses' pay. The resources allocated to the NHS continued to rise ahead of inflation, but the demands and costs of the service raced ahead of the resources – and, as always, the fact that so many of the middle classes used the service gave an extra articulacy to its defence. This was reflected in extensive media coverage. The government clearly had to respond, and in particular let people believe that it would implement whatever recommendations the review body on nurses' pay put forward when it reported in April 1988. This duly happened; the government undertook to accept the award, and in due course to fund it in full, without any of the cost falling on the district health authorities. Even so, there was a good deal of argument about the restructuring entailed in the nursing profession and its pay implications; but overall nursing undoubtedly became a more financially attractive career.

There was also one piece of legislation that caused considerable difficulty within the party during 1988, a Health and Medicines Bill. This measure introduced for the first time charges for dental and optical tests. There were substantial exemptions, but they did not, for instance, cover pensioners, for whom optical tests were held to be particularly important, nor young adults who are at an age when teeth problems are prevalent. The government met with considerable opposition during the Report stage of the Bill in the summer, and with even more when it came back to the Commons from the Lords in the Autumn with the charges effectively abolished. A group led by Dame Jill Knight, and ranging across the spectrum of the party, did all they could to get the government to accept the Lords changes, and by the time it came to eye tests the government's majority was down into single figures.

By then another significant event had occurred. It had been argued for some time that the massive Department of Health and Social Security was too great for any single minister to handle. Its share of public expenditure was enormous and its share of political problems at least as large. Even a Secretary of State more on top of his form than Moore had been would undoubtedly have found the 1987–8 session remarkably taxing. In an unexpected reshuffle shortly before the summer recess, the Department was split. A former Minister of State for Health, the lively yet relaxed debater Kenneth Clarke, became Secretary of State for Health, which included the personal social services. Moore took the reduced Department of Social Security. It was Clarke therefore who had to pick up the problems over nurses' regrading and eye and teeth tests. At least he had the advantage of a substantial further increase in funding for the health service in the Autumn Statement.

He also took over departmental responsibility for the review of the structure of the NHS which had been under way since the election under Mrs Thatcher's chairmanship. Although the outcome of the review falls outside the scope of this book the fact of it, and the reports of the course it was taking, had aroused great interest.

The problems were not essentially different from those which had been diagnosed long before by people like Dr D. S. Lees: the open-ended nature of the service; the difficulty of controlling costs; the ever-increasing needs of the mounting population of old people; the managerial difficulties of such a large-scale organisation; the tendency of the interests of the providers to come (sometimes) before the consumers or patients – all these and other factors led to the feeling that a review was necessary. Certainly it could not be said that the NHS was causing Britain to spend more on health care than other comparable countries: the question was rather whether we were using the money to best effect, and whether alternative systems might make it easier to win more resources for health care.

It was argued, for example, that a method of funding through which people felt a more direct stake in their own care than they did in a tax-funded system might be preferable. This led back to the long-held view that the right answer lay with some kind of compulsory insurance. This could be run by either the government or the private sector. An alternative would be to convert national insurance into a scheme for funding health care, leaving social security to be funded by taxation. But insurance-based systems clearly have their drawbacks. For a start, a substantial proportion of geriatric, psychiatric and acute illnesses may prove very unattractive to insurers. Insurance, too, carries the risk that both doctors and patients will feel tempted to maximise treatment: the insurance companies already find it increasingly necessary to keep a tight control on treatment and 'hotel' charges.

Reports suggested that the review was turning away from the insurance approach – which might, of course, include tax concessions for those relying on private care – towards an attempt to see whether more of an 'internal market' could be built up. This was based on the notion that there might be more buying and selling of services between one health authority and another, as well as more buying in of services from private hospitals, nursing homes and clinics. There was interest, too, in the possibility of 'health maintenance units' by which groups of general practitioners might buy in hospital and specialist services for their patients, in effect as if from a market, with the funding coming either from the state or from insurance schemes. It was also argued that the monolithic hospital structure set by by Aneurin Bevan should be fragmented, with a variety of different bodies, statutory, voluntary and private, managing hospitals and offering greater competition than exists at present.

Although ideas abounded, and the various 'think-tanks' were hard at work, as the review progressed it looked likely that the more radical changes were being discarded. Kenneth Clarke was known to be a more enthusiastic supporter (and user) of the NHS than his predecessor, and the Prime Minister was probably still cautious about provoking any furore in what still seemed to be a popular institution. For all the readiness to challenge the past that marked the Thatcher period, conservatism had not disappeared from the Conservative hierarchy.

11 The Evolving Agenda

There was a time when people talked about the 'unfinished business of the welfare state'. The assumption was that there were a few more areas of need to be identified and problems to be solved; the edifice would then be complete, with only the cost of maintenance to worry about. That view was always naive, and the passing of the years has only served to confirm that social policy has to evolve continuously, just as society itself evolves. Needs change, expectations change, resources change, ideas change – and in each case the verb 'change' has both a passive and an active meaning.

So far, this book has been an attempt to record what happened, without too much intrusion of my own views. In this and the next chapter the subject matter is the future – what is likely to happen and to some extent what ought to happen.

But first let me try to summarise the main themes in Conservative social policy since the Second World War. I have accepted earlier that it is a mistake to regard the early post-war period simply in terms of consensus: moving on parallel lines seems a better description. But there is no doubt that the shared experiences of government during the war-time coalition, accompanied by a national mood that was strongly sympathetic to the idea of the welfare state, meant that Conservative–Labour rivalry in this field in the post-war years was more about who could do the job more effectively than about the principles of social provision. It was accepted that resources had to be switched through the tax system from the better-off to the less well-off to provide the latter with health care, cash benefits, education, housing and so on – though this process was more palatable to the middle class because they too received 'free' health care, education and family allowances, as well as the government's contribution towards national insurance.

This broadly egalitarian concept was coupled with another one – the notion that the social services were there to enhance human potential. There was argument about the comparative desirability of absolute equality as against equality of opportunity, but either way it was clearly the job of the education and training system to make the best use of human potential, whichever social class it came from. Even the argument about comprehensive schools was partly, though not wholly, about this. Where there was more divergence was on the place of the private sector and the freedom to receive private provision; but interestingly Labour never quite brought itself to abolish private medicine, private education, private pensions or private rented accommodation. Indeed, it never even fully implemented its plans to end the paybeds in the hospitals, which Aneurin Bevan had reluctantly allowed.

For a long time, when it came to the crunch of election times, the emphasis on both sides was on how much they had done and how much more they proposed to do: Labour would trumpet the Act creating the NHS, the Conservatives the achievement of 300 000 houses, and so on. And even when attention began to shift to administrative structures and institutional change around the time of Edward Heath there was no very great ideological divide to be discerned.

But gradually significant changes began to make themselves felt. For a start, the growing awareness that Britain was lagging further and further behind the other Western (and Far-eastern) economies, coupled with the escalation of inflation, led to the view that too much of our wealth was going into the social services and too little into investment, savings and incentives. First the oil crisis of 1973 and then the rude shock of the IMF settlement in 1976 – together with a host of attendant factors – led both parties to accept that public expenditure *had* to be controlled more rigorously, and that automatic inflation-proofing *had* to give way to cash limits. Inevitably, in a democracy, this was more easily said than done, and the surge in unemployment did not make it any easier; but however erratically monetarism came on the scene.

Then, as the Thatcher years moved on, other interrelated factors came to the fore which particularly impressed Conservatives. One was a reaction against the mass-scale public providers – the nationalised industries, local government and (though less consistently) central government. This was a compound of various elements. The big battalions were seen as deadening, incompetent, unresponsive to consumer or individual choice, unadaptable, prone to empire-building, hostile to enterprise and intrinsically likely to be socialistic in their ways. (Socialists, though, were also increasingly concerned abut the problem of bigness.) In the industrial sector, privatisation provided a ready made answer, even if the extent to which privatisation has brought in competition has varied. In some areas of both central and local government, the privatisation of specific services has also been possible, and often successful. But the questions about who should actually *control* services have been more profound and more difficult.

Central government has not relinquished much of its actual power over the social services, and in some respects has increased it. In the health service, it has made various attempts to decentralise further to regions, and indeed to work through an overall management board at arm's length from government; but the first attempt to have a non-ministerial businessman chairman of that board failed, because of the high political content of the NHS, and there are sharp limits to the extent of regional decentralisation. Parliament will not easily let the Secretary of State for Health forget that he is the only democratically elected accountable authority in the NHS.

The January 1989 white paper, *Working for Patients*, really falls outside the scope of this book, but it envisaged significant changes in the organisation of the health service.[1] They include some delegation of functions from region to district and from district to hospital. More radically, the white paper set out a scheme for self-governing hospitals within the NHS, for more buying and selling of services across administrative boundaries and for larger general practitioner practices to have their own budget and both buy certain services from hospitals and compete for patients. Moreover, at national level, a two-tier board system was proposed, with the Secretary of State chairing the policy board and a management executive under a chief executive working to the policy board. But it is doubtful if any of this would really lessen the Secretary of State's ultimate authority – try as Ministers may to escape the burden of accountability for all that happens in the NHS!

There are however areas where more significant change in the locus of power is to be seen: they generally have to do with local government. In some cases, power is passing out to the consumer, in some to a more localised management, in some back to central government. There are those who argue that our constitution requires a balance between central and local government, but in fact central government through Parliament holds the cards: there is no constraint on the power to legislate. We may see the outcome. Central government now has the power to cap local spending, both in general and specifically on housing; it will determine the business rate, as well of course as the revenue support grant; and it severely limits the spending of capital receipts. In housing, council tenants are being encouraged to transfer their dwellings to other landlords or, of course, to buy them for themselves. In education, schools are able to opt out of local authority control, city technology colleges are developing outside the local government system, assisted places have been brought back, parental rights of choice of schools have been strengthened, budgets are being devolved to schools and governing bodies have gained power at the expense of education authorities.

There is one other major change in the current Conservative philosophy of welfare: the growing commitment to the view that the social services have created a 'culture of dependency' and that the sense of individual responsibility has been seriously diminished over the years. (I shall come back to this later.) The sentiment is by no means new – there have always been those to complain of the 'nanny state' and the diminution of self-reliance; but over the past decade what was an instinct has been intellectualised and to some extent quantified by the radical right and indeed others. In social security, housing and local government finance the first steps have been taken to reverse the trend of four decades and social policy has become more politically controversial than it has been for many years. The radical right is no doubt moving ahead of the country as a whole, but sooner or later a process of rethinking on these lines was probably inevitable.

Let us now look a little more closely at certain specific policy areas. Clearly one of the main themes will derive from demography. In 1951, 5 332 000 people in the United Kingdom were aged over 65, of whom 218 000 were over 85. In 2025, there are expected to be 9 956 000 over 65, with 1 230 000 over 85.

This represents an enormous growth in the size of the potentially dependent elderly population, with substantial demands for retirement pensions, health care, home helps, sheltered housing, retirement homes and provision for disability.

As we have seen, the government has taken certain steps to help deal with this problem. It has taken two in particular to limit the financial call of pensions. The breaking in 1980 of the link between the level of retirement pensions and whichever was higher between earnings or prices meant that the actual rate for a single pension in April 1989 was to be £43.60 as opposed to a putative rate of £54.65. The addition for an adult dependant was to be £26.20 as opposed to £32.65. The government has now been able to abolish the Treasury supplement to the national insurance fund, which used to constitute 18 per cent of it.

Obviously this development has been attacked by the opposition, particularly since national insurance is financed on a pay-as-you-go basis, rather than through a true fund. It can be argued that today's pensioners should not have to suffer to solve tomorrow's problems. But the cost of social security as a whole has soared – from £16.2

million in 1978–9 to an estimated £46.9 million in 1989–90 at current prices – and retirement pensions have been the biggest single ingredient.

The other major reduction in expected expenditure on the old is the severe pruning of SERPS, the state second pension scheme, which I have already described. There have also recently been attempts to control the soaring costs of residential care and of housing benefit.

These in a sense are negative measures: the main positive line of policy is the drive to increase private pension provision over and above the state basic retirement pension. This is making headway. The majority of pensioners have some form of pension in excess of the basic entitlement. In March 1988 some 18 per cent had pension increments as a result of delayed retirement, some two-thirds had graduated pensions arising from the pre-1975 earnings-related scheme and some 23 per cent were receiving additional SERPS pension. In many cases, however, the amounts received were very small. The main thrust is outside the state scheme. Data for 1985 suggest that of private households consisting solely of pensioners 51 per cent had occupational pensions and some 71 per cent had some form of investment income. It is significant that in 1971 pensioners represented about half of all households in the bottom fifth of households by income. By 1985 this had dropped to just over a quarter.

In some ways, the strategy for dealing with the financial problems of the old is relatively clearcut, even though it will take years to come to full fruition. Its essence is insurance or the contributory principle. Whether in due course it will be possible to shift the great bulk of retirement pensions on to private and occupational schemes remains to be seen. From a public expenditure point of view it might not matter, so long as contributions cover pensions. But any scheme to curtail or means-test pensions for which full contributions have been made would understandably run into enormous opposition. And for the time being the state has to make a substantial contribution to cover the cost of topping up the basic pensions of somewhere near two million pensioners. The January 1988 public expenditure white paper put the cost of supplementary pensions in 1987–8 at £1260 million, going to 1 875 000 people.

If the hope, nevertheless, is that insurance can eventually take care of the great bulk of the income needs of the retired, it would be unrealistic to assume that pensions and insurance will be adequate to take over anything like the full cost of the other services needed by the old. The health care of the elderly, which is so unattractive to the insurance companies' actuaries, is likely to remain indefinitely a major demand. Residential accommodation is unlikely to become cheap, particularly where nursing or active care are required, and the cost of housing generally looks full of complications. Recent legislation in both the public and the private rented sector predicates higher rents, to be met where necessary by higher housing benefit, while the community charge will also tend to increase the cost of housing benefit.

Housing benefit raises the critical issue in social security policy today: the balance between selective or means-tested and universal benefits. I say 'balance' because virtually no one argues that all benefits should be universal or all should be selective. There is no pressure, for instance, to means-test war pensions. Conversely, income support is bound to be selective.

The issue crystallises in child benefit. Child benefit at £7.25 per child was planned to cost £4528 million in 1988–9, and to go to 12 015 000 children in 6 745 000 families. It was pegged at the same rate as in the previous year (and there was to be no increase in 1989–90).

The case for not uprating it, and either abolishing it or allowing it to fade away through inflation, is a simple one. Since it is a universal benefit with almost complete take-up it is clearly going to a great many families who have no need for it. Money spent on supporting families with children through family credit and income support can, it is argued, be much more effectively targeted on needy children. To spend £200 million on uprating child benefit is seen as much less cost-effective than it is to spend the money through the selective benefits, particularly as under the present system any additional money received is deducted from the income support or family credit entitlement.

But selectivity, as we have seen earlier, has its drawbacks and there are particular factors of importance relating to child benefit. For a start, selectivity all too easily leads to disincentives. If you go out to work, or improve your job, you will lose benefit; and even though the system may be designed so that you lose less benefit than you gain through pay or higher pay, this gain may easily disappear with the cost of going to work and particularly where there are a number of children in the family.

Means-testing itself is still an unloved process, while the task of conveying information as to entitlements to benefit is complicated. Not surprisingly, some means-tested benefits have a low take-up – family credit was running at about 30 per cent of the estimated number eligible some months after it was launched in 1988. There is a welcome certainty about child benefit, and no delay in receiving it. And if means-testing takes the form of taxing a universal benefit, then there is the phenomenon of churning – of paying out with one hand, only to collect with another – repudiated by the Fowler review. Taxing child benefit would anyway be difficult with the separate taxing of husbands and wives. Would the wife who received the benefit be taxed, even though she would normally be on the lower income? Or would the husband have to pay tax on a benefit he had not received? The notion of depriving those on the higher rate of tax of it has the drawback that tax demands are often not finished until long after the year to which they relate has begun.

But beyond that there are deeper questions. Do we accept that the state should give special help to those who carry the burden (if also the pleasures) of bringing up children? We have done so for a very long time. Tax allowances for children stretch well back for nearly a century, and indeed have their origins in the days of the Younger Pitt. At the end of the Second World War, as we have seen, family allowances were added – tax allowances were no use to those who did not pay tax. Later the two were amalgamated in the tax-free child benefit: to end it would be to end a long tradition of accepting that having children, like being old or buying a house, should lead to special help without a means test.

But child benefit recognises too that the task of bringing up children imposes special strains, especially on the mother. It may mean that she cannot go to work; it may be that her family is only just above the line where the selective benefits come into play – the not-quite-poor can be hard-pressed by selectivity. It may even become the case that the decline in family sizes means that Britain should adopt a positive population policy of encouraging more rather than fewer births, so that there are enough young to look after the ever-increasing numbers of old. But in the meantime the argument persists: is it the universal or the means-tested benefit that really leads to the culture of dependency?

History has shown the difficulty of bringing about a major change in the system of non-contributory benefits. The most ambitious schemes for change continue to be in the realm of tax credits.

In recent years, the most ardent Conservative advocate of a merging of the tax and benefits systems was Sir Brandon Rhys Williams. When he died in 1988, he left in draft a pamphlet which was edited and completed by Hermione Parker under the title of *Stepping Stones to Independence*.[2] He replaced the term 'tax credit' by 'Basic Income

Guarantee' (BIG), and stressed that for practical reasons the scheme could only be introduced gradually.

The essence of the scheme is that every legal resident would be credited with a small BI, which would replace existing income tax allowances and would be deducted from existing benefit entitlements. In time, the BIs would be age-related, with adults receiving more than children, and elderly people, as well as the disabled and carers, receiving special supplements. The target amount of the BI would be £26.00 at 1988 prices, but the scheme might start on an initial partial BI of £10.50.

These BIs and the first slice of earned income would be free of income tax: for those without income against which to offset the BIs, they would convert into cash. There would be no restrictions on earnings and no means testing. Child benefit would be absorbed as children would qualify for BIs. Husbands and wives would be taxed separately. As Hermione Parker puts it:

> People without jobs would be free to take whatever work was available, to study or to train without fear of prosecution or loss of benefit. Employers would be able to take on trainees without having to pay wages competitive with income support grossed up for tax. Gone would be the status of 'claimant', gone the degradation of signing on, gone the complexities of PAYE codes, 24-hour rules, 21-hour rules, earnings rules, cohabitation rules, and so on.[3]

Since BIs would serve as fixed-amount credit against tax, there is obviously a heavy cost in providing them at a substantial level. To lift everybody off existing benefits could entail BIs of about £65.00 a week, requiring an impossibly high tax on all other income. (Income tax and national insurance contributions would be merged.) But very much lower levels of BI would still serve to reduce means testing and bolster family life through the certainty of provision which would be available for mothers at home and their children, while the fact that BIs were not means-tested would mean that poorer families would have every incentive to earn more through work, rather than to remain unemployed. The effect would be equivalent to a substantial increase in tax thresholds, and reverse the post-war tendency for tax to be imposed on more and more of the less well-paid.

What are the snags in all this? A major administrative upheaval would be entailed and the scheme could not be brought in until the computers were ready for it. Clearly administrative costs are an important factor. But the government's green paper of March 1986, *The Reform of*

Personal Taxation, also put forward objections in principle.[4] It argued that the payment of a substantial basic benefit to everyone, irrespective of their financial circumstances, would not only mean unacceptable increases in public expenditure and taxation, but that at the same time automatic generous benefits would undermine the incentive to work. Instead, the Chancellor of the Exchequer claimed that transferable allowances between husbands and wives would reduce the number of people both paying tax and receiving income-related benefits; that paying both housing benefit and the new family credit on net rather than gross income would end marginal tax rates of 100 per cent or more; and that paying family credit through the pay packet would reduce the 'churning', by which one member of the family might pay tax while another received family income supplement. (In the event, as we have seen, family credit was changed so that it normally goes to the mother, rather than through the pay packet to the father.)

Obviously these are points which have to be taken seriously and it is clear that no more than a limited scheme could be introduced initially. But at any foreseeable level the amount of income produced would not be enough to encourage idleness: on the contrary, the incentive to work would be greater than it is with the present means-tested systems. For all the improvements brought in by Family Credit, it cannot be said that the 1986 Social Security Act has abolished the poverty or employment trap.

Rhys Williams thought that a scheme that would not impose additional burdens on the Exchequer, and which would be based on a partial BI of £26.00 and a tax-cum-national insurance rate of 35 per cent, might be possible at the end of the century. He recognised that there were many economic imponderables and favoured the phasing out of mortgage tax relief and commuted pension tax-free lump sums as part of the system – clearly very sensitive political points. But he was surely right to claim that the stimulus to work, the simplified administration following the merger of income tax and national insurance, and the clearing up of much of the present jungle of benefits, means-tests, grants, allowances and subsidies should be highly beneficial, both in terms of administration and even more important of support for the family. At the very least, it would be a grave error to reject the whole concept as flawed and fit only for the history books.

In the meanwhile, we clearly have to rely on a combination of contributory and non-contributory benefits, the latter including some with means tests and some without; and experience of the implementation of the 1986 Social Security Act – as we have seen earlier – shows just how difficult any change other than the distribution of more resources really is.

Housing benefit in some ways presents the most difficult problems of all. At least national insurance is now broadly self-funding. Income support and family credit are not, of course, but so long as unemployment tends to fall the pressure on income support is lessened. Disability benefits are now, rightly, a substantial call on the Exchequer, but the numbers of the disabled are not subject to erratic fluctuations. But housing benefit is peculiarly different to manage. It cannot be standardised and brought within income support because of variations between regions and between different types of tenure. Moreover, because it is open-ended it would be difficult to cash-limit it. On top of this, government policy in the field of rented housing is based on generally higher rents, which will in turn mean higher housing benefit for the less well-off. This applies alike to privately rented housing, housing association tenancies and council housing. The 1988 Housing Act is the vehicle for higher rents for the two former categories: the Local Government and Housing Bill brought in in the 1988–9 session is the instrument for raising council rents. To some extent the aim of this legislation is to protect the public purse by further reducing the amount of housing subsidy; but it has to be said that the success of the government's overall housing policy rests heavily on housing benefit and, of course, tax relief on mortgages. Moreover, as we have seen, the introduction of the community charge has had to be eased by more generous housing benefit. No wonder the benefit is reputed to be causing the Treasury considerable alarm, even though any fall in unemployment reduces the numbers on housing benefit.

Obviously the government is right to take steps to see that housing benefit is not used to support exorbitant rents or over-housing, but the scope for structural limitation of the benefit seems restricted. National or regional limits on the amount of benefit that can be paid would raise considerable problems. It seems more likely that there will be an attempt to squeeze the benefit – but again the experience of Spring 1988 shows how difficult in both political and human terms that can be. There may also be mounting pressure for transferring the responsibility for housing benefit from the Department of Social Security to the Department of the Environment, on the grounds both that it is the latter's policies that largely determine its level and that the essential components of housing benefit – rents and the new community charge

– fit naturally into the local government-based housing system, rather than the DSS. It is already the case that although housing benefit comes under the DSS budget it is largely handled through local government.

But this in turn raises one of the major questions for social policy in the next decade: what exactly should be the role of local government?

Early in 1988 Nicholas Ridley wrote a pamphlet called *The Local Right*: it was sub-titled *Enabling not Providing.*[5] Ridley describes the new role of the councillor as he sees it in words which sum up the essence of his argument:

> His role will shift from the role of the manager to the role of the enabler and decider of local priorities, always conscious of what his decisions will cost his charge-payers.

Earlier in the pamphlet he applies this philosophy to housing. He describes how the sale of council houses, the 1988 Housing Act's stimulus for private renting and for the transfer of ownership of council properties to other landlords, and the creation of Housing Action Trusts, should mean a substantial break-up of the local authorities' near-monopoly of rented housing.

> But there will still be a key role for local authorities. Freed from having to be managers and providers of general housing, with all the day-to-day problems that that entails, they can concentrate on ensuring that those who are genuinely in need, and unable to get adequate housing on the open market, are properly catered for. To do this they will need to retain a range of clearly defined powers and responsibilities ... They will be able to devote more attention to the tasks of ensuring an adequate supply of sites for housing, for example through planning decisions; for channelling grants and subsidies towards the people and areas in greatest need; for carrying out the roles of monitoring and inspection, for instance of fitness and safety regulations; for ensuring that there are adequate arrangements – perhaps through contracts with the providers – for housing the homeless, and vulnerable groups such as those released from institutions for care back into the community.[6]

Behind this philosophy there lies a strong sense that local government has failed. The worst Labour authorities 'have lost touch with the beliefs and attitudes of ordinary people'. Some Conservative authorities have 'taken up the challenge of accountability and competition', but Ridley clearly sees the system as a whole as in a state of failure, caused by a kind of elephantiasis.[7]

Not surprisingly, this policy is unpopular among a good many Conservatives in local government, as well as among socialists. As Ridley himself points out, many of them have come into local government believing that they have managerial skills to apply (often intruding into territory once regarded as the domain of officers); even among those who have not, there is the natural tendency to become sympathetic to, and involved in, the services for which you have responsibility. Conservative councillors may be committed to the virtues of cost effectiveness, but they are as likely to be proud of their council's services as are their opponents. Though, like Tony Crosland, they would generally accept that 'the party's over', and that the days of general expansion had come to an end, they do not for the most part accept the sharp contraction of their role any more readily than they took to rate-capping and penalties for what the government deemed over-spending.

As I have suggested already, our unwritten constitution does not offer much practical succour to those wishing to defend the powers of local government against a central government that is in control of Parliament. The issue becomes primarily one of argument. How exactly can local authorities fulfil their responsibilities for the homeless, except through bed-and-breakfast accommodation, if they do not have housing of their own to offer? Will the notion of contracting out work effectively? And, for that matter, will large numbers of council tenants in fact choose to switch landlords or see Housing Action Trusts take over? In some ways the strategy is even more radical than the diversification taking place in the running of schools. It is crucial that it is effectively monitored – not least to see that the new role does not deter able people from coming into local government, whether at elected or official level.

Another instance of the same problem is raised in the report to the Secretary of State for Social Services by Sir Roy Griffiths on community care.[8] In this report, Griffiths – a senior director of Sainsbury's – came to the view that the primary responsibility for implementing the government's programme for moving, where possible, the mentally ill, the mentally handicapped and other disabled people into the community, should lie with local government social services authorities. It would be for them to identify those with needs and for them to make sure that they were met by the appropriate authority.

The report was signed in February 1988, but the government was slow to respond to it. It was reported to be reluctant to hand over increased power to local government (and of course many people in the medical world were loath to see local government in the lead 'over' them). But it could be argued that the local authority role would be in line with Ridley's philosophy of 'enabling' and monitoring – though in truth a significant amount of management would have to be involved, especially in the early stages. Perhaps the particular merit of the Griffiths report was its acceptance that there had to be a clearly identified and accountable body for making sure that policy was implemented. Surely one of the lessons of recent years – in all sorts of spheres – has been the need to identify responsibility, rather than to disperse it.

The notion of the enabling rather than the managerial role may well make headway in other social services. In health, it seems likely that the monolithic hospital service may fragment, with health authorities or general practioners 'buying' hospital care from a variety of different sources. In education, the pattern may be somewhat different, with central intervention sometimes replacing local government control but also more genuine decentralisation to schools and colleges. At the higher level there is the increasing possibility that the universities may seek to loosen their bonds with government, perhaps using their ability to fix their own fees, and select their own students, as a mechanism for launching this change. Whether this can be achieved without damaging access to the universities would of course be crucial: much could depend on the extent to which government would be willing to support students in paying the full fees, offsetting the reduction in direct funding of the universities (and polytechnics) which the development would make possible.

Even as I write, there is movement on all these fronts. A challenging period clearly lies ahead in all the main social services, and the pattern of social policy may continue to change more and more rapidly.

12 Responsibility and the Underdog

Over the whole post-war period, social policy has been dominated by one factor, the redistribution of wealth. Indeed, some would say that the welfare state is simply a mechanism for redistribution, whether through cash or through services: in this view, social policy is egalitarian or it is nothing.

And of course if we look at social policy over the period covered in this book there is a great deal of truth in that view. The insurance principle has counted for something, but the driving force of social security has been the transfer of resources from richer to poorer. If it is also from people without children to people with children or from able to disabled, or from those who are working to those who have retired, that is primarily because these latter are groups with particular needs. If we look at housing, the same is broadly true – though *fiscal* policy, through tax relief on mortgages and pensions, has given a different slant. If we look at education, the emphasis for many years was on equality of provision. The National Health Service too, for all the extent of middle-class use of it, has been based on the redistributive mechanism of taxation – in contrast to private medicine.

The consequence of this is that public expenditure has been the fuel that makes social policy work. Indeed, given the difficulty of testing effectiveness or results in many areas, the scale of public spending has often been taken as the main yardstick of social policy, by politicians and experts alike. The answer to most social problems has been predominantly seen in terms of more resources.

It has also predominantly been seen in terms of social or collective action. From wartime days onwards, the sense of community has lain firmly at the heart of social policy. In a sense, taxation in itself is an expression of communal action; but on top of that the responsibility for what goes wrong has been seen to lie with society rather than with individuals.

In the last few years, however, there has been a significant change in the picture. While some continue to hold tenaciously to the 'welfarist' view which I have just described, others have increasingly sought to challenge it. They have argued that the basis of the social problems that face us is increasingly often not a matter of the equitable distribution of resources, but to do with the diminution of personal responsibility and with forms of breakdown in behaviour and relationships which cannot simply be solved by stepping up social provision. Indeed, they would say that social provision often feeds or reinforces exactly those actions which cause social problems. It is not new to argue that welfare makes people irresponsible, but the argument has intensified.

The areas where social change can broadly be seen to have thrown up an increasing quantity of social problems are crime and breakdown in family life. (I do not of course equate the two.) The rise in the crime figures, as indicated in the appendix, is clearly a matter of great concern; and it is difficult not to be equally concerned by what has been happening to family life. There may be different views about the extent of fault or blame, but one cannot write off the significance of some of the figures. Illegitimate births in England and Wales rose by just under 39 per cent between 1974 and 1986, and from around 5 per cent of live births in the 1950s to over 20 per cent in the mid-1980s. The number of one-parent families rose from 474 000 in 1961 to 960 000 in 1985. Even where illegitimate children are registered as having a father and mother at the same address, such unions are considerably more likely to break down than formal marriages. As I have already remarked, the introduction of the Abortion Act in the late 1960s and the provision of family planning by the NHS in the early 1970s were anything but followed by the decline in 'unwanted' births which they were intended to produce. At the same time, it is difficult to shrug off the estimate that some 80 per cent of the young offenders aged up to 21, at an establishment which deals with the worst of them, Aylesbury, come from broken homes.

The reason for concern at all this is not simply that what has been happening to family life indicates a large-scale abandonment of traditional morality: it is that both crime and family breakdown can lead to great hardship and misery. The point is all too evidently true with crimes of violence and drug abuse and indeed theft; and there is no need to stress what a high proportion of the victims of crime come from the less well-off. Similarly, the spread of divorce and one-parenthood leave a trail of problems in their wake. Of course divorce can relieve great unhappiness, and one-parenthood is very often not a voluntary condition, let alone a culpable one. But both are likely to produce financial hardship, very often (though not always) a more deprived life for the children concerned, and particular problems in the field of housing. The burdens and worries of parenthood are normally heavier if there are not two parents to share them. The splitting of families often means that two homes are needed instead of one and a significant proportion of homelessness and the housing to meet it derives from single parenthood or family breakdown. Similarly with incomes: in 1984, 55 per cent of one-parent families depended on supplementary benefit, as opposed to 7 per cent of two-parent families.

If I may quote anecdotally from my own experience, which I believe to be shared by other Members of Parliament, there has been a substantial shift over the past two decades among those who come to 'surgeries' from young married couples with housing problems to cases where the marriage has broken down or where there is no husband. There also seems to be a higher proportion of cases involving financial disputes following the breakdown of marriage, while such mercifully rare cases of child abuse as I have encountered involve second unions.

The legal replacement of the term 'illegitimacy' by 'non-marital' may do something to remove a stigma, but it is unlikely to affect the real hardships that flow to the children concerned. But this brings us to one of the crucial dilemmas in policy in these areas: should it essentially be designed to rescue the casualties, particularly the young who cannot be responsible for their condition, or should it also be involved in 'laying down the law' – or indeed literally laying down the law – in a way designed to prevent these things happening? Should the state simply take a morally neutral attitude about behaviour in this realm? Should not 'responsibility' be reinforced? Is it right for example that the single parent should leapfrog the housing list? Is it possible that by ending the stigma of illegitimacy we may expose more children to what seems the almost inescapably greater risk of hardship that goes with the condition? The alternative view, that ever-increasing social provision could eradicate those hardships, does not carry much conviction. Even if generous financial benefits dealt with the poverty concerned, there are still psychological risks which would be likely to persist.

There is also the concern, as I have mentioned, that providing benefits may lead people into the condition in which they become available. Homelessness and lone parenthood have increased since the legislation tackling homelessness and the introduction of a special benefit (in 1988 £3.70 a week, on top of income support) for single-parent families – though as always in social policy research proving cause and effect is remarkably difficult.

The ability of the law to set social norms has been much argued over the years: can it affect attitudes? Divorce raises this point. The Morton Commission of 1956 considered that less restrictive divorce laws contribute to 'an increasing disposition to regard divorce, not as the last resort, but as the obvious way out when things go wrong'.[1] The Law Commission discussion paper in 1988, *Facing the Future* did not, however, go along with the idea that the law can buttress the stability of marriage.[2] It was particularly concerned that the divorce process should be morally neutral – and that issues of fault should not be reintroduced. But it is difficult to shake off the feeling that divorce has in fact been increasingly seen as the quick way out, with a damaging effect on people's determination to make their marriages work. It is particularly high nowadays in the lower socio-economic groups – those who are by definition likely to be the least able to cope with the financial problems which divorce throws up. Overall one in three marriages are now being dissolved: and Britain has the highest divorce rate in the European Community.

Divorce raises another difficult question: how far should the state be seen as the upholder of moral values, and how far should that role rather lie with other bodies, notably the churches? The tension that has arisen in recent years between church and state (or the Conservative party) is very much an aspect of this question. Many Conservatives have tended to feel that the churches have plunged with too little thought into social and economic policy at large, while speaking with too faint and uncertain a voice on questions of personal and especially family morality.

The issue came to a head early in 1988. Speaking at the inauguration of the Moderator of the Free Church Federal Council on 18 March, the Archbishop of Canterbury, Dr Runcie, argued that there had been a deep Christian consensus

> having a good deal to do with the Christian economics of R. H. Tawney. And this was until recently accepted by a majority of politicians of all parties. Conservatives like Rab Butler and Harold Macmillan had no major difficulty with the idea of the Welfare State. Christian leaders such as Archbishop Temple spoke for almost all Christians and almost all parliamentarians in welcoming the Welfare State's common Christian philosophical principles. But the Churches today, while they still hold to these convictions, find the wider political consensus has disappeared. The retreat from the middle ground has left the Churches united but also often isolated.

By the time Dr Runcie spoke one leading Conservative, the Home Secretary Douglas Hurd, had already challenged the churches. In a speech at Robert Peel's old constituency town of Tamworth on 5

February 1988, Hurd talked of the problems of violence, vandalism and diminished discipline and respect for the law to be found not only in deprived inner cities but in more affluent areas. He asked:

> What has become of the influence, never complete but once strong, which the churches of all denominations used to exercise over the manners and morality of the people? We should not resent comments of churchmen on political and social affairs. They have every right to intervene and have a long tradition of such intervention behind them. Equally, those who are involved in politics have an equal right to comment on the presence or the absence of the churches and their sometimes bizarre choice of priorities for discussion. It is not a political but the individual gospel, the building of a foundation for individual behaviour and values which desperately needs preaching today.

Hurd went on to ask, talking of young criminals and hooligans: 'above all, where were the parents of these youths and what influence have they had on the way their children conduct themselves?'

This theme of responsibility was at the heart of the next major contribution to the debate, the highly publicised speech of Mrs Thatcher to the General Assembly of the Church of Scotland at Edinburgh on 21 May 1988. In it she made clear that 'the only way we can ensure that no-one is left without sustenance, help or opportunity, is to have laws to provide for health and education, pensions for the elderly, succour for the sick and disabled. But', she added, 'intervention by the State must never become so great that it effectively removes personal responsibility.' Earlier in the speech she had stressed that we are all responsible for our own actions. 'We cannot blame society if we break the law. We cannot simply delegate the exercise of mercy and generosity to others.' And she reminded her audience how St Paul had said that 'If a man will not work he shall not eat' and that anyone who neglects to provide for his own house (meaning his own family) has disowned the faith and is 'worse than an infidel'.

This speech, and a comment by Mrs Thatcher questioning whether there was such a thing as 'society', led to a vigorous argument. In a letter to her, printed in *The Times* of 1 June 1986, the chairman and secretary of the Church of England's Board for Social Responsibility, the Bishop of Gloucester and Prebendary John Gladwyn, asked whether it was possible to understand personal responsibility without stressing also the essentially social character of human life. They stressed the latter, and the need for social provision. They also picked up remarks that Mrs Thatcher had made at Edinburgh about the legitimacy of wealth creation. They said that there were bound to be searching questions about how wealth is gained and distributed, and on the effects of wealth on those who possess it. And they asked 'Is it not unrealistic to think that the needs of the poor can be met in our sort of world by individual charity alone?'

Mrs Thatcher had not, of course, said that they could be; the essence of the argument on both sides was really whether the current need is to tip the balance more strongly in the direction of personal or of collective responsibility, rather than to plump absolutely for one or other. But it is true that the prevailing Conservative view would include the belief that a greater stress on individual responsibility would include a greater stress on charitable action. Charities have benefited considerably by tax changes since 1979, and it is significant that certain beneficiaries under the new Social Fund have to show that they have tried to gain help from charities before they can receive help from the fund. There is also a feeling that some voluntary agencies have tended to move too much from the direct provision of services to becoming pressure groups for *government* action.

All this ties in naturally with the argument that social provision may too easily reward anti-social behaviour – and perhaps also that human behaviour tends to be more 'rational', more conscious of punishment and reward, than many social policy-makers and observers have tended to think.

Of course their view is not dead. To give one example, there was a passage in a review of the life of Bertrand Russell by Alan Ryan in the *Observer*[3] in which the reviewer David Marquand writes:

Today, the most serious threat to individuality comes from the erosion of community, not from the excesses of collectivism. The symbol of our nightmare is the emotionally starved football hooligan, not the grey-suited power-hungry bureaucrat, or, for that matter, the jackbooted secret policeman. The question that matters now is how to maintain the ties of community in the face of a debased definition of individualism, how to reassert man's social nature against the onward march of the yuppie.

Conservatives cannot duck this challenge – either the facts of the Heysel football stadium disaster or the mounting crime figures (which may or may not show some signs of slackening). But they do not easily accept the simple notion that a type of *laissez faire* 'erosion of community' leads to an emotional starvation which in turn leads to hooliganism and worse. Their concern is rather that the stress on social action, operated through the agencies of the welfare state, may allow the individual to engage in a form of buck-passing as far as his responsibility for his family, his fellows and himself are concerned.

The word 'community' should not simply be equated with government or statutory social action. Those who stress individual responsibility would certainly also recognise the importance of the community, as a means both of providing more reinforcement to the individual in his behaviour and of giving practical help to those in need. Individual responsibility implies both responsibility for your own action and responsibility for other people, and the latter may be given either directly or through the vehicle of the community – church, voluntary agency or less formal actions. Again the essence of those who stress individual responsibility is that, coupled with the duty of the individual to try to look after himself and his family, there is also the duty to care actively for his neighbour, rather than simply leave it to the social services. Greater wealth is not justified if it simply means greater selfishness.

As to crime, it must be said that there is a singular lack of consensus today about its causes and cures. On the left, crime is seen in the sort of terms which Marquand uses, and as a product of an acquisitive society. Unemployment, and lack of opportunities are seen as particular causes. The marxist historian, George Rudé, has put a slightly different slant on this when he writes about

the 'acquisitive' type of criminal who, far from turning his back on the norms of society he lives in, is the one who ... exploits these norms, including the competition for property and profit, in order to enrich himself and become more securely entrenched in a form of society that he patently admires and wishes he belongs to.

Conservatives may accept that the existence and promotion of increasing quantities of material goods can lead to more of them being stolen. They may also go along with the implication of Rudé's remarks, that we should not reject 'rational' explanations of crime but with a different emphasis. In *Losing Ground* Charles Murray[4] uses a telling quote from the distinguished American sociologist James Q. Wilson:

People are governed in their daily lives by rewards and penalties of every sort. We shop for bargain prices, praise our children for good behaviour and scold them for bad, expect lower interest rates to stimulate home building and fear that higher ones will depress it, and conduct ourselves in public in ways that lead our friends and neighbours to form good opinions of us. To assert that 'deterrence doesn't work' is tantamount to either denying the plainest facts of everyday life or claiming that would-be criminals are utterly different from the rest of us.[5]

Murray himself quotes the experience in Cook County, which includes Chicago. At a time of soaring juvenile crime rates between 1966 and 1976 the number of juveniles committed to the Illinois state system of training schools fell from 1200 to less than 400. By the mid-1970s the average number of arrests of a Cook County youth before he was committed to a reform school was no less than 13.6.[6] In Murray's view, the situation was made worse by the fact that the juvenile's record was either increasingly restricted in its use or completely expunged, so that there was no record that he had been in trouble with the courts, and therefore less incentive to refrain from criminal acts.

If much crime is, to this extent, a 'rational' matter then we must clearly look to 'rational' solutions based on effective punishments and rewards. But no one would dispute that there is also plenty of 'irrational' crime, together with crime provoked by sexual urges. A community that does nothing for the destitute, or for those who have left long-term pyschiatric or mental handicap units without then receiving community care, is also going to find 'criminals' on its hands – and 'criminals' to whom 'rational' notions of crime clearly cannot by and large apply. To accept that there is much force in the rational approach does not absolve the state of any action beyond the penal or deterrent role. Probation, community service, good prison education and so on are all needed, as is the apparatus of prevention which has recently been strengthened.

But there is another element in the campaign against crime that is also vital – the moral dimension. Sociological explanations of crime tend to be determinist. Clearly rootlessness, family breakdown and poor schools are more likely to breed it than are their opposites. But individuals can still make choices. It is therefore necessary to stress that nearly all crime means hurt, sometimes grave hurt, to others; that the old often live in deep fear because of it; that the places where it is most prevalent are being ruined by it. This has to be translated into vivid words and images. They cannot alone do this job, but they can help to dissuade at least those who are on the margins of criminality, particularly if they can plausibly also convey the message that crime is not a rewarding activity. A war on crime that does not employ a strong moral element is as unlikely to succeed as a campaign against Aids that relies solely on the need for condoms. The 'rational' criminal may not be impressed by moral arguments, but those who bring up or influence the young often need the reinforcement derived from public morality, as well as from persuasive evidence that crime leads to punishment. A wise penal policy does not neglect individuals; it makes them more aware of the consequences of their actions.

The relationship between crime and unemployment has been much argued about. Certainly unemployment in itself does not seem to lead inexorably to crime: the inter-war years were years of high unemployment but exceptionally low recorded crime. But it seems indisputable that there is in Britain (as in the United States) an 'underclass' among the young where formal employment at least is low and the rate of crime against both persons and property, as well as drug abuse, is high. In the United States, more than in the United Kingdom, the problem is particularly to be found amoung young blacks. The one-parent family is prevalent; the more successful black middle-class families move out from the areas where the underclass are to be found; the decline in semi-skilled labour is making it harder to escape from the bottom of the economic pile; and the combination of welfare and the black economy makes it possible to survive without a job. Thus in 1980 the US Government asked inner-city unemployed 16–24-year-olds in Chicago, Boston and Philadelphia how hard they thought it would be to get a minimum-wage job: 46 per cent replied 'very easy', 25 per cent 'somewhat easy'. None had any intention of looking.

One answer to many Americans, and an increasing number of people in Britain, lies in some form of workfare – a requirement for those of working age that benefits should lead to a liability to work. In Britain young people who have neither jobs nor training may lose their income support. It is claimed that workfare is working in America: Ohio's tough provisions have resulted in a 17 per cent drop in female welfare recipients over a four-year period, and a 60 per cent drop in families where a father is present.[7]

Characteristically, the particular emphasis in the American approach is on work as a solution to social problems: a Bill before Congress required women with children only a year old to work in return for welfare benefits.

But the problem is very much harder to solve among families headed by women. The whole question of the position, rights and duties of women remains one of the major issues of social policy today. Indeed, nothing illustrates more vividly the interaction between social policy and social change.

The most striking development lies simply in the increase of employment among women. The civilian labour force in Great Britain rose by 1.8 million between 1971 and 1986 entirely because of an increase in the number of women in the labour force.[8]

But even more striking than what has happened to date is the likely trend in the future. On the one hand, women are increasingly seeking work, whether for more money, from a desire to escape from the drudgery, loneliness and tedium of housework (and sometimes the stresses of childcare), or for less easily defined reasons to do with status and fulfilment. On the other hand, the demand for their labour in many areas looks set to grow, not least because of the greatly reduced number of 18-year-olds coming on to the labour market round about 1990 – together, of course, with gradually greater acceptance that women should not be confined to 'women's jobs'.

The problem in all this, of course, is what happens to the children. One answer is improved childcare, daycare, nursery education. These clearly have to be considered very carefully. But first we have to think about what exactly is happening. In the United States, where the pressure for daycare is mounting rapidly, it is argued that mothers *have* to work for financial reasons. It is often said that it is not 'possible' to live on the man's income alone – anyway at what is seen as an acceptable standard. But on top of this the *right* of women to work is stressed. In Europe the same view is there. It is significant that when the European Commission launched a study of childcare, it did so from the standpoint of equal opportunities for women, rather than specifically of the child's interests.[9] The report indicated that the United Kingdom is one of the lowest providers for the children of working parents among the Community countries.

But there are those in most western countries, certainly in Britain, who are concerned about the spread of daycare, for very young children in particular: they feel that it may not be an adequate alternative to being with the mother, that the working mother anyway may be under pressures of time and energy that prevent her giving adequate attention to the child even when they are at home, and that the childcare setting frequently does not have the stability and continuity of staff that are necessary if the child is to be away from its parent. The younger the child, the more, naturally, these arguments are held to apply. Moreover, where there is provision for under-five children, the fact that it is, rightly, very often part-time means that it does not solve the problems of the working parent.

This is an important and difficult problem. It may well be true, as Professor Judy Dunn argues on the basis of her research[10] that 'whether children have a good or a bad childhood depends on how satisfied the mother is with her life, *not* on whether she works or not', but that does not quite solve the matter; we have to deal with all sorts and conditions of both parents and children.

The aim, perhaps, should be to concentrate on *availability*, on a full choice of different forms of pre-school or childcare provision where the parents want it. This essentially was the conclusion of the House of Commons Select Committee on Education's report on *Educational Provision for the Under Fives*.[11] Its focus was on the ages between three and five, and its emphasis was on making sure that the education provided for that age group was both appropriate and good; but the objective of providing well-run nurseries and other forms of daycare applies equally to younger children – so long as access is based on choice rather than any kind of pressure. What gives grounds for concern at the moment is the way that some mothers feel that to be at home with the child is to be somehow second-rate, inadequate and stereotyped – a feeling of inferiority compounded by the fact that the mother who works at home is likely to be less well-off than the mother who goes out to work.

There are limits to the extent to which governments can change attitudes in this sort of respect: but it is open to them to use the tax system and child benefit to support those mothers who stay at home instead of tipping the tax system in favour of the couple where both work. For the latter, bringing up children can be made easier by the encouragement of effective job-sharing schemes and reasonable flexibility about working hours.

In all the areas discussed in this chapter, the common ground has been (as I suggested at its beginning) that although resources continue to be important they are only a part of what has to be done, and that the crucial requirement is a sense of responsibility and concern. Certainly this embraces concern by society, by government; but it does also emphatically mean a stronger sense of direct responsibility by the individual for his own actions and by the family for what goes on within its membership. It implies giving less reinforcement to behaviour that breeds trouble and misery, more to marriage and the care of children and to effort – if you like, more to respectability *so long as there is a real meaning to it*, rather than simply censoriousness towards others.

Overall, comparative abundance has gradually replaced comparative scarcity in the post-war years; but if absolute poverty has diminished, hardship – above all that associated with family breakdown – still exists in plenty.

I have tried in this and the previous chapter to sketch some of the elements in Conservative thinking that seem to be developing at the present time. Conservative ideas, in Britain anyway, have never settled easily into either a libertarian or a paternalistic straitjacket. The doctrine of the free market has certainly had a substantial impact. Conservatives generally look for a shift in the frontiers between public and private provision in pensions and housing, as well as perhaps health care and education. Nevertheless they do not sense that the market will solve all the questions of behaviour and hardship that face us. Individual *choice* is anyway too crude without a strong sense of individual *responsibility* – hence the emphasis in this chapter. And there are some Conservatives who would argue that man's greatest problems may be too deeply embedded in the human condition for politics to be able to offer more than limited, transient solutions.

But in spite of all this, and the changing nature of our social problems, it seems inconceivable to suppose that the historic Conservative view of government as an active agency for the improvement of the condition of the people will fade away. The disabled, the mentally and chronically sick, the destitute, many of the aged, will all greatly depend on government for succour and support; the care and education of the young, the health of the population, the support of housing for the needy, and indeed the sad task of salvaging the wreckage of family breakdown – all these are reasons why we will continue to need social services. Social policy is not only about the social services, and the social services are not the only way of meeting social need. New approaches are necessary and inevitable. But the day has not yet arrived when Conservatives can or should forget all the wartime ideals – or their duty to the poor.

Appendix

This book has essentially been an exercise in narrative history, though the last two chapters are speculative. But there are questions which narrative alone cannot answer – where we have to turn to the statistics if we are to make any attempt at objectivity. Among these questions, the crucial one for the purpose of this book must be: what difference did it make whether or not a Conservative government was in power? The only alternative in the period covered by this book (since the wartime coalition) has been a Labour government. How do the records of the two compare?

But of course comparison is a complicated matter: the circumstances in which each government found itself in office varied, sometimes greatly. The international economic picture, wars and rumours of war, oil prices and revenues may all greatly influence the context of government. On top of this, governments should be judged by the *totality* of their policies – social policy cannot be looked at in isolation from economic policy, what happens to benefits must be intimately linked to what happens to taxes, measures designed to achieve equality do not necessarily point in the same direction as measures designed to create more overall wealth, and so on. Policies to increase employment and decrease inflation can look particularly perverse: increased output per worker and higher interest rates can appear anyway in the short term to have exactly the opposite to the desired effect. Moreover, even though we can take the effect on inflation into account when we examine how much different governments spend on social services, spending levels do not tell us much about quality or opportunity costs.

So the difficulties are all too obvious; but over the years the quantity of data has mounted, and for this appendix I have selected a number of graphs and tables which reflect the subject matter of this book. For the most part, the material covers the full period since the Second World War, but in some cases it seems useful to offer statistics over more limited periods. Such statistics may in any case be the only ones readily available. The selection is by definition selective, and others would have chosen differently; but at least the facts are there, drawn from official sources and I believe honestly presented. As with almost any series of figures over time, there will be changes, qualifications and nuances of which scholars will wish to take note. I do not begin to list them all, but I am confident that the overall picture is valid. The graphs and tables cover population, inflation, unemployment, cash benefits and incomes, housing, health, education, crime and divorce and illegitimacy.

What do they show? Essentially, my aim is to let the reader supply for himself the link between the statistics which follow and the policies which I have described in earlier chapters. But a few comments are worth making.

One is a very broad generalisation. The graphs suggest that for much of the time there were basic trends and movements that seemed to override the question of which party was in power. If we look at the simple graphs showing public expenditure between 1949 and 1988 on our four main areas of health, education, social security and housing we find that a steady upward movement has broadly been the picture for social security and health, that it was so until the late 1970s in education, but that housing presents an altogether more erratic scene. In the case of education, demography was clearly very relevant: the number of school pupils fell appreciably in the mid-1980s. But in housing, changes in policy and the growth of home ownership were highly significant – and, of course, tax relief on mortgages does not count as public expenditure.

But what can we say about the fundamental overall question of the creation of wealth and its distribution among different social classes? In crude terms, it can be said that the Conservative objective is to concentrate on the creation of wealth, in the belief that all will tend to benefit, though not necessarily proportionately or to the relative advantage of the worse off. The socialist objective places great stress on equality: in their case, relative wealth seems even more important than absolute wealth. And of course wealth embraces services as well as cash.

The graphs which follow – and indeed, to the best of my knowledge, the available evidence – do not really answer the question. A table in the Central Statistical Office's *Economic Trends* (December 1988, HMSO) indicates that between 1975 and 1986 the share of final income (after taxes, benefits etc.) of the first or bottom quintile fell from 7.1 per cent to 6.3 per cent, while the share of the top quintile rose from 38 per cent to 42 per cent. The second and third quintiles also fell; the fourth remained the same. On the other hand, *Economic Trends* of July 1984 and November 1987 indicates that between 1978/9 and 1984/5 the average income after deduction of income tax of the top 1 per cent rose by 136 per cent, of the next 9 per cent by 105 per cent, of the next 40 per cent by 78 per cent, of the next 50 per cent by 77 per cent, and of the bottom 20 per cent by 82 per cent. The overall average was 85 per cent. During this period, prices rose by 77 per cent. However, these figures do not include the cost of national insurance contributions, where the increases would probably have adversely affected those in the middle: nor do they include the effect of benefits. The least well-off appear to have become clearly better off in real terms, but it is difficult to say more than that.

This book anyway has not been directly concerned with Treasury policy. I have included graphs showing unemployment rates and consumer price inflation, but otherwise the material in this appendix relates specifically to the subject matter of this book.

Table A.1   *Benefit levels, 1948–87 (all at equivalent value of April 1987 prices)*

Year (month varies with benefit changes)	Standard Rate Retirement Pension for man or woman on own insurance (under 80) (£)	National Assistance or Supplementary Benefit scale for single householder (short term) (exclusive of housing costs) (£)	Levels of support for 2-child family on average earnings (benefit and tax allowances) (£)
1948	16.71	14.27	8.24
1949	—	—	9.08
1950	—	14.67	8.17
1951	16.28	14.92	9.52
1952	16.53	16.11	7.38
1953	—	—	8.96
1954	—	—	9.50
1955	18.92	16.34	10.50
1956	—	16.57	10.84
1957	—	—	11.09
1958	20.93	17.39	11.07
1959	—	19.39	10.66
1960	—	—	11.24
1961	22.97	19.96	11.34
1962	—	20.43	11.19
1963	25.02	22.04	12.22
1964	—	—	12.70
1965	28.03	25.02	13.07
1966	—	24.95	13.41
1967	28.96	26.24	13.21
1968	—	26.25	12.90
1969	28.85	26.20	12.28
1970	—	26.36	11.74
1971	29.72	27.20	13.31
1972	30.82	28.55	12.52
1973	32.20	28.33	11.29
1974	36.61	29.22	12.57
1975	36.08	28.60	12.01
1976	37.06	28.85	12.22
1977	37.50	29.05	10.89
1978	38.67	28.94	12.11
1979	39.37	29.16	15.00
1980	39.78	29.94	13.92
1981	38.73	29.55	13.74
1982	40.46	30.66	14.41
1983	40.00	30.53	15.27
1984	40.07	30.77	15.33
1985	40.65	30.86	14.86
1986	40.40	30.72	14.82
1987	39.50	30.40	14.50

Source: *DHSS Abstract of Statistics* for index of retail prices, average earnings, social security benefits and contributions, 1987.

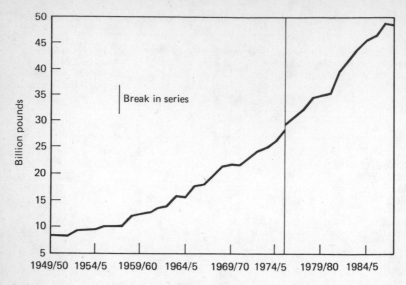

Figure A.1 Expenditure on social security (£bn at 1987/8 prices). (*Source:* CSO *Annual Abstract of Statistics*, 1989, and earlier editions.)

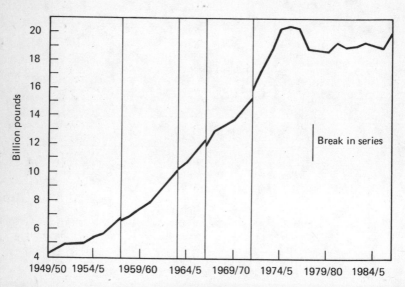

Figure A.2 Expenditure on education (£bn at 1987/8 prices). (*Source:* CSO *Annual Abstract of Statistics*, 1989, and earlier editions.)

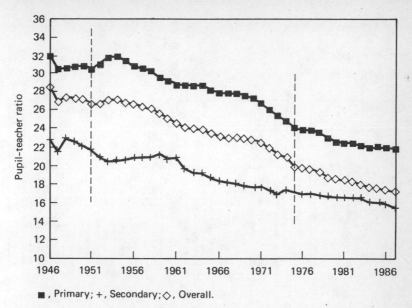

Figure A.3 Pupil–teacher ratios, maintained schools, England and Wales 1946–87. ■, Primary; +, Secondary; ◇, Overall. (*Source:* CSO *Annual Abstract of Statistics*, 1956, 1963, 1970, 1974. DES *Statistics Bulletin*.)

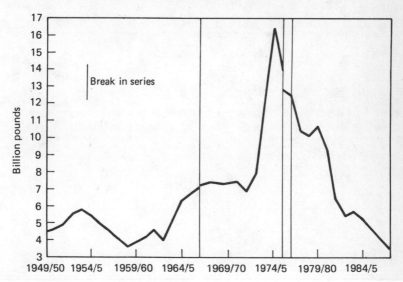

Figure A.4 Expenditure on housing (£bn at 1987/8 prices). (*Source:* CSO *Annual Abstract of Statistics*, 1989, and earlier editions.)

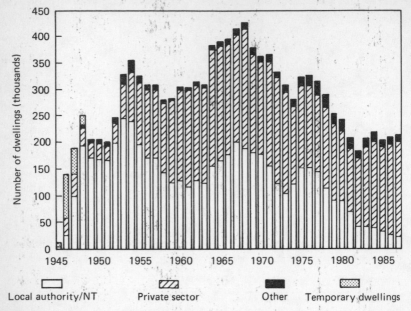

Figure A.5   New dwellings completed, United Kingdom, 1945–87. (*Source:*
Annual Abstract of Statistics, 1956, 1963, 1970, 1980, 1986, 1988; DoE
Housing and Construction Statistics, 1977–87.)

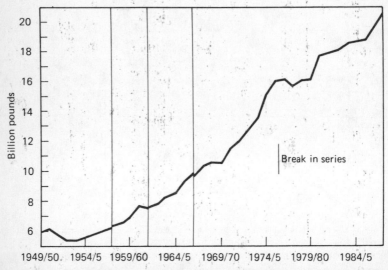

Figure A.6   Expenditure on health (£bn at 1987/8 prices). (*Source:* CSO
Annual Abstract of Statistics, 1989, and earlier editions.)

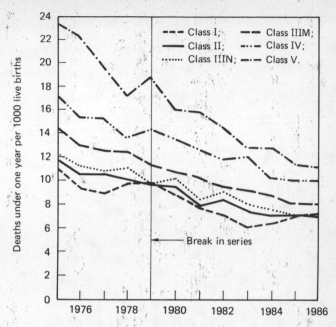

Figure A.7 Infant mortality rates in England and Wales, by social class, 1975–86. --------- Class I; ———— Class II; ········· Class IIIN; ––––– Class IIIM; -·--··· Class IV; -··-··- Class V. (*Source:* OPCS *Mortality Statistics*, OPCS *Monitor* DH3 88/1.)

Table A.2 United Kingdom National Health Service hospital summary: all specialities

	1971	1976	1981	1984	1985	1986	1987[1]
All in-patients							
Discharges and deaths (thousands)	6 437	6 525	7 179	7 666	7 884	7 959	8 088
Average number of beds available daily[2] (thousands)	526	484	450	429	421	409	392
Average number of beds occupied daily (thousands)							
Maternities	19	16	15	14	13	13	13
Other patients[3]	417	378	350	333	327	316	304
Total–average number of beds occupied daily	436	394	366	347	341	330	317
Patients treated per bed available (number)	12.3[3]	13.6	16.0	17.8	18.7	19.4	20.6
Average length of stay (days)							
Medical patients	14.7[4]	12.1	10.2[4]	9.1	8.7	8.5	—
Surgical patients	9.1[4]	8.6	7.6[4]	6.9	6.7	6.5	—
Maternities	7.0[4]	6.7	5.6[4]	4.9	4.7	4.5	—
Percentage of live births in hospital[4]	89.8	97.6	98.9	99.0	99.1	99.1	99.2[8]
Private in-patients[5] (thousands)							
Discharges and deaths	115	95	98	79	71	—	—
Average number of beds occupied daily	2	2	1	1	1	—	—
Day case attendances (thousands)	—	565[4]	863	1 081	1 166	1 288	1 207

New out-patients[6] (thousands)						
Accidents and emergency	9 358	10 463	11 342	12 279	12 492	12 682	12 797
Other out-patients	9 572	9 170	9 816	10 376	10 604	10 758	10 350
Average attendances per new patient (numbers)[7]						
Accidents and emergency	1.6	1.6	1.4	1.4	1.3	1.3	1.3
Other out-patients	4.2	4.0	4.4	4.3	4.3	4.3	4.2

[1] 1987 figures for England relate to the financial year ending 31 March 1988.

[2] Staffed beds only.

[3] Out of the 233 thousand in-patients in England in 1987, 86 thousand were mental illness/handicap patients who occupied 40 per cent of available beds.

[4] Great Britain only.

[5] England and Wales only.

[6] The 1971 and 1976 figures for out-patients in Scotland include ancillary departments.

[7] Patients attending out-patient clinics in England solely for attention of a minor nature and not seen by a doctor, eg to have a dressing changed, are no longer counted.

[8] United Kingdom.

(*Source: Social Trends*, 19, HMSO).

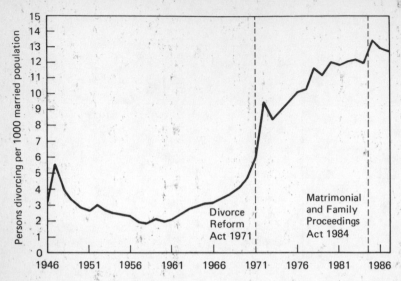

Figure A.8   Divorce rate in England and Wales, 1946–87. (*Source:* OPCS *Marriage and Divorce Statistics*; Series FM no 18; OPCS *Monitor* FM2 87/2 dated 18.10.87; OPCS unpublished tables; Registrar-General's *Statistical Review of England and Wales 1946 to 1950.*)

Table A.3   *Live births outside marriage (thousands and percentages)*

	United Kingdom		England and Wales
	Live births outside marriage (thousands)	As percentage of total live births	Percentage registered in joint names
1961	54	6	38
1971	74	8	45
1976	61	9	51
1981	91	12	58
1986	158	21	66
1987	178	23	68

Source: Social Trends 19.

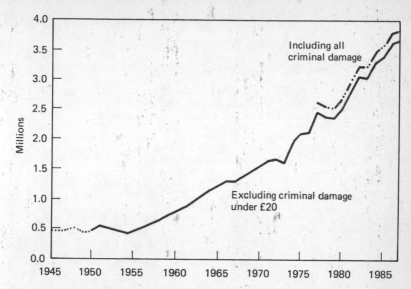

Figure A.9 Notifiable offences recorded by the police in England and Wales. (*Source: Criminal Statistics Annual Command Papers; Home Office Statistics Bulletin.*)

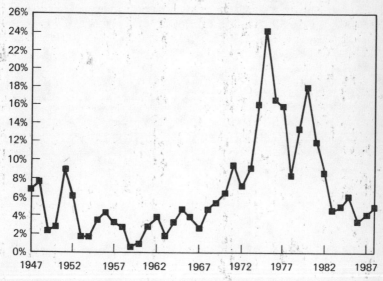

Figure A.10 Consumer price inflation (% change over previous year). (*Source:* CSO press notice.)

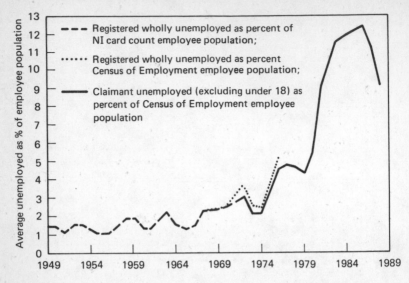

Figure A.11 Great Britain unemployment rates, 1949–88. Employee population based annual average unemployed (excluding school leavers) as per cent of employees in employment and unemployed at June). – – – Registered wholly unemployed as per cent of NI card count employee population; ······ Registered wholly unemployed as per cent of Census of Employment employee population; —— Claimant unemployed (excluding under 18) as per cent of Census of Employment population. (*Source: British Labour Statistics Historical Abstract 1886–1968;* Department of Employment Statistics; *British Labour Statistics Year Book.*)

References

1 1939–45: Coalition

1. J. Ramsden, *The Making of Conservative Party Policy* (London: Macmillan, 1980) p. 91.
2. H. Macmillan, *The Middle Way* (London: Macmillan, 1938) p. 29.
3. R. M. Titmuss, *Problems of Social Policy* (London: Longman, 1950) p. 507.
4. J. Harris, *William Beveridge* (Oxford: Clarendon Press, 1977) pp. 381–2.
5. *Social Insurance and Allied Services*, Cmd 6404 (London: HMSO, 1942).
6. C. Barnett, *The Audit of War* (London: Macmillan, 1986) p. 27.
7. Ibid., p. 33.
8. *Social Insurance: the Government's Policy, Part I,* Cmd 6550 (London: HMSO, 1944).
9. *Social Insurance: the Government's Policy, Part II (Workmen's Compensation)*, Cmd 6551 (London: HMSO, 1944).
10. *A National Health Service*, Cmd 6502 (London: HMSO, 1944).
11. Ramsden, *The Making of Conservative Party Policy*, p. 96.
12. A. Howard, *RAB: The Life of R. A. Butler* (London: Jonathan Cape, 1987) p. 107.

2 1945–51: Parallel Lines

1. P. Hennessy and A. Seldon, *Ruling Performance* (Oxford: Blackwell, 1987) pp. 310–11.
2. J. and S. Jewkes, *The Genesis of the British National Health Service* (Oxford: Blackwell, 1961) p. 48.
3. *The Industrial Charter* (London: CPC, 1947 Report of the Industrial Committee, Chrd R. A. Butler).
4. Q. Hogg, *The Case for Conservatism* (Hardmondsworth: Penguin, 1947) p. 256.
5. Ibid., p. 259.
6. *The Right Road for Britain* (London: CPC, 1949) p. 9.
7. Ibid., p. 37.
8. Ibid., p. 39.
9. Ibid., p. 41.
10. Ibid., p. 42.
11. Ibid., p. 46.
12. I. Macleod and A. Maude (eds), *One Nation: A Tory Approach to Social Problems* (London: CPC, 1950).
13. Ibid., p. 9.
14. Ibid., p. 18.
15. Ibid., p. 19.
16. Ibid., p. 37.
17. Ibid., p. 64.
18. J. E. Powell, 'Conservatives and Social Services', *Political Quarterly*, XXIV (1952) pp. 156–66.

19. R. A. Butler, *The Art of the Possible* (London: Hamish Hamilton, 1971) p. 155.

3 1951–6: Back in Government

1. H. Macmillan, *Tides of Fortune* (London: Macmillan, 1969) p. 363.
2. Ibid., p. 376.
3. Ibid., p. 456.
4. N. Fisher, *Iain Macleod* (London: André Deutsch, 1973) p. 87.
5. Ibid., p. 93.
6. *Report of the Committee into the Cost of the National Health Service*, Cmd 9663 (London: HMSO, 1955).
7. White Paper *Technical Education*, Cmd 9703 (London: HMSO, 1955).

4 1957–64: The Middle Ground

1. H. Macmillan, 'The Middle Way: 20 Years After' (Lecture, March 1958) (London: CPC, 1958).
2. J. Boyd-Carpenter, *Way of Life* (London: Sidgwick & Jackson, 1980).
3. B. Cooper, *Minds Matter* (Bow Group pamphlet) (London: CPC, 1959).
4. Lord Hailsham, *The Conservative Case* (Harmondsworth: Penguin, 1959).
5. One Nation Group, *The Responsible Society* (London: CPC, 1959).
6. B. Sewill, 'Reshaping Welfare', *Crossbow* (Summer 1959) p. 57.
7. Hobart Paper, *Health Through Choice* (London: IEA, 1961).
8. G. Howe, 'Reform of the Social Services', *Principles in Practice* (London: CPC, 1961) p. 58.
9. *Report of the Royal Commission on London Government*, Cmnd 1164 (London: HMSO, 1960).
10. '15–18 year olds', Report of the Central Advisory Council on Education, (London: HMSO, 1959).
11. 'Half our Future', Report of the Central Advisory Council on Education, (London: HMSO, 1963).
12. 'Higher Education', Report of the Committee chaired by Lord Robbins, Cmnd 2154 (London: HMSO, 1963).
13. 'Children and Their Primary Schools', Report of the Central Advisory Council on Education, (London: HMSO, 1967).
14. Conservative Party *Manifesto 1964*.
15. *Penal Practice in a Changing Society 1959*, Cmnd 645 (London: HMSO, 1959).
16. *Homosexual Offences and Prostitution*, Cmnd 247 (London: HMSO, 1959).
17. *Housing in Greater London*, Cmnd 2605 (London: HMSO, 1964).

5 1964–70: Heath in Opposition

1. D. Howell, *Efficiency and Beyond* (London: CPC, 1965).
2. T. Raison, *Conflict and Conservatism* (London: CPC, 1965).
3. G. Howe, *In Place of Beveridge* (London: CPC, 1965).

4. J. MacGregor, *Housing Ourselves* (London: CPC, 1965).
5. *Housing in Greater London*, Cmnd 2605 (London: HMSO, 1965).
6. *Putting Britain Right Ahead* (London: CPC, 1965).
7. J. Ramsden, *The Making of Conservative Party Policy* (London: Macmillan, 1980) p. 248.
8. Ibid., p. 272.
9. *Crime Knows No Boundaries* (London: CPC, 1966).
10. Ramsden, *The Making of Conservative Party Policy* p. 252.
11. *Daily Telegraph*, 20 October 1969.
12. C. B. Cox and A. E. Dyson (eds), *Fight for Education* (London: Critical Quarterly Society, 1969).
13. E. Boyle, A. Crosland and M. Kogan, *The Politics of Education* (Harmondsworth: Penguin, 1971) p. 88.
14. H. Sewill, *Auntie* (London: CPC, 1966).
15. B. Hayhoe, *Must the Children Suffer?* (London: CPC, 1968).
16. Conservative Manifesto 1970, *A Better Tomorrow*.

6 1970–74: Heath in Government

1. *Tax Credit Scheme (Arthur Cockfield)*, Cmnd 4653 (London: HMSO, 1971).
2. *Report of the Royal Commission on Local Government in England* (London: HMSO, 1969).
3. *Local Government in England: Government Proposals for Reorganisation*, Cmnd 4548 (London: HMSO, 1971).
4. *Education: A Framework for Expansion*, Cmnd 5174, (London: HMSO, 1972).
5. M. Rutter and N. Madge, *Cycles of Disadvantage* (London: Heinemann, 1976).
6. *Firm Action for a Fair Britain*, (CCO, 1974).
7. *Putting Britain First* (CCO, 1974).

7 1974–9: The Coming of Thatcher

1. *Reversing the Trend* (London: Barry Rose, 1975).
2. A. Seldon 'Keith Joseph interview', *Contemporary Record*, Col. 1, No. 1, 1987.
3. *Stranded on the Middle Ground?* (London: CPC, 1976).
4. R. Lewis, *Margaret Thatcher* (London: Routledge & Kegan Paul, 1975).
5. *The Right Approach* (London: CPC, 1976).
6. *The Right Approach to the Economy* (London: CPC, 1977).
7. *Land*, Cmnd 5730 (London: HMSO, 1974).
8. *Campaign Guide 1977* (CPC).
9. Lord Blake and J. Patten (eds), *The Conservative Opportunity* (London: Macmillan, 1976).
10. *Conservative Manifesto* (CCO, 1979).

8 1979–83: Thatcher in Government

1. H. Young and A. Sloman (ed.), *The Thatcher Phenomenon* (London: BBC, 1986) p. 135.

2. *Government Expenditure Plans 1980–81/1983–84*, Cmnd 7841 (London: HMSO, 1980).
3. *Brixton Disturbances Enquiry (Scarman Report)*, Cmnd 8427 (London: HMSO, 1981).
4. P. Riddell, *The Thatcher Government* (Edinburgh: Martin Robertson, 1983).

9 1983–7: The Tempo Mounts

1. C. Taylor, *Bringing Accountability Back to Local Government* (London: CPS, 1985).
2. A. Henney, *Trust the Tenant: Developing Municipal Housing* (London: CPS, 1985).
3. C. Murray, *Losing Ground* (New York: Basic Books, 1984).
4. *Streamlining the Cities*, Cmnd 9063 (London: HMSO, 1983).
5. *Better Schools*, Cmnd 9469 (London: HMSO, 1985).
6. *Reform of Social Security*, Cmnd 9517, 9518, 9519 (London: HMSO, 1985).
7. *Reform of Social Security*, Cmnd 9691 (London: HMSO, 1985).
8. *Conduct of Local Authority Business*, Interim Report of the Widdicombe Committee, Cmnd 9797 (London: HMSO, 1986).
9. *Review of the University Grants Committee*, Cm 81 (London: HMSO, 1987).
10. *Higher Education: Meeting the Challenge*, Cm 114 (London: HMSO, 1987).

10 1987–8: The Flagships Launched

1. 'Our First Eight Years' and 'The Next Moves Forward' *Conservative Manifesto* 1987 (CCO).
2. *Housing: the Government's Proposals*, Cm 214 (London: HMSO, 1987).
3. *Paying for Local Government*, Cmnd 9714 (London: HMSO, 1986).
4. *Alternatives to Domestic Rates*, Cmnd 8449 (London: HMSO, 1981).

11 The Evolving Agenda

1. *Working for Patients*, Cm 555 (London: HMSO, 1989).
2. B. R. Williams in H. Parker (ed.), *Stepping Stones to Independence* (Aberdeen University Press, 1989).
3. H. Parker, 'A Mission to Beat Poverty', *Independent,* 13 June 1988.
4. *Reform of Personal Taxation*, Cmnd 9756 (London: HMSO, 1986) p. 32.
5. N. Ridley, *The Local Right: Enabling not Providing* (London: CPC, 1988) p. 34.
6. Ibid., pp. 20–21.
7. Ibid., p. 9.
8. *Community Care: Agenda for Action* (London: HMSO, 1988).

12 Responsibility and the Underdog

1. *Report of the Royal Commission on Marriage and Divorce*, Cmnd 9678 (London: HMSO, 1956).

2. *Facing the Future*, Law Commission discussion paper (London: HMSO, HC 479, 1988).
3. D. Marquand reviewing '*Bertrand Russell* by Alan Ryan', *Observer*, 10 July 1988.
4. C. Murray, *Losing Ground*, (New York: Basic Books, 1984) p. 170.
5. J. Q. Wilson, *Thinking About Crime* (New York: Basic Books, 1983) p. 131.
6. Murray, *Losing Ground*, p. 170.
7. A. Sullivan, 'Below the Bottom Line', *Daily Telegraph*, 13 July 1988.
8. *Social Trends*, 1988 edition, p. 65 (London: HMSO, 1988).
9. *Childcare and Equality of Opportunity*, Report of the European Commission, 1988.
10. J. Dunn, 'A Double Act', *New Society*, 5 February 1988.
11. *Educational Provision for the Under Fives*, First Report of the Commons Select Committee on Education, Science and the Arts (Session 1988/89) (London: HMSO).

Index